[9—0]
Pieris japonica

[9—0a]
**Swiss Stone Pine
(Pinus Cembra)**

[9—1]
Blue Spruce (Picea pungens)

NEW *ILLUSTRATED* ENCYCLOPEDIA OF GARDENING

UNABRIDGED

EDITED BY T. H. Everett

Assistant Director (Horticulture) and Curator of Education
The New York Botanical Garden

WITH CONTRIBUTIONS FROM

TWENTY HORTICULTURISTS AND AUTHORITIES
IN THE UNITED STATES AND CANADA

Growers, Breeders, Exhibitors, Plantsmen, Writers, Lecturers, Professors, Editors and Superintendents of Famous Estates, who are Experts in all Fields of Horticulture, including Pests and Their Control.

VOLUME NINE—Pic-Pro

GREYSTONE PRESS • NEW YORK

Transplanting Seedlings. The seedlings may be removed from the seedbed when one year old, or left for a second year. They are planted in lines, usually about 2-3 in. apart in rows 12 in. from each other, and after one or two years they are set out in their permanent places.

When small numbers of plants are wanted it is usual to sow the seeds in prepared soil in pots or flats in a frame or greenhouse. As soon as the young plants are large enough to handle they are either potted singly or set out in a nursery border. Transplanting is carried out every second year until the plants are placed in permanent positions.

Grafting is carried out under glass in winter or spring, the stocks having previously been established in pots and taken into a warm greenhouse two or three weeks before they are to be worked. Erect shoots should be used for scions when possible and ordinary side grafting may be practiced. As soon as the union between stock and scion is complete, they should be placed in a cold frame and eventually planted out in a nursery border.

When to Take Cuttings. Cuttings of the various dwarf kinds of the common and Oriental Spruces can be rooted during late summer and autumn. They are made from short shoots about 2 in. long and dibbled in a sand bed in a propagating case in a greenhouse. They should be left untouched until they have rooted, when they should be potted individually in small pots and later set out in a nursery bed the way seedlings are. When Spruce plants are very small it is an advantage to arrange for a light covering, a foot or so above the ground, that can be used as a protection against hot sun in the day and frost at night.

Layering is not, as a rule, practiced with the Spruces, although they root quite well from layers; in fact, the lower branches of some kinds, particularly of Picea mariana and P. Abies, often take root when in contact with the ground, and form new trees. One form of P. Abies growing on one of the mountains in Sweden renews itself by means of naturally layered branches.

Pruning. Trees growing under forest conditions are expected to lose their lower branches early in life but the garden owner may like to see his decorative trees covered with branches to the ground line. In such a case, little pruning will be necessary.

There is another item in pruning that needs attention; that is keeping the trees to single trunks. There is a decided tendency for some trees to form several leaders, particularly after injury to a leader and, if these are not reduced to one, the tree is soon spoiled.

Pruning may be carried out at almost any time, June to fall perhaps being better than spring. On old trees that have been allowed to branch low down, the lower branches may show signs of deterioration; they should be removed, for the trees are much better without them.

The Norway Spruce. Picea Abies (P. excelsa), the Norway Spruce, is a common tree from the mountains of central Europe, where it ascends to an altitude of 6,000 ft., almost the limit of tree growth in northerly regions. At its best it may grow 150-200 ft. high, with a girth of 15-20 ft., although the average is less, and in the more exposed and northerly regions it dwindles to a bush. In cultivation in North America it is usually smaller than these maximum dimensions. It is very variable in habit, in having hairy or hairless shoots, and in the length of the leaves. The leaves usually persist for several years. The pendulous cones are cylindrical and 4-6 in. long. The seeds ripen in autumn.

The tree is well adapted for planting in moist places and for shelter. As a decorative tree it is surpassed in beauty by some of the rarer kinds, but it is one of the most generally useful Spruces. It is a comparatively fast grower.

Dwarf Spruces for the Rock Garden. Variety names have been given to many forms of P. Abies of distinct habit. These are increased by grafting or by cuttings. Some of them are only of interest in general collections of trees, but the dwarf kinds are very useful for planting in rock gardens and as subjects to use in foundation plantings and other places where permanently compact plants are needed. Some distinct ones are: conica, pygmaea, parviformis, compacta, Clanbrasiliana, procumbens, tabuliformis, and pumila. These make dense, compact bushes of very slow growth.

Spruces with Colored Leaves and Interesting

One of the many compact, dwarf varieties of the Norway Spruce, Picea Abies.

Growth Habits. Varieties of P. Abies with colored leaves are argenteo-spica, with young shoots creamy-white; aurea, with golden leaves when young. Varieties of stiff erect habit are pyramidata and columnaris. Varieties with weeping branches or of grotesque habit are pendula, with weeping secondary branches; inversa, of drooping habit; viminalis, with long, slender, almost prostrate branches; virgata, commonly called Snake Spruce, a tall tree with long branches and few branchlets; monstrosa, a most curious tree with very few branches.

The Oriental Spruce, P. orientalis, a native of the Caucasus and Asia Minor, forms a large tree, over 100 ft. high, and bears small, dark green leaves in profusion on graceful branches. As a decorative tree, under ideal growing conditions, it is superior to P. Abies. It is not hardy as far north as P. Abies, although it will grow in central New England. It thrives best in fairly sheltered locations.

The cones of the Oriental Spruce are smaller than those of the Norway Spruce, being about 3 in. long and 1/2-3/4 in. in diameter. The variety aurea has golden leaves in early summer; nana and pygmaea are of dwarf compact habit, and aureo-spicata has golden young shoots and leaves.

Siberian Spruce, P. obovata, is a tree of northern Europe and northern Asia that is closely related to P. Abies, but less generally useful in American gardens.

The Himalayan Spruce, P. Smithiana (Morinda), is an excellent decorative tree with long, weeping branchlets clothed with dark green leaves. It is hardy in sheltered places in southern New England. An allied but quite distinct tree is the Sikkim Spruce, P. spinulosa (morindoides), also a good decorative kind, but hardy in the far South and in other mild climates only.

The White Spruce, P. glauca, native from Labrador to Alaska and southward to northern New York, Michigan and Minnesota, is a handsome tree, long-lived and of imposing appearance. Its foliage is strongly aromatic and the tree thrives on a variety of soils. It is excellent for use as a windbreak and may be sheared to form a good hedge. This Spruce thrives best in the northern part of North America and cannot be expected to grow well south of New York City.

The White Spruce has many distinct varieties. The one known as variety densata, the Black Hills Spruce, is much better than the northern

Rarely reaching more than 8 ft., Picea glauca variety albertiana is of dense, compact growth. It is a useful evergreen where slow growth is desirable.

type for planting in regions where summer droughts occur, such as in Nebraska, Minnesota, Iowa and the Dakotas. The variety named conica is a dwarf, compact, conical form that is useful for planting in rock gardens. Variety albertiana, the Alberta Spruce, grows naturally from British Columbia to Montana and is distinguished by its more crowded growth.

The Red Spruce, P. rubens, is not common in cultivation but it is of great importance as a source of wood pulp for papermaking. It occurs as a native from Nova Scotia to the mountains of North Carolina. It is not a long-lived tree and seems to thrive only in the North and further south at considerable elevations. P. rubens variety virgata has long, slender branches without lateral branches.

The Black Spruce, P. mariana, is not a very ornamental kind. It grows slowly and is of untidy appearance by reason of the old cones which remain attached to the branches for several years. This tree grows from Labrador to Alaska and southward to New Jersey, Michigan and Minnesota. It is most often found growing in bogs in the southern part of its range.

The Sitka Spruce. From western North America, the Sitka Spruce, P. sitchensis, is a most valuable kind. It there grows to a height of 160-180 ft., with a very large trunk girth, and produces valuable timber. It is hardy as far north as Massachusetts but does not thrive in the eastern states.

A closely allied kind is P. Engelmannii, a handsome tree, one of the finest and hardiest of the Spruces. P. Engelmannii is native from British Columbia to New Mexico. Its variety argentea has silver-gray leaves, variety glauca steel-blue leaves, and variety Fendleri drooping branches.

The Blue Spruces. P. pungens, the Colorado Spruce, is closely related to P. Engelmannii but has more rigid spiny leaves. Some varieties have very attractive blue-green leaves and, when well grown, are among the most beautiful evergreens of the garden. Unfortunately some of the colored-leaved kinds have been planted at times in unsuitable places and have suffered in popularity as a result. Several have been given variety names, notably glauca, caerulea, argentea, and Kosteriana, all of which are very beautiful.

P. Breweriana is a western North American Spruce that is only found in southern Oregon and northern California. It is remarkable for its long, slender, drooping branchlets, which sometimes hang six or more feet from the branches.

Some Other Spruces. A very useful and interesting European Spruce is P. Omorika, the Servian Spruce. It grows well and maintains a slender pyramidal habit. The Japanese Spruces are generally useful. A few are P. bicolor, a tree 80 ft. high in Japan; P. Glehnii, a tree up to 100 ft. high in Japan; P. jezoensis and its variety hondoensis; P. Maximowiczii, a small, densely branched tree; and P. polita, the Tigertail Spruce, a small tree with very stiff, sharp-pointed leaves, the latest Spruce to break into growth in spring. There is also P. Schrenkiana, a central Asiatic tree hardy to New England.

Newer Spruces. In addition to these older kinds many others have been introduced during the present century, chiefly from China, with one from Formosa and one from Japan. Some of them give promise of becoming excellent decorative trees. Notable among them is P. asperata, a densely branched tree of variable habit, growing to a height of 100 ft. in western China and hardy in the North.

P. brachytyla is a handsome Chinese tree, 35-80 ft. high, with flattened leaves. P. Koyamai is a free-growing and handsome Spruce that was found on the mountains of central Hondo, Japan, and introduced about 1911. P. likiangensis, a free-growing kind with spine-tipped leaves, was brought from western Szechuan, China, early in the present century.

P. morrisonicola is a Formosan kind related to the Japanese P. Glehnii and probably not reliably hardy in the North.

Economic Uses. The timber of the Spruces is easily worked and much used in carpentry. That of the Sitka Spruce, P. sitchensis, is the best of all and, although light, is strong in comparison to its weight. The resonant properties of the wood cause it to be used in the manufacture of violins and other musical instruments. Burgundy Pitch is the purified resin extracted from P. Abies, and the bark of various kinds contains tannin. Spruce Beer is partly made from an essence extracted from the leaves and shoots of the European Spruce. Spruces are much used as sources of wood pulp.

PICK-A-BACK PLANT. Tolmiea Menziesii, which see.

PICKERELWEED. Pontederia, which see.

PICOTEE. This is a term used in describing those varieties of Border Carnation in which the edges of the petals are of a different color from the rest of the flower. See Carnation.

PIE PLANT. Rhubarb, which see.

PIERIS: HANDSOME SHRUBS

Good Flowering Evergreens for Acid Soils

Pieris (Pi'eris). Evergreen or deciduous shrubs which are of considerable decorative value. They are very free-flowering, some opening their flowers in spring, others in early summer. The flowers are usually white and pitcher-shaped, large numbers being produced together in dense or loose clusters according to the kind.

These shrubs are natives of China, Japan, Formosa, the Himalayas, and North America. Several kinds bear richly colored red or rose-shaded young leaves. Some are hardy, others tender, in the North. Some are very old plants in gardens, others are among the more recent introductions. Pieris belongs to the Heath family, Ericaceae, and the name is taken from Pieria, the abode of the Muses in Greek mythology. Pieris are often called Andromedas.

When to Sow Seeds. Propagation may be carried out either by seeds or by cuttings. Seeds should be sown, as soon as ripe, on the surface of sandy peat in a flat or flowerpot placed in a cold frame or cool greenhouse and kept shaded until seedlings appear. Gradually accustom the seedlings to the light and, when the young plants are large enough to handle, transplant them into a bed of peaty soil in a cold frame or in flats. They should be about 1 in. apart and be allowed to remain until the plants touch. Then move them to a nursery border. Growth is usually slow for two or three years, but they grow faster afterwards.

Taking Cuttings. Cuttings should be made of short, half-ripe shoots from July to September. They should be about 3 in. long and set in a

The hardiest Pieris (Andromeda) is P. floribunda, a native of the southeastern United States which is hardy in southern New England.

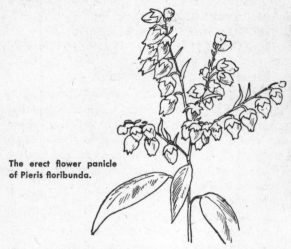

The erect flower panicle of Pieris floribunda.

Pieris japonica is a favorite evergreen shrub. Its flower panicles droop.

bed of sandy peat in a cold frame, which should be kept close, or in a greenhouse.

Flowering Shrubs for Lime-free Soil. These shrubs require a moist soil that is somewhat acid in reaction, and they succeed in sun or in a little shade. Sandy peat forms a very good rooting medium, but, where peat does not exist, do not excavate large holes and fill them with peat. Provided your soil is free from lime, dig it over, fork some leaf mold or peat into the upper 9 in. and set the plants.

Firm planting is necessary, and this is best done in early autumn or spring. As the plants root near the surface, mulching with peat moss or leaf mold is very beneficial.

The early spring-flowering kinds should be planted in a position sheltered from cold, sweep-ing winds. If possible, they should have a dark background in order that the white flowers may be seen to advantage.

No Regular Pruning Is Required. Even young plants grow into shapely specimens with little or no pruning. However, it is an advantage if the old flower heads are removed before seeds are matured. When old plants become weak and sickly, it is wise to destroy them and begin again with young stock, for old, worn-out plants do not respond very readily to treatment.

The Hardiest Kinds. The following kinds are all excellent garden shrubs: P. floribunda is a rounded, evergreen bush, 3-6 ft. high, with small, ovate leaves 1½-3 in. long and ½-1 in. wide, and short, erect, branched heads of white flowers produced in early spring. It is one of the two commonest kinds, is hardy, and is a native of the southeastern United States.

Flower cluster of Pieris taiwanensis, a lovely evergreen shrub from Formosa.

P. japonica is equally well known and widely grown. It is a native of Japan and not quite so hardy as P. floribunda. At its best it is a shapely bush, 6-10 ft. high, though often little more than 4 ft. Its evergreen leaves are larger and glossier than those of P. floribunda and in their young stages are bright coppery red. Its white flowers are borne in much larger, drooping clusters. Both plants are in flower at about the same time, but the flowers of P. japonica may be injured by late frosts and cold winds. There is a variety, variegata, in which the leaves are much smaller than those of the type, and margined with white. It is not a particularly handsome plant.

Suitable for Mild Regions Only. P. formosa is a Himalayan shrub or small tree, exceedingly handsome when at its best, but rather tender and, in cold districts, subject to injury by cold, or to killing in winter. In favorable climates it may grow 20 ft. high, but is often less. The broadly lance-shaped, evergreen leaves are 5 or 6 in. long and 1¼ in. wide, leathery in texture, and dark, glossy green. In a young state they are of a brilliant rose or red shade. The white flowers are borne in very large, drooping panicles in May. It is an excellent shrub for milder parts of the country.

The variety Forrestii, from China, grows freely and will eventually form a large bush. The evergreen leaves are variable in shape and size, and the white flowers, which are sometimes flushed with pink at the base, are borne in large clusters in May. In some respects it suggests affinity with P. japonica, but the leaves are smaller. The leaves are brightly colored when developing.

P. taiwanensis is a very beautiful evergreen kind introduced from Formosa in 1918. It grows into a large bush bearing thick, leathery, dark green leaves up to 4 in. long and 1 in. wide, and large inflorescences of white flowers from the ends of the shoots in May. It seems to be rather tender, and there can be little doubt but that the best results can only be looked for in gardens in the mild parts of North America. For such gardens, however, it is an excellent shrub. It is said to grow 8-10 ft. high in its native country, where it is found at an altitude of 8,500-11,000 ft. The young leaves are very highly colored.

PIGEONBERRY. See Duranta.

PIGEON PEA. See Cajanus Cajan.

PIGGYBACK PLANT. Tolmiea Menziesii, which see.

PIGNUT. Carya glabra, which see.

PILEA (Pi'lea). Tender, evergreen, ornamental foliage plants from tropical America, Jamaica, China, and Indo-China. They belong to the Nettle family, Urticaceae. The name is derived from *pileus,* a Roman cap, and refers to the caplike covering of the seeds. Although there are numerous kinds of Pilea, few are in general cultivation.

Excellent Window Plants. When grown in pots, Pileas make excellent window plants, provided the atmosphere is not excessively dry. The pots are half-filled with crocks and these are covered with the rough siftings from the compost.

The Artillery Plant, P. microphylla (muscosa), grows 4-8 in. in height and forms a mass of fernlike foliage. The tiny, ovate leaves, which are light green, are arranged on gracefully arching, tapering sprays. The reddish flowers are very minute and inconspicuous and are produced abundantly in summer.

The common name, Artillery Plant, refers to the fact that the unexpanded flower buds, when moistened, forcibly discharge their pollen in a visible dustlike cloud.

P. microphylla is often grown as an edging for benches in greenhouses and conservatories

Pilea Cadierei, the Watermelon Pilea.

The Panamiga or Pilea involucrata was introduced from South America some years ago by a florist in New Rochelle, New York. Its deeply veined leaves form a handsome pattern and so do its lacy flowers when they are fully out. Here they are shown in the bud stage. This is a fine plant for terrariums.

and as a window plant. It thrives in terrariums. Its cultivation presents no difficulties. If the bench is covered with cinders or gravel, all that is necessary is to break off small portions of the branches and plant them in the cinders or gravel. By damping the cinders or gravel twice a day with a fine spray, roots will quickly be induced to form and in a few months a compact, continuous growth of greenery will result.

Throughout the year the plant can be kept growing vigorously by nothing more than this daily damping of the ashes or gravel. No soil is required. If desired, it can be clipped with scissors into a symmetrical Box-edge-like form. After a few years, when the growth becomes

The Artillery Plant, Pilea microphylla.

ragged, the plants should be pulled up and fresh young tips of shoots laid down to form a new edging.

Cultivation in Pots and Baskets. If desired, the Artillery Plant can be grown in pots or hanging baskets. If in a hanging basket, the latter is first lined with moss and then filled with light, sandy compost. Sufficient tips of shoots are first rooted in sand and are then inserted in the top of the basket and all around the sides, 1 in. or 2 in. apart. The soil is moistened and the basket hung in the shade until the plants are established. Then the basket is suspended in a light position and the soil is kept moist.

Eventually the basket becomes a mass of delicate feathery foliage. The tips of the shoots should be pinched out when they are 2 in. in length to keep the plants compact and bushy.

The Watermelon Pilea, P. Cadierei, sometimes called the Aluminum Plant, was introduced to the United States from Europe in 1952. It is a native of Indo-China, where it was discovered in 1928. It grows a foot or 18 in. tall and has ovate, green leaves handsomely marked with silver on the upper surface. It is easily propagated by cuttings, grows well in any well-drained, fertile soil, and flourishes as a window garden plant. This kind bears attractive clusters of white flowers, each cluster carried on a long stalk, in late summer.

The Panamiga, P. involucrata, is popular as a window garden plant and very useful for growing in terrariums. It is a native of South America. This kind grows to a height of a few inches only and branches freely. Its stems are thick and succulent, and its leaves are 1½-2 in. long, somewhat less in width, and short stalked. They are in opposite pairs and have deeply indented veins that provide pleasing leaf surface patterns. The upper sides of the leaves are rich greenish brown, beneath they are purplish. The tiny pinkish cream-colored flowers are in sprays that lie flat on the top sides of the upper leaves. The Panamiga is a charming low foliage plant.

Creeping Charlie, P. nummulariaefolia, is a native of the West Indies that forms a tight, ground-hugging mass of nearly circular, light green leaves. It thrives best in moist soil in shade. This kind is a good low ground cover for use in greenhouses and conservatories and also thrives splendidly and forms a handsome specimen when grown in a hanging basket. If it receives too much sunshine its foliage turns yellowish.

PILLBUG. See Pests and Diseases.

PILOCEREUS. An obsolete name of several Cacti now classified as Cephalocereus.

PIMELEA—*Rice Flower* (Pimel'ea). Tender flowering shrubs from Australia which belong to the family Thymelaeaceae. These dainty little shrubs are very free-flowering and useful for ornamenting the greenhouse or conservatory in early summer and for planting outdoors in mild climates. They are slow-growing and take several years to reach their maximum height of 3-4 ft. Their slender, wiry branches are clothed with small, ovate, smooth, evergreen leaves and are terminated by large clusters of small, four-petaled, white, pink or red flowers in May and June. The name Pimelea is derived from *pimele*, fat, and refers to the oily seeds.

Free-flowering Shrubs for the Greenhouse. When grown indoors, they require a minimum winter temperature of 45 degrees. The best compost consists of four parts of peat to one

Pimelea, an attractive shrub for a cool greenhouse.

part of sand. Repotting is done when the plants have finished flowering. The shoots are first pruned back to one third of their length and are then placed in a warm corner of the greenhouse. They are syringed several times a day to encourage new shoots to form. When these are ¼ in. in length, the plants are taken out of the pots, and the crocks removed from the roots without seriously disturbing the ball of soil, but a few of the main roots are loosened so that they may more readily enter the new compost.

Repotting the Plants. The new pots should be one size larger than the old ones and well drained with crocks; over these a layer of coarse leaves is laid, to prevent the soil from washing into and clogging the drainage. The new soil must be packed firmly, as this ensures the production of short-jointed, free-flowering shoots.

After potting, the plants must be shaded from bright sunlight. The soil is not watered until it becomes moderately dry, and this system of watering is continued until the roots have freely entered the new soil. It is then kept moist during the remainder of the summer.

Autumn and Winter Management. Less water is needed as autumn approaches, and during the winter the soil is moistened only when it becomes moderately dry. During the winter, great care must be taken in watering, for if the soil becomes dust-dry the leaves will fall; a waterlogged condition is equally injurious.

Except for a few weeks after the plants have been repotted (when they are kept in a moist atmosphere and shaded from the hottest rays of the sun), they must be exposed to full sunlight, especially at the end of the summer when the shoots are ripening and the flower buds are forming. Ventilation should be free in suitable weather throughout the year.

Propagation. Cuttings of side shoots, 2 in. in length, are taken off with a "heel" in spring. The leaves from the lower half of the stems are removed and the "heel" is pared smooth. The cuttings are then inserted in a firmly packed bed of a mixture of peat moss and sand under a bell jar or in a propagating case in a greenhouse where a temperature of 55-60 degrees at night is maintained.

Each morning the bell jar is removed, and the moisture wiped from the inside. This treatment is continued until roots are formed, when the plants are potted separately in 2-in. pots and subsequently in larger pots.

The tips of the main shoots should be pinched out when they are 3 in. high, and the side branches are similarly treated; afterwards an annual pruning after flowering is sufficient.

The Chief Kinds. P. ferruginea (P. decussata), 3 ft., rose; P. spectabilis, 4 ft., pink and white; P. rosea, 2 ft., pink; P. ligustrina, 5 ft., white; P. hispida, 2 ft., pink; and P. sylvestris, 2 ft., pink.

PIMENTA—*Wild Clove, Allspice* (Pimen'ta). Tropical evergreen flowering trees with aromatic foliage. They grow up to 40 ft. in height, have large, leathery lanceolate (lance-shaped) leaves, which are on long stalks and are dotted with black beneath. The flowers, which resemble those of the Myrtle, to which Pimenta is closely related, are small, white, with four or five petals and many stamens, and are produced in loose clusters in the axils of the leaves. These plants are natives of tropical America and belong to the Myrtle family, Myrtaceae.

The two principal kinds are P. acris and P. officinalis. These are grown for their economic properties. The fruits of P. officinalis (Allspice) are aromatic and are used as spice; they are also used in medicine as a stimulant, and Oil of Pimento is made from the fruits. From the leaves of P. acris (Wild Clove) an oil is obtained which is used in the manufacture of Bay Rum, a preparation extensively employed as a hair tonic. The name Pimenta is derived from the Spanish name *pimento*, allspice. The flavor of the fruits was supposed to resemble that of the nutmeg, clove and cinnamon.

Cultivation. These trees are adapted for outdoor cultivation in warm, frost-free climates only. In temperate climates they are sometimes grown in collections of economic plants in botanical gardens. When cultivated indoors, the plants require a minimum winter temperature of 55 degrees and a compost of two parts of loam, one part of leaf mold, and a sprinkling of sand. They are grown in large pots or tubs, or planted in a prepared bed, and the shoots are trained to wires or a trellis.

After potting or planting, no water is given until the soil becomes fairly dry, and then it is well moistened. This system of watering is followed until the plants are well established and during the remainder of the summer the soil is kept moist. Throughout the winter it is only moistened when it becomes quite dry. Pruning consists of shortening straggling shoots in March.

Propagation Is by Cuttings. Well-ripened shoots 6 in. in length are taken off in late summer. They are rooted in pots of sandy soil and covered with a bell jar.

PIMENTO BUSH. Pimenta officinalis. See Pimenta.

PIMPERNEL. Anagallis, which see.

PIMPERNEL, BOG, Anagallis tenella. See Anagallis.

PIMPINELLA—*Aniseed* (Pimpinel'la). A large group of hardy perennial and annual plants, of little horticultural value. They are found wild in the Himalayas, China, Africa and Europe. From P. Anisum, a native of Greece, Aniseed is obtained. An oil is extracted from the seeds, which is used in the manufacture of medicines and for flavoring.

PINANGA (Pinan'ga). Tropical ornamental foliage plants, which belong to the Palm family, Palmaceae, and are found wild in Malaya. These Palms grow up to 30 ft. in height, have bamboo-like stems and terminal tufts of pinnate (feathery) leaves. The bases of the leaves sheath the stems, and the clusters of inconspicuous flowers are produced from the nodes below the leaves. Young plants are very ornamental in small pots but fully grown specimens are only suitable for lofty conservatories or for growing outdoors in southern Florida and other frost-free, warm climates. Pinanga is the old Malayan name.

Summer and Winter Treatment. When grown in greenhouses, the plants require a minimum winter temperature of 55 degrees. The best soil compost consists of two parts of peat and one part of turfy loam with sand freely added. Plants growing in small pots are repotted annually in March. The pots are well drained with crocks and these are covered with a layer of rough siftings from the compost. When potting, the soil is made firm with the potting stick.

The soil is not watered until it becomes

moderately dry and then it is thoroughly moistened. The atmosphere is kept moist by damping the floor and benches between the pots, and the foliage is syringed two or three times daily.

When the plants are well rooted, the soil is kept moist throughout the summer, but in winter it is watered only when it becomes fairly dry. Less atmospheric moisture is also needed in winter but the air must not be allowed to remain dry for long, as red spider mites and thrips will infest the foliage.

When these Palms are fully grown, they are planted in large tubs, in which they are kept in a healthy state by top-dressing with fresh compost in spring.

Propagation is by Seeds. These are prepared by chipping a tiny piece out of the side of the outer hard coat or by filing a nick through it; then they are soaked in tepid water for several days. They are sown in deep, well-drained pans or pots of finely sifted porous soil at a depth of 1 in. and spaced 2 in. apart. After sowing, the soil is soaked with a fine spray of water and the seed pot or pan is plunged in a propagating case with a bottom heat of 75-80 degrees.

The seeds are slow in germinating, but when the first leaf is 1 in. in length the seedlings are potted separately in 3-in. pots, and subsequently in larger ones.

The chief kinds are P. disticha, P. Kuhlii, P. lepida, P. maculata and P. Sanderiana.

PINCHING. A term used by gardeners to describe the removal of the growing tip of a shoot to ensure the development of side shoots. Sometimes the terms "pinching back," "pinching out" are used with the same meaning.

The term "pinching out" is also used to

Pinching a Chrysanthemum plant to induce it to grow bushy.

Pinching out unwanted side shoots of Dahlias.

describe the complete removal of small side shoots, as is done when Tomatoes are trained with single stems and when the stems of Chrysanthemums, Fuchsias and other plants are trained to form the "trunks" of standard (treeform) specimens.

PINCUSHION FLOWER. See Scabiosa.

PINCUSHION PLANT. See Pterocephalus.

PINE. The common name, used with various prefixes, for the different kinds of Pinus. Thus the Scots Pine is Pinus sylvestris; the Cluster Pine is Pinus Pinaster; the Swiss Mountain Pine is P. Mugo (P. montana).

PINEAPPLE. The cultivation of the Pineapple (Ananas comosus) is practicable outdoors in the United States only in southern Florida. Elsewhere, however, it may be grown in tropical greenhouses as an object of interest.

When grown in a greenhouse, the Pineapple thrives best in loamy soil in large pots. The minimum temperature in winter should be 65 degrees; during the summer months hot, moist conditions are required; the temperature may then rise to 80 degrees or higher.

The plants are propagated in spring by detaching suckers or side shoots and placing them in 5-in. pots filled with sandy, loamy soil. When well rooted, they are repotted in large pots. The leafy top of a Pineapple fruit will form roots if set in a pot of sandy soil and kept in a warm propagating case or under a bell jar.

During the summer months Pineapple plants require an abundance of water; during the winter months the soil should be watered only when it is moderately dry.

Outdoor Culture. In southern Florida Pineapples are grown on porous, well-drained soils that are generously fertilized. They are planted in the open or under slat shades. Planting is done in August or September. Fruits are harvested the second year after planting.

PINEAPPLE FLOWER. Eucomis, which see.

Pineapples thrive outdoors in moist tropical climates.

PINEAPPLE, GUAVA. See Feijoa.

PINE, AUSTRALIAN. Casuarina, which see.

PINE, CELERY-TOPPED. See Phyllocladus.

PINE, CYPRESS. See Callitris.

PINE, DAMMAR. Agathis, which see.

PINE, GROUND. Lycopodium obscurum, which see.

PINE, NORFOLK ISLAND. See Araucaria excelsa.

PINE, RUNNING. Lycopodium clavatum, which see.

PINE, SCREW. See Pandanus.

PINETUM. A term used for an area of ground set apart for the cultivation of the different kinds of Conifers.

PINE, UMBRELLA. Sciadopitys verticillata, which see.

PINGUICULA—*Butterwort* (Pinguic'ula). An interesting group of hardy and tender perennials belonging to the family Lentibulariaceae; they are natives of the Northern Hemisphere and the Andes of America and extend to the Antarctic regions. The name Pinguicula is from *pinguis*, fat, and alludes to the greasy texture of the plants.

For the Bog Garden. All are bog plants, requiring constantly damp conditions. They may be propagated from seeds sown in spring in a cold frame or cool greenhouse in pots filled with leafmold, sand, and a large proportion of chopped sphagnum moss.

Propagation. Another method of propagation is by offsets. At the end of the summer the leaves disappear and the plant resolves itself into a fleshy tuber or bulb; at the base of this will be found a number of much smaller bulbs which may be detached and grown separately.

The plants have a curious greasy or buttery surface on leaf and stem—hence the popular name Butterwort. Small insects stick to the leaves, as to flypapers, and die. The products that result from the decay of their bodies are possibly absorbed by the plant. The flowers are extremely pretty, being carried singly upon erect stems. They resemble little Gloxinia flowers, but are spurred.

The Alpine Butterwort. Pinguicula alpina, which is common in damp places throughout the Alps, grows 2-3 in. tall, and has pretty white

The Common Butterwort, Pinguicula vulgaris.

flowers with yellow throats. There is a pale yellow-flowered form, lusitanica. P. flavescens is akin to these, but has deeper yellow flowers and is from the eastern Alps.

The Best Kind. Pinguicula grandiflora is the best of the hardy kinds, and is a very beautiful plant indeed. It grows wild on the west coast of Ireland, and also in the western Pyrenees. It is 6-9 in. high, with very large violet-colored flowers in May and June.

P. grandiflora is well worth growing in the rock garden, where it needs rich loamy soil and constant moisture. It does well in the alpine house (which see).

The Common Butterwort. Pinguicula vulgaris, which is native to North America, Europe and Asia, is an extremely pretty plant, and well worth a place in the rock garden. It grows 3-4 in. tall, and has violet-colored flowers. P. elatior, with flowers purple to white, and P. lutea, with yellow flowers, are natives of the southeastern United States and are worth growing where they are hardy. Both are about a foot tall.

Pinguicula Bakeriana (caudata), from Mexico, is a very beautiful greenhouse plant, growing 6-9 in. tall, with large, deep pink flowers. It does best in pots of peat and sphagnum moss and is often grown in an orchid house.

There are several other kinds of Pinguicula, but few if any of them are in cultivation. (See also Insectivorous Plants.) Pinguiculas are sometimes known as Bog Violets.

PINGUIN. Bromelia Pinguin, which see.

PINK. Pinks are handsome, fragrant garden flowers that are much more popular in Great Britain and in some other parts of Europe than they are in America. They are types and varieties of Dianthus that have descended chiefly from D. plumarius, which has given rise to various free-flowering, single and double kinds. It should be noted that the word Pink in combination with other words is the common name of a number of distinct kinds of plants—thus we have the Swamp Pink, Helonias; the Fire Pink, Silene; the Moss Pink, Phlox; and the Sea Pink, Armeria. These and others are all distinct from the true Pinks. See also Dianthus.

Garden Pinks. A Pink is not a miniature Carnation although it bears a superficial resemblance to one. Lightness and daintiness of flowers is appropriate to a Pink, and great size is not desirable except in single-flowered varieties if size does not give an impression of heaviness. The Pink is essentially a garden plant. It should preferably not exceed 18 in. in height and should be compact and cushion-like. Foliage should be firm and glaucous (covered with a waxy, blue-green coating). The stem should be strong and proportionate in length and thickness to the size

of the flower which it is intended to support.

Show Pinks. Some varieties have a tendency to burst their calyces, while the Allwoodii, Show and Herbertii types have non-splitting calyces, and these are naturally preferred by exhibitors and, indeed, by most Pink lovers. The old split calyx varieties, however, of which Mrs. Sinkins, Sam Barlow, and Earl of Essex are popular examples, are excellent for edging beds and borders, giving an immense quantity of blooms when established.

A Pink without scent is not considered an asset, and a scentless variety will appeal only if it has other attributes of outstanding value.

Show Pinks should have round and symmetrical flowers. The outer or guard petals of a double and all the petals of a single should be flat, at right angles to the calyx. Petals should be firm without being clumsy, flat, and regular in shape. The edges should be either (a) perfectly smooth, or (b) regularly and evenly serrated (saw-toothed). Serrations should be distinct and clear, and should be flat in the plane of the petal.

In double flowers the inner petals should lie regularly and smoothly over the guard petals, diminishing in size as they near the center of the flower. Generally they should form a flat rosette,

A vase of Allwoodii Pinks. They come in a wide range of colors.

but where the petals are very numerous the center of the flower may be raised and the center petals stand up somewhat. Single-flowered varieties should have five evenly shaped petals, which should overlap sufficiently to prevent any space from appearing between them.

Sections of Pinks. Pinks are divided into sections, or groups, according to their coloring.

Selfs, as the word implies, are of one distinct, even color, with no marks of any other color, except possibly a very light shading at the center of the flower.

Bicolors should have two colors in concentric rings, the inner one of which may be either small or large. The boundary between the two colors should be distinct and clear and it is desirable for the two colors to contrast with each other. A bicolor with a sharply defined, very dark eye on a white ground is known as a "black and white" Pink.

Laced Pinks are most attractive. There are two kinds: (a) white ground and (b) other than white ground. Double flowers and smoothly laid petals are essential in this class. The lacing color should form a well marked eye in the center of the flower, from which a narrow, even band of color should extend around the petal, leaving a clear patch of the ground color in the center of the petal. Those flowers in which the band of ground color is equal in width to the lacing color are considered very desirable.

Fancies include all those pinks which are not Selfs, Bicolors, or Laced—for example, those which are speckled or have radial strips, or have some petals of one color and others of a different color.

Fringed Laced Pinks. Show Pinks popular a hundred or so years ago were of the type known as Fringed Laced Pinks. They were similar to modern Laced Pinks, except that the edge of the petal was fringed with fine indentations.

Cultivation. Pinks love a sunny position, and the most suitable soil for them is a deep, crumbly loam, but they are very accommodating and it is surprising how well the garden varieties thrive on a wide variety of soils.

Both overlight and overheavy soils are improved by well-decayed farmyard manure, compost or other well-decayed humus-forming material. Ground limestone at the rate of 8 ounces to the square yard for light soils, hoed in after the ground has been spaded, is beneficial. For heavy soils hydrated lime at 4 ounces to the square yard is best. It is well to wait for three or four weeks and for rain before planting Pinks in soil so treated. Wood ashes are good for light soils, and heavy soils are improved by digging in sand, sifted, gritty coal cinders or old limestone rubble. Make sure the soil is not acid, but do not overdo the liming. Pinks, although lime lovers, do best when only a moderate amount is present.

Pinks will not thrive in a waterlogged soil, and to make sure there is adequate drainage it may be advisable to raise the beds 4-6 in. above path level.

Planting. A good time for planting in well-drained soils is early fall. Spring planting is advised for heavy soils. Excellent blooms may be had from spring planting. Do not plant too deeply. Set the plants 9-12 in. apart.

Propagation. The propagation of Pinks is by pipings (cuttings) and by layering, which process is similar to that of layering Border Carnations (see Carnations).

Cuttings should be taken from mid-May to mid-July. Take them from strong, healthy plants, choosing medium-sized, vigorous shoots with three or four pairs of fully developed leaves. Do not select shoots which are beginning to go into bloom. Pull off, with a downward pull, the bottom pair of leaves on each cutting, then cut through with a sharp knife immediately below the joint. Insert the cuttings in a well-packed bed of sand in a cold frame. After the cuttings have been inserted, they should be given a light watering to settle them in the sand. The frame should be in a cool and somewhat shady situation and should be kept close until rooting has taken place.

Raising Seedlings. Seed can be sown in flats or pots containing well-drained sandy soil in a cold frame or cool greenhouse from mid-March to mid-April. When they have made their first pair of true leaves, the seedlings should be transplanted to other flats or to a bed of soil in a cold frame, a distance of 2-3 in. being allowed between them. When the young plants begin to crowd each other, they are transplanted to the open garden in nursery rows; the rows should be 12-18 in. apart, with a distance of 8-9 in. allowed between the plants in the rows. The nursery bed should be spaded, fertilized and limed before the young plants are set out. Seedling Pinks bloom freely in their second season.

Dianthus Allwoodii. A wonderful race of modern Pinks, continuous-flowering, with silvery foliage that remains attractive throughout the winter, is known as Dianthus Allwoodii. There are over fifty highly selected varieties grown in Europe but few are available in the United States or Canada.

Chinese Pinks, or Indian Pinks, as they are often called, are descended from Dianthus chinensis. They are very showy plants which bear large, fringed flowers of various bright colors in the summer months and are often used for planting in summer flower beds. They are treated as annuals or biennials and are raised fresh from seeds each year. The seeds are sown in a cold frame in June to provide plants that will bloom the following year, or in a greenhouse in February to bloom the same year.

These plants reach a height of 9-12 in. and bloom freely from early summer until autumn. A packet of mixed seeds will provide plants bearing richly colored flowers in variety.

Japanese Pinks, varieties of D. chinensis Heddewigii, grow 8-9 in. high and bear a profusion of large fringed flowers of varied coloring from July until autumn. They are usually treated as annuals and raised from seeds sown in a greenhouse in January or early February—minimum temperature 50-55 degrees. The seedlings are set 3 in. apart in flats of loam, leaf mold and sand, hardened off in a cold frame and planted out of doors when it is assured that the danger of frost is past.

PINK, CUSHION. Silene acaulis, which see.

PINK, FIRE. Silene virginica, which see.

PINK, GROUND. Phlox subulata and Gilia dianthoides, which see.

PINK, MOSS. Phlox subulata, which see.

PINK, MULLEIN. Lychnis coronaria, which see.

PINK, SEA. Armeria, which see.

PINK, SWAMP. Helonias bullata, which see.

PINK, WILD. Silene carolinianum, which see.

PINNATE. A botanical term applied to compound leaves (those composed of a number of distinct leaflets) when the leaflets are arranged in two rows on either side of a common axis (rachis or stalk). The leaves of the Ash, Rose and Wisteria are examples of pinnate leaves. The term is also used to describe the arrangement of leaf veins when the side or lateral veins spread from the central vein or mid-vein and are parallel to each other. Examples of pinnate-veined leaves are those of Beech, Elm and Oak. Pinnate actually means feather-like, but the possession of pinnate leaves or of pinnately veined leaves does not necessarily give a feathery appearance to plants possessing them.

PINNATIFID. A botanical term used to describe leaves in which the indentations between the lobes do not reach to the midrib or vein; the lobes occur in two rows on either side of the midrib, much like the leaflets of a pinnate leaf.

PIN OAK. Quercus palustris, which see.

PINUS or PINE
A Wide Variety of Beautiful Evergreen Trees

Pinus (Pi'nus). Evergreen trees and shrubs of decorative and commercial importance, widely distributed through the Northern Hemisphere, some being found in Europe, Asia, North and Central America, northern Africa, the Canary Islands and the Philippine Islands. Most grow wild in temperate and cold temperate climates; a few are warm temperate or subtropical trees.

Those growing in the warmer countries are usually mountain trees, although in the southeastern United States they occupy considerable areas of ground at little if any elevation above sea level. The Pines give their name to the family Pinaceae.

Pinus is the classical Latin name for the Pine tree, and was probably used by the ancients on

Loblolly Pine, Pinus Taeda, is a native of the southeastern United States. It has very attractive, bright green foliage.

account of the resinous properties of the tree.

Pines Have Two Types of Leaves. As is the case with many other genera of the Coniferae, there is a good deal of difference between the juvenile and mature leaves. On seedling trees and trees a year or two old, the leaves are soft, produced singly, and surround the shoot; very soon, however, the mature or adult type of leaf appears. This type is longer and stiffer, sometimes rigid and sharp-pointed. The leaves vary a good deal in length on different kinds and are usually arranged in twos, threes or fives; only in rare cases are other numbers found.

How Different Kinds Are Distinguished. Each cluster of leaves is bound at the base by a sheath. This sheath varies in length in different kinds, and in some kinds it falls very soon after the leaves are developed; in others it lasts until they fall, which may be at the end of two, three, four or five years. The number of leaves produced together, the length of the sheath, and the time it lasts, are all characteristics that are taken into consideration in the identification of the different kinds. There is also another type of leaf that may pass unnoticed. These leaves are small

scalelike bodies, dull in color, and they fall early.

Flowers of the Pines. The terminal buds of mature shoots also provide distinguishing characteristics, the shape, length and the closeness of the covering scales all being points that are given consideration. Male and female flowers are found on the same tree in spring or early summer, usually May or June. The male flowers are usually produced in cylindrical cones or catkins about the base of the young shoots. They are usually yellow or reddish in color, and produce large quantities of pollen.

The female flowers are generally reddish, sometimes pale pink or other colors, and they appear as tiny cones, usually from the ends of young shoots, but sometimes below the ends. Pollen is conveyed by wind to the female flowers, but actual fertilization is a long process, and is not completed until the following year. In most kinds the seeds ripen the second season after the flowers, but in a few instances another year is required.

The Cones Vary in Size, Shape and Hardness. Those of Pines in which the leaves are in groups of five have softer scales than the two- and three-

[9—2]
White Pine
(Pinus Strobus)

[9—2a]
Scots Pine
(Pinus sylvestris)

[9—2b]
Austrian Pine
(Pinus nigra)

[9—2c]
Swiss Mountain Pine
(Pinus Mugo Mughus)

[9—3]
Polygonum sachalinense

[9—3a]
Espaliered Peach trees in greenhouses at Longwood Gardens, Kennett Square, Pa.

A branch of the Japanese White Pine, Pinus parviflora, bearing a cone.

leaved kinds, and in most of them the scales open and the seeds are shed soon after they ripen. The cones of the two- and three-leaved kinds are often quite woody. The scales are sometimes armed with stiff prickles and remain closed longer than the cones of the five-leaved kinds; in fact, there are some, such as Pinus muricata, P. radiata and P. attenuata, in which the cones remain tightly sealed for many years; the seeds remain sound throughout that time.

When seed is to be extracted from the cones of Pines it is not unusual to submit them to heat. This causes the resin which holds the scales together to soften and the scales open out.

Raising Pine Trees from Seeds. All the species of Pine must be increased by means of seeds, but varieties that do not come true from seeds are grafted on stocks of their respective types. Grafting, however, should be avoided whenever possible, for grafted plants are less satisfactory than seedlings. Seeds of the hardier and commoner kinds are best sown in a bed of well-drained soil out of doors in April or early May, the object being so to direct the sowing that all danger of late spring frosts shall have passed by the time the seedlings appear. From the time of sowing, germination may take place in from two to five weeks, according to the prevailing conditions. The ground chosen for the seedbed should have been thoroughly well cleaned of weeds the previous season.

The seeds should be sown thinly, either broadcast or in drills, and covered by a quarter of an inch of light soil or sand, the seeds having previously been rolled in red lead as a protection against vermin. Not on any account should the

A cold frame containing seedlings of Pinus Thunbergii.

seedbed be made on ground subject to flood-ing, even for a short period, for standing water or waterlogged ground is fatal to the seedlings.

Seeds may also be sown in pots or flats in a greenhouse or cold frame in light, loamy soil containing peat moss or leaf mold and sand; they may be sown as early as February. As soon as the seedlings are large enough to handle, they should be placed singly in small pots and transferred to a nursery bed in May. Named varieties should be grafted under glass in late winter or spring on stocks previously established in pots.

Trees for Dry Land. Most Pines give best re-sults when planted on dry or well-drained land; it is a waste of time planting them where the ground is waterlogged or sour. There are some kinds that succeed in wet ground but these are not of great garden importance. They do not require rich soil, although they grow well in good loam, and are often seen luxuriating on sand and sandy peat. Some can be grown at considerable elevations and they also succeed at sea level. A few kinds only are suitable for alka-line soils.

Planting. Pines for forest planting should be set in their permanent places while quite small, say about 9-12 in. high. Larger specimens can be transplanted in gardens for other ornamental purposes but it is not wise to attempt to move trees more than 3-4 ft. tall, unless they have been grown in a nursery where they have been transplanted every 2-3 years or unless they are carefully root-pruned a year before they are moved. Pines tend to form long, straggly roots. It is not always easy to dig them up with a good soil ball about roots, yet this is important to the successful transplanting of all except very small specimens.

Planting time is early fall or in spring, just be-fore new growth begins. Trees for forest plant-ing are often set in very small holes or in notch-es cut in the ground.

More trouble is taken with those that are to be grown as ornamental specimen trees. Holes should be dug for them, 1½-2 ft. deep and at least 1 ft. wider all around than the size of the root ball. When the holes are dug, the topsoil is kept aside and separate from the subsoil. After the transplanted tree is set in position in the

A shapely, nursery-grown specimen of Pinus nigra dug with a good ball of soil which has been wrapped in burlap and laced tightly with rope, in readiness for transporting to its planting site.

hole, this soil is used for packing around the roots. If the location is an exposed one, plant with the heads of the trees leaning a little into the wind. If there is any danger of wind loosen-ing the trees at the collar (the point where the trunk joins the mass of roots at about ground level) before they have become well rooted, they should be staked or supported by guy wires.

Pruning Pine Trees. Trees grown under forest conditions need little pruning. Ornamental trees require more and very careful pruning, for there is a general tendency for them to produce large branches low down on the stem; if these are not removed, they will take the food material that should have gone to build up the trunk.

The gardener must make up his mind early whether he wishes to produce bushy trees branched to the ground line, or whether he de-sires the trees to appear with a definite length of trunk clear of branches, and he must act accord-ingly. If he does not wish for a clear trunk there is no need for regular pruning. If, however, he wishes to clear a space of trunk, he must begin by removing the lower branches while the trees are very young. He must also watch for any branch that appears to be more vigorous than its neighbors and cut it back to check excessive growth.

When removing the branches from vigorous young Pines, do not cut them quite back to the bark of the trunk but to a slight swelling that appears about the base of the branch; if that swollen part is left, the wound will be covered with new wood more quickly than if the cut is made close to the trunk; this is one of the few cases where the close cut is not the best.

The gardener must also be on the lookout for rival leaders and remove them when necessary. Any such pruning may be done during summer, autumn or winter. The appearance of older trees can be improved by removing dead and poor branches.

Usually Two-leaved Pines

The Scots Pine. An important tree in the group with two leaves in a sheath is the Scots Pine, Pinus sylvestris, a tree common in central and northern Europe and in Siberia, and a na-

A fastigiate Scotch Pine, Pinus sylvestris variety fastigiata, is thoroughly hardy and grows easily.

tive tree in Scotland. It is one of the hardiest of the Pines and forms a picturesque tree at maturity. In eastern North America it does not grow so large as in its native range, and it is likely to be comparatively short-lived, a life of some forty years being about average.

A number of well-marked types are known, which have developed peculiar characteristics according to the conditions to which they have been exposed for many centuries. The old Scottish forest form has bright orange bark and rather short branches. This is one of the best types.

The Golden-leaved Scots Pine. A number of fancy forms have been given variety names, such as aurea, with golden leaves; nana, of dwarf compact habit; fastigiata, with stiff erect branches and narrow habit of growth; globosa, of dense, low, rounded appearance; Watereri, with silver variegated leaves, and so on. Then there are the types found in various well-defined regions, such as scotica, the type from the old Scottish forests; engadinensis, from the Engadine; nevadensis, from southern Spain, and so on.

The Corsican and Austrian Pines. P. nigra (P. Laricio) includes the Corsican and Austrian Pines, trees that take the place of P. sylvestris in

The bright orange-colored bark on the upper trunk and branches is an attractive feature of the Scottish form of Pinus sylvestris, the Scots Pine.

The Austrian Pine, Pinus nigra, is one of the best kinds for adverse conditions. It forms an excellent windbreak and thrives near the sea and on alkaline as well as acid soils.

ous growth, with longer and darker green leaves than the Scots Pine. They produce timber of very good quality.

Although these Pines grow more rapidly than the Scots Pine, their timber matures more slowly, heartwood taking a long while to form. They give good results when planted in sandy places near the sea.

A Splendid Shelter Tree. The Austrian Pine, Pinus nigra, is a much coarser tree than the Corsican Pine, P. nigra Poiretiana (calabrica), but it is in demand for shelter purposes. It branches low down and has very heavy foliage; it succeeds in exposed places and will grow on lime soils. Another useful sort is the Crimean Pine, P. nigra variety caramanica. There is also a distinct type in the Pyrenees, P. nigra variety cebennensis. Several other distinct types of P. nigra exist including the dwarf varieties Hornibrookiana and pygmaea.

The Cluster Pine, P. Pinaster, is a vigorous tree from the Mediterranean region, with long, dark green leaves and hard, woody cones, 3-7 in. long, sometimes produced in large clusters. It has been widely planted on the sand dunes of western France, where it is valued for its resin and also as a timber tree. This Pine is conspicuous by reason of the rough, red bark. It is not suitable for colder parts of North America and is liable to be blown about when young.

The Bishop Pine, P. muricata, a native of California, is peculiar because the cones remain

southern Europe and various parts of the Mediterranean region and that have proved valuable evergreens for planting in North America. They are hardy and are perhaps the most satisfactory Pines for city conditions. These are of vigor-

This is a good specimen of the dwarf form of the Austrian Pine, Pinus nigra variety Hornibrookiana.

A magnificent specimen of Pinus muricata, the Bishop Pine, a native of California. Its cones remain unopened on the branches for many years.

on the branches unopened for many years, sometimes thirty to forty, and yet the seeds stay good throughout that time. It is a decorative tree.

The Aleppo Pine, P. halepensis, is a tree from the Mediterranean region, where it luxuriates on hot, sunny mountainsides, establishing itself better than most kinds of trees in places where there is light rainfall. This kind usually has its leaves in groups or bundles of twos; rarely, they are borne in bundles of threes. It is adapted for cultivation only in the milder parts of the United States.

The Mugo or Swiss Mountain Pine, P. Mugo, is a European kind that sometimes forms a tree 40 ft. tall but more often is of dwarf, bushy growth and does not exceed 10-12 ft. in height. This kind exists in several distinct varieties, one of the most popular of which is named Mughus by botanists.

Both P. Mugo and P. Mugo variety Mughus are hardy into Canada and are easy to cultivate.

The latter is especially desirable where a low-growing evergreen that will stand full sun and rather dry soil conditions is needed. It is very useful for foundation plantings because, unlike some evergreens that are often used for that purpose, it develops slowly and does not grow out of scale and obscure windows.

When raised from seeds, as these Pines commonly are, there is much difference among individual plants. Some are low and spreading, others more rounded and bushy; some have dense foliage, in others the leaves are more loosely arranged on the branches; certain individuals have rich green leaves, in others they are more yellow-green.

Because of this tendency to vary, it is well, when purchasing Pines of these types, to go personally to the nursery and pick out the particular specimens that you need for your own special site and purpose.

The Red Pine. P. resinosa, the Red Pine, is

The dwarf Swiss Mountain Pine, Pinus Mugo variety Mughus, is a low-growing, bushy kind that is excellent for landscaping use in small gardens.

sometimes known as the Norway Pine. This name has no very logical application because the tree is not a native of Europe but of North America, where it covers a natural range from Newfoundland to Manitoba and southward to Pennsylvania, Michigan, Wisconsin, and Minnesota.

The Red Pine is a fast-growing kind, much valued for its timber and as an ornamental. It is one of the hardiest of evergreens and is excellent for planting as a windbreak.

At maturity the Red Pine forms a conical tree up to 100 ft. tall. A dwarf variety named globosa, that is of rounded habit of growth, was discovered in New Hampshire in 1910.

The Japanese Black Pine, P. Thunbergii, is a very adaptable Pine that is hardy as far north as New England and southern Ontario. It is especially suitable for planting near the seashore and will live and thrive in almost pure sand. It withstands wind well and is a good shelter tree.

At maturity, under favorable conditions, the Japanese Black Pine grows to a height of 100 ft. or more. At maturity it assumes a picturesque form with a wide-spreading head of horizontal branches.

P. Thunbergii is closely related to the Austrian Pine, P. nigra. Under cultivation, however, it grows much faster than the Austrian Pine.

The Japanese Red Pine, P. densiflora, is a round-headed tree that attains an eventual height of 90 ft. It is hardy into southern Ontario and New England.

In the normal form the leaves are blue-green, but several varieties with differently colored foliage are known. These include variety alboterminata, in which the tips of the leaves are yellowish; variety aurea, in which the leaves are yellow; and variety oculus-draconis, which has each leaf marked with two yellow bands.

An especially interesting form is P. densiflora variety umbraculifera, the Japanese Umbrella Pine or Tanyosho. This tree grows slowly and does not exceed 10-12 ft. in height. It has many more or less upright branches that diverge like the supports of an umbrella and make a dense, rounded head of foliage.

The Chinese Pine, P. tabulaeformis, is not consistent in having two leaves in each bundle; frequently the leaves appear in threes. It is closely related to both the Japanese Black Pine and the Japanese Red Pine but is less hardy. In favored positions this Pine lives as far north as Boston, Massachusetts. The Chinese Pine was introduced into western cultivation in 1910 by the late E. H. (Chinese) Wilson. It is a native of northern to central and western China.

This tree attains an ultimate height of 70 ft. but under some conditions it forms a low specimen with a flat, table-like top, for which characteristic the name tabulaeformis (table-form) was applied. P. tabulaeformis variety densata has its leaves almost always in twos.

The Italian Stone Pine, Pinus Pinea, is one of the characteristic trees planted in the Mediterranean region. In North America it is hardy only in the southern states and in California. Its seeds are edible and are valued as a food.

At maturity the Italian Stone Pine is of picturesque form and carries a fine head of spreading branches towards the top of a gnarled, naked trunk. It approaches a height of 80 ft.

Other two-leaved Pines are P. contorta, the Shore Pine or Western Scrub Pine, which occurs along the coast from Alaska to California. This Pine is not much planted and is not hardy in the Northeast.

A variety of P. contorta named latifolia is the Lodgepole Pine of the Rocky Mountains and the Black Hills. The Lodgepole Pine is hardy into New England and southern Ontario.

P. Heldreichii, the Graybark Pine, is a hardy kind that is a native of the Balkan Peninsula. Its variety leucodermis is characterized by having whitish bark and twigs.

The Jack Pine, P. Banksiana, occurs naturally from Nova Scotia to Minnesota and New York. It is a scrubby kind well adapted for planting in poor, dry, sandy and gravelly soils. Despite the fact that mature specimens are often picturesque, this Pine is not generally valued as an ornamental. It is extremely useful for planting in cold regions. No other native American Pine withstands more cold.

The Table Mountain Pine or Poverty Pine, P. pungens, grows 30-60 ft. tall and inhabits naturally the region from New Jersey to eastern Tennessee to northern Georgia on mountains and rocky places. Its leaves are commonly in bundles of twos, more rarely in threes. It is seldom planted as an ornamental.

Another Pine that is not much planted but that is of some usefulness for setting in poor, rocky or sandy soils is the Scrub Pine, P. virginiana. This kind is found naturally from southern New York to Mississippi and Alabama.

Most usually not growing more than 30-40 ft. tall, the Scrub Pine sometimes attains a height of 70 ft. It is of open, straggly growth.

Usually Three-leaved Pines

The Monterey Pine. A useful tree in the group of Pines that usually have three leaves in a sheath is P. radiata, often called P. insignis, the Monterey Pine of California. In that state it is confined to a very limited area. Under cultivation, however, in other countries it has given wonderful results, particularly in New Zealand, Australia and South Africa. In those countries it has been known to grow to a height of 90-100 ft. in twenty-five years, and to form timber at a very rapid rate. It is not hardy in the colder parts of the United States. It grows rapidly and is easily recognized by its bright, grass-green leaves and woody cones, which remain on the branches unopened for many years. This Pine sometimes has its leaves in bundles of twos.

The Big-Cone Pine, P. Coulteri, is a striking tree by reason of its long (6-12-in.) leaves and its large, woody cones, which bear strong, claw-like hooks from the ends of the scales. It is a native of California but is hardy in sheltered places as far north as southern New England. The Digger Pine, P. Sabiniana, is a closely allied tree, from California, with somewhat smaller but similar cones. Both are worth planting as decorative trees.

The Western Yellow Pine, P. ponderosa, is a vigorous tree of western North America, where it has considerable commercial value. It is hardy as far north as southern New England but is generally better adapted to western than to eastern conditions. It is very variable in length of leaves and in the size of its cones. The number of leaves in each bundle is usually three but it varies from two to five.

The Lace-Bark Pine. P. Bungeana, the Lace-Bark Pine of China, is a very interesting kind that is constantly shedding small plates of bark. In China, old trees are said to have white trunks and branches. Under cultivation it grows slowly and appears to succeed best in a dry and sunny position. It is decorative by reason of its handsome, multicolored trunks and major branches, which show a patchwork pattern of reds, lavenders, greens, grays and white. It is quite hardy and should be more commonly planted.

The Mexican Stone Pine or Pinyon, P. cembroides, and its varieties constitute a group of variable small-growing Pines that are known collectively as Nut Pines because the seeds are edible. They are natives of western America. P. cembroides usually produces its leaves in threes, occasionally in pairs. P. cembroides variety edulis usually bears its leaves in pairs, occasionally in threes. In P. cembroides variety monophylla the leaves are usually borne singly, sometimes in pairs, and in P. cembroides variety Parryana the leaves are usually in fours, rarely fives, and occasional shoots appear which bear the juvenile type of leaves.

These trees usually do not exceed 20-40 ft. in height and form round-topped specimens. They are densely branched and slow growing. P.

A picturesque old Scots Pine, Pinus sylvestris.

cembroides is hardy only in mild climates but its varieties edulis and monophylla may be grown as far north as Massachusetts.

The Longleaf Pine or Southern Pine, P. palustris, is native from Virginia to Florida, Mississippi and Texas. It mostly inhabits sandy soils along the coast, and is planted sometimes for ornament in the South. It attains a maximum height of 100-120 ft. and is much valued as a source of lumber, turpentine and resin.

The Loblolly Pine, P. Taeda, is another south-ern Pine that yields excellent lumber and is used to some extent as a source of turpentine. Occurring natively from New Jersey to Florida, Texas and Arkansas, this species is hardy as far north as southern New York. It is not much planted for ornament. It grows to an ultimate height of 100 ft. or more, and specimens as tall as 170 ft. are recorded.

The Pitch Pine, P. rigida, grows natively from Maine to Ontario and Ohio to Georgia, usually on poor, rocky soils. It makes rapid growth when

A young specimen of the Longleaf Pine, Pinus palustris, a fast-growing native of the southeastern United States.

young and develops into a picturesque tree when mature. Its maximum height is 70-80 ft. This tree is useful because it can be established in dry, rocky places.

The Canary Island Pine, P. canariensis, is a handsome kind that makes rapid growth in mild climates. It is not hardy in the North but is suitable for planting in California and in the South. This picturesque, long-leaved Pine does well even in dry and rocky places.

The Chir Pine, P. Roxburghii, of the Himalayas, is often known as P. longifolia. It is hardy only in the South and in California. It is a handsome kind with long, drooping leaves of a light green color.

Other Three-leaved Kinds. The Chilghoza Pine, P. Gerardiana, is another native of the Himalayas that is hardy only in mild parts of North America.

The Mexican P. Teocote is a three-leaved Pine that attains a height of 90 ft. Little-known in cultivation, this Pine is hardy in mild regions only.

P. patula is an exceedingly graceful Pine, from Mexico, with long, light green leaves. It is not hardy in the North but may be grown in mild climates.

P. leiophylla is a native of New Mexico, Arizona and northern Mexico. It is not hardy in the North.

Closely related to P. leiophylla is P. Jeffreyi, a tree that in its native forests grows 120 ft. tall. This species is much hardier than P. leiophylla and can be grown as far north as Massachusetts. It is native from Oregon to Lower California. This long-leaved Pine is very handsome. Its foliage is blue-green.

The Pitch Pine, Pinus rigida, has horizontal branches and is picturesque when mature. It grows rapidly when young and thrives in poor soils and exposed locations.

Five-leaved Pines

The White Pine. The best-known Pine of the group having five leaves in a sheath is the White Pine, Pinus Strobus, a magnificent native tree of eastern North America which produces excellent timber. Under ideal conditions this useful and popular Pine attains a height of 150 ft. There are many varieties of the White Pine, including variety aurea, with golden leaves; variety nana, of dwarf habit; variety fastigiata, of narrow, conical growth; and variety prostrata, which has low, spreading branches.

The Western White Pine, P. monticola, of western North America, is very similar to P. Strobus but is somewhat narrower. It may grow 100-150 ft. high and live 200-500 years. It is hardy as far north as Massachusetts.

The Mexican White Pine, P. Ayacahuite, has very long cones. In its native country it attains a height of 100 ft. and it grows into a fine tree in the milder parts of the United States. In many respects it resembles the Bhutan Pine of the

The White Pine of eastern North America, Pinus Strobus, is one of the most magnificent and valuable of coniferous trees.

Himalayas, P. nepalensis (P. excelsa), differing chiefly in the fact that its shoots are downy and the lower scales of its cones are reflexed (turned outwards). This Pine is not hardy in the North.

The Himalayan White Pine or Bhutan Pine, P. nepalensis (P. excelsa), forms a fine decorative tree of rather open or loose habit of growth, with graceful, drooping foliage. Unfortunately its top is easily damaged by wind and so it should not be planted in exposed locations. In sheltered places it is hardy as far north as southern New England.

The Japanese White Pine, Pinus parviflora, is one of the most ornamental of Pines. It is a native of Japan, where it attains a maximum height of about 80 ft., but in cultivation in North America it is much lower. It is a truly lovely tree and is excellent for planting in small gardens. It is a slow-growing, hardy kind and has bluish-green leaves that are usually more or less twisted and are borne in dense clusters towards the ends of the twigs. The branches of this species spread comparatively widely. As it ages this tree assumes very picturesque forms.

The Sugar Pine. This handsome species, P. Lambertiana, in its native Oregon and California may grow 200 or more ft. high with a trunk up to 40 ft. in girth. Its branches are spreading and slightly pendulous; its foliage dark green. In the eastern United States it is hardy to central New England but grows slowly. It bears cones that are longer than those of any other Pine; they are sometimes 18 in. long.

The Limber Pine or Rocky Mountain White Pine, P. flexilis, grows natively from Alberta to Texas and westward to Oregon and California. It also occurs in Lower California. It is hardy into southern Massachusetts and is of attractive appearance. This species normally attains heights of 40-70 ft.

P. flexilis variety reflexa, which is a native of Arizona, grows to a height of 100 ft. It is probably not hardy in the North.

The Swiss Stone Pine, P. Cembra, is hardy in the North but is extremely slow growing. It forms a narrow, dense pyramid and has dark green foliage. It is symmetrical when young and usually becomes very picturesque after it attains

The Swiss Stone Pine, Pinus Cembra, at the Morris Arboretum, Philadelphia.

maturity. This Pine is a native of central Europe and Siberia. It grows to a height of 70-100 ft. or even more. Varieties of the Swiss Stone Pine are aurea, with yellowish foliage; columnaris, of narrow, column-like growth; and sibirica, which has shorter leaves and bigger cones.

The Korean Pine, P. koraiensis, an especially useful Pine for small gardens, is hardy in the North. It grows slowly and forms a tree of broad, dense, pyramidal shape, with dark green foliage. This is a native of Japan and Korea and, in its native habitat, attains a height of up to 100 ft. In cultivation in North America it is not known to grow as large.

The Hickory Pine or Bristlecone Pine, P. aristata, a native of the western United States as far north as Colorado, Utah and Nevada, is hardy in cultivation in Massachusetts. In cultivation this kind is usually a low shrub with erect branches. It is handsome.

Other Five-leaved Pines. Closely related to the Hickory Pine is another westerner, the Foxtail Pine, P. Balfouriana. This grows at considerable

A columnar form of the Swiss Stone Pine, Pinus Cembra variety columnaris, at the Morris Arboretum, Philadelphia.

elevations in California and becomes 40-90 ft. tall. It is hardy in sheltered locations as far north as Massachusetts.

A rare kind of Pine is the Torrey Pine, P. Torreyana. This Pine occurs as a native in a very restricted area in California. It thrives well by the sea and grows 40-90 ft. tall.

Uses of Pine

Pine Lumber. The wood of many kinds of Pine trees is of the utmost importance in commerce. Of the eastern American Pines greatly valued for lumber are P. echinata, Shortleaf Pine; P. Strobus, White Pine; and P. palustris, Longleaf Pine. Western American Pines much valued for the lumber they produce are P. Lambertiana,

Sugar Pine; P. monticola, Western White Pine; and P. ponderosa, Western Yellow Pine.

Abroad, the following Pines are of great importance for the wood they provide: P. sylvestris, Scotch Pine; P. nigra, Austrian Pine; P. Thunbergii, Japanese Black Pine; and P. densiflora, Japanese Red Pine.

Resin and turpentine are other important products of the Pine. Trees are tapped for this purpose in several parts of the world, the three most important areas being western France, the southeastern United States and the Himalayas. The most important resin-yielding tree in France is Pinus Pinaster; in the United States, P. palustris; and in the Himalayas, P. longifolia. Other Pines, however, yield resin in smaller quantity. The distilled resin yields turpentine and resin.

Pine Kernels. Pine seeds are widely used in a fresh and roasted state under the name of pine kernels. Large quantities of the seed of the Stone Pine, Pinus Pinea, are exported from Italy. The seeds of P. Cembra are used for food in Switzerland, and there is a big home and export business in food seeds of the same kind in Siberia. The seeds of P. Gerardiana are widely used in Afghanistan and are also exported, and seeds of various North American Pines are used for food, particularly those of P. cembroides and its varieties.

PINXTER FLOWER. See Azalea nudiflora (Rhododendron nudiflorum).

PINYON. Pinus cembroides, which see.

PIP. A name given to the seeds of Apple, Orange and other fruit trees, and to the single growth buds, with roots attached, of Lily of the Valley.

PIPER—*Pepper* (Pi'per). A large group of plants, most of which are shrubs or shrubby climbers. They grow wild in tropical America, Ceylon, Peru, Malaya, and other tropical countries and belong to the family Piperaceae. A few kinds are grown in greenhouses for their ornamental foliage, and those of economic importance are cultivated in botanical collections.

Piper is the ancient Latin name for these plants. For the Peppers of the vegetable garden, see Pepper.

The Peppers of Commerce. Those kinds which are of economic importance are grown extensively in India, Malaya, the Straits Settlements, and other countries for the seeds, which yield most of the various kinds of pepper. Black and white pepper are both obtained from P. nigrum; black pepper is made from the unripe fruits, and white pepper from the ripe fruits, after the rind has been removed. The leaves of P. Betel are chewed with the Betel Nut by the natives.

The ornamental-leaved kinds require a minimum winter temperature of 55 degrees and a soil compost of two parts of loam, one part of peat moss or leaf mold and a liberal admixture of sand.

These kinds are repotted annually in March. The shoots are lightly pruned to make the plants shapely, and the latter are syringed several times a day to encourage the development of new shoots. When these are ½ in. in length, the plants are taken out of their pots, and the crocks and the loose soil removed from the roots with a pointed stick. The new pots are drained with crocks which are covered with a layer of rough leaves; the plants are then placed in them and soil is filled in about the roots and pressed firm.

After repotting, the plants are again frequently syringed and the atmosphere is kept moist by damping the floor and benches twice a day.

Summer and Winter Treatment. The soil is not watered until it is moderately dry, and then it is

The Japanese Pepper, Piper Futokadsura, is the hardiest member of its genus. When grown in pots, it is an excellent house plant and it thrives outdoors provided it is not subjected to excessive frost.

thoroughly saturated. This system of watering is continued until the plants are well rooted, then the compost is kept moist during the remainder of the summer. During the winter months much less water is required, and the soil is then moistened only when it approaches dryness. During the summer the plants must be shaded from bright sunlight.

Propagation Is by Cuttings. Shoots 3 in. in length are removed in April. The leaves are removed from the lower half of each shoot and a cut is made below the bottom joint. The cuttings are then inserted in a bed of sand or sand and peat moss or vermiculite in a propagating case.

The case is kept close to prevent the cuttings from wilting. Once a day it is opened and the moisture wiped from the underside of the glass to prevent the cuttings from rotting. When roots are formed, the case is gradually ventilated, and after a week the cuttings are potted and are returned to the case for a week or so before being transferred to the greenhouse benches.

The Principal Kinds. P. nigrum, Pepper, is a woody climber with aerial roots and large ovate to nearly orbicular leaves; the flowers, which are small and inconspicuous, are produced in catkins and are succeeded by red berries, which become black.

P. excelsum aureum pictum has ovate leaves, 3-5 in. long, green with yellow blotches. P. porphyrophyllum, a climber, has roundish leaves, bronze-green, spotted with pink.

P. Futokadsura, Japanese Pepper, is a fine climber that resembles P. nigrum but is very much hardier. It may be expected to prove hardy outdoors in climates as mild as that of Virginia. In addition to its value for outdoor cultivation it is also an excellent house plant when grown in pots. P. Futokadsura has oval-lanceolate leaves that are 4-5 in. long and up to 3 in. wide. They are glossy green.

P. ornatum is an attractive vine with leaves marked with a network of pink or white.

A plant grown as P. magnificum is cultivated in greenhouses. It is a tropical vine with dark green leaves and conspicuously winged leaf-stalks.

PIPING. A name used by gardeners to describe

the top of a shoot of a Pink, which is pulled out and used as a cutting. It is inserted without further preparation.

PIPSISSEWA. Chimaphila, which see.

PIPTANTHUS (Piptanth'us). Leaf-losing (deciduous) or subevergreen shrubs with soft, pithy growths and three-parted leaves. The flowers are yellow and produced in short, laburnum-like clusters, but individual flowers are much larger than those of Laburnum. The few kinds are not hardy; they are best suited for growing in the South. Piptanthus belongs to the Pea family, Leguminosae, and the name is taken from the Greek *pipto,* to fall, and *anthos,* a flower; the flowers last a very short time in good condition.

A Quick-growing Flowering Shrub. P. laburnifolius (nepalensis) is the best-known kind. It is a native of the Himalayas. Growing at least 12 ft. high, it forms rather long, soft branches and grows very fast when young. The yellow flowers are borne during May and June, and any pruning necessary to shape plants should be done as soon as the flowers fade.

This kind is easily increased by seeds sown in a frame as soon as ripe, the young plants being kept in pots in a cold frame throughout the first winter. Ordinary good garden soil is suitable.

Two other rather similar kinds have been introduced from western China, P. concolor and P. tomentosus.

PIQUERIA (Piquer'ia). Tender, perennial flowering plants, one of which is grown in greenhouses under the name of Stevia. It is distinct from the plants named Stevia by botanists. The name commemorates a Spanish botanist, A. Piquer.

Piquerias are natives of Mexico and Central America, and belong to the Daisy family, Compositae. The principal kind, P. trinervia (Stevia serrata), has slender stems and opposite, lanceolate leaves with serrate edges, and produces terminal clusters of small, white, fragrant flowers, very similar in appearance to those of Eupatorium. There is a variety with variegated leaves which is sometimes grown as a summer bedding plant, the ends of the shoots being pinched out to induce compact growth.

A Winter-flowering Plant for the Greenhouse. If given correct treatment, the plants will flower in a greenhouse in winter. Cuttings of young shoots, 2 in. in length, should be taken from April to June. The leaves from the lower parts of each shoot are cut off and a cut is made below the bottom joint. The shoots are inserted in a sand propagating bed in a cool greenhouse.

The rooted cuttings are potted separately in 3-in. pots, then into 5-in., and later, possibly, into 6- or 7-in. pots. When established in the final pots, they are placed out of doors on a bed of ashes until the autumn, when they are taken into a cool greenhouse, or they may be grown in the greenhouse throughout.

The shoots should be pinched occasionally until September, when they are allowed to develop and will produce flowers in winter. A night temperature of 40-50 degrees is ample. Full sunshine is needed.

PISTACHIO NUT. See Pistacia.

PISTACIA (Pistac'ia). Evergreen or leaf-losing (deciduous) trees and shrubs, natives of the Mediterranean region and China. Some are of considerable decorative and economic importance in subtropical countries, but are not suitable for cultivation out of doors in the North. Pistacia belongs to the family Anacardiaceae, and the name is derived from the ancient Greek name for the plant, *pistake.*

The leaves are compound and made up of three or more leaflets, the evergreen kinds being distinctly ornamental. The flowers, however, are not showy, but the fruits of some kinds are of value. They are sun-loving trees and shrubs and give the best results in open places.

Most of the kinds are increased by seeds, but some sorts are grafted. This is the case with Pistacia vera, the Pistachio Nut, which is often grafted on stocks of Pistacia Terebinthus and grown as a commercial crop. Male and female flowers are found on different plants.

The hardiest kinds are P. chinensis, the Chinese Pistachio, a leaf-losing tree up to 80 ft. high in China, with compound leaves 9 in. long. It was introduced in 1908, and appears to be hardy to Philadelphia and perhaps further north. P. Terebinthus is also a leaf-losing tree.

This tree grows about 30 ft. high in Asia Minor.

PISTIA STRATIOTES—*Water Lettuce* (Pist'-ia.). A tropical floating aquatic plant, native to tropical America and the southernmost United States. The leaves, which grow in attractive rosettes, are 2 in. long, pea green, velvety, and somewhat wedge-shaped. The small green arum-like flowers are inconspicuous. The name is presumably from *pistos,* the Greek for watery, and refers to the plant's habitat. It belongs to the Arum family, Araceae.

Aquatic Plants for a Greenhouse. These plants are grown in tanks or aquaria in the hothouse, where a minimum winter temperature of 60 degrees is maintained. Tubs 18 in.–2 ft. in depth are used and a 6-in. depth of loam is placed in the bottom. They are then filled with water and, when this becomes the same temperature as the greenhouse, the plants are placed on the surface. The slender feathery roots grow downward and penetrate the soil, which serves as an anchorage and a source of food supply.

Very little attention is required except that the plants must be shaded from sunlight, and the water replaced as it evaporates.

Pistias may be grown permanently in outdoor pools in warm, frost-free regions, and in outdoor pools in summer elsewhere.

Propagation Is by Runners. These plants send out long runners on which small plants are formed. These are detached and put in separate tubs when it is desired to increase the number of plants.

PISTIL. That part of a flower which comprises the female organs, the stigma and ovary.

PISUM. The botanical name of the genus of which the edible green Pea, Pisum sativum, is a member. Its cultivation is dealt with under Pea.

PIT. A term used by gardeners to denote a low-built greenhouse, usually with a path below ground level, which is used for forcing or propagating purposes or for the storage of plants over winter. The term is also used to describe the seeds of "stone" fruits—for example, Peach pits and Cherry pits.

PITCAIRNIA (Pitcair'nia). A large group of hothouse evergreen plants, with ornamental flowers and foliage. They are natives of South America and belong to the Bromelia family, Bromeliaceae.

These plants form rosettes of stemless leaves close to the soil. The leaves are sword-shaped, green, brown or scaly, and vary from 1½ in. to 3 ft. in length. The small tubular flowers are in upright spikes which rise from the center of the rosettes in summer. They are either red, yellow or white. The name Pitcairnia commemorates W. Pitcairn, a London physician.

Flowering Evergreens for a Hothouse. A minimum winter temperature of 55 degrees is required. The best soil compost consists of equal parts of turfy loam, orchid peat (osmunda fiber) and leaf mold with sand and crushed brick freely added.

Repotting is carried out in February and March. Large pots are not needed; when repotting, only slightly larger pots should be used. These should be filled to one quarter with crocks, upon which a layer of rough leaves or orchid peat is laid. The plants are then taken out of their pots, the crocks and as much as possible of the loose soil being removed from the roots with a pointed stick. The plants are set in the new pots and the soil is made firm.

After potting, the plants are placed in a warm greenhouse, which is kept moist by frequently damping the floor and benches, and the plants are lightly syringed twice a day. The soil is not watered until it becomes moderately dry and then it is well moistened. By following this method of watering and keeping the atmosphere moist, the roots will quickly enter the new soil.

Summer and Winter Management. For the remainder of the summer the compost must be kept moist. When autumn approaches, the water supply is gradually lessened, and during the winter the soil is only moistened when it approaches dryness. Less atmospheric moisture is also required in winter, but the greenhouse should not be allowed to remain dry for long, as a dry atmosphere encourages thrips and red spider mites. Very little shading is required.

Raising Plants from Seeds. Propagation is by seeds or division. Seeds are sown in pots of light soil in spring or early summer in a propagating case with a bottom heat of 70-75 degrees. Every morning the glass sash must be wiped dry.

As soon as the seedlings appear above the soil, the glass is removed and they are exposed to the light. When 1 in. in height, they are planted, 1 in. apart, in a well-drained pan filled with the potting compost, which has been sifted through a fine sieve. When large enough to be potted separately, they are set in small pots and subsequently are potted in larger ones.

Propagation by Division. Division is carried out at repotting time. Plants with several shoots are taken out of their pots, and the crocks and all the soil removed from the roots. The plants are then either pulled apart or separated with a sharp knife. The pieces are potted in the smallest possible pots and, when established in these, are repotted.

The Chief Kinds. P. Andreana, 20 in., yellow and red; P. fulgens, 18 in., red; P. corallina, 36 in., red; and P. aphelandraeflora, 12 in., red. All bloom in summer.

PITCHER PLANT. See Nepenthes and Sarracenia. For California Pitcher Plant, see Darlingtonia. For Australian Pitcher Plant, see Cephalotus. See also Insectivorous Plants.

PITHECELLOBIUM (Pithecello'bium). Tender trees and shrubs, suitable for planting in tropical and subtropical regions only. They belong to the Pea family, Leguminosae. Some species are of economic importance as sources of tannin and lumber. In many, the aril that surrounds the seed is edible. The name, sometimes spelled Pithecolobium, is derived from *pithecos*, an ape, and *lobos*, the lobe of the ear, and alludes to a native name meaning Monkey's-Ear.

These plants are normally propagated by seeds. They succeed under a variety of conditions.

Kinds that are grown in North America include P. dulce, (Manila Tamarind, Guaymochil, Opiuma), a native of Mexico, tropical America, the Philippines and the East Indies. This species grows to 50 ft. tall and bears whitish flowers. It was once popular as a street tree in Florida but is much less used now because of its susceptibility to storm damage. P. guadelupense (Ram's-Horn) occurs as a native from southern Florida to northern South America and forms a shrub or small tree 15-20 ft. tall. Its flowers are greenish-yellow. P. Unguis-cati (Cat's-Claw, Black Bead), a native of Florida, the West Indies and northern South America, grows 15-20 ft. tall and has greenish-yellow, purple-stamened flowers. P. Junghuhnianum, a native of Java, is a tree that has decorative orange-yellow flowers.

PITTOSPORUM (Pitto'sporum; Pittospo'rum). Small evergreen trees or large shrubs which vary a good deal in leaf and flower. In some kinds the foliage is very decorative and in others the flowers are fragrant. They are very definitely conspicuous in the native floras of Australia and New Zealand, but some are found wild in China and in other countries.

In mild parts of the United States many kinds may be grown out of doors. Some are useful as pot or tub plants. Pittosporum gives its name to the family Pittosporaceae. The name is derived from the Greek *pitta*, pitch, and *sporos*, seed, and alludes to the soft resin-like coating of the seeds.

When to Take Cuttings. Cuttings of half-ripe shoots, about 4-5 in. long, taken with a slight heel of old wood in July, and dibbled in a propagating case in a greenhouse or even in a cold frame, root readily; those placed in a cold frame should be left undisturbed until the following spring. Either pot the young plants singly and keep them in a cold frame until they can be planted in permanent places, or plant them in a nursery border.

Suitable for Mild Climates. These shrubs are not hardy in the North. They thrive in ordinary well-drained loamy soil, or, in fact, in almost any good garden soil where the climatic conditions are suitable, and they grow into shapely bushes with hardly any attention to pruning. What little pruning is necessary may be carried out in summer. As a rule they are cultivated for their foliage rather than as flowering shrubs, but a few kinds have both advantages.

Hedge Shrubs for Seaside Places. Some of the more vigorous kinds are good hedge plants, particularly in maritime gardens. A few, such as P. eugenioides, P. Colensoi, and P. tenuifolium, provide useful foliage for cutting to use in floral arrangements.

A young plant of Pittosporum Tobira. This is an attractive flowering evergreen shrub suitable for outdoor culture in mild climates and for growing in pots and tubs.

The Hardiest Kinds. Possibly the hardiest of all is P. tenuifolium. This is a native of New Zealand, where it forms a tree 30 ft. high with a dark-colored trunk up to a foot in diameter. It has black or dark purplish shoots covered with light glossy green leaves, 1-1½ in. long, with wavy margins. The flowers are dark purple and are usually produced singly from the leaf axils, the flowering time being May. The variety Silver Queen has very attractive silver foliage.

P. eugenioides is also a New Zealand tree. The glossy, light green leaves are oblong, up to 5 in. long and 1 in. wide, with wavy margins. There is a variety, variegatum, with silvery margined leaves.

P. crassifolium is a large shrub, 12-18 ft. high, with thick leathery leaves, dark green above and covered beneath by a dense grayish felt. The leaves grow to 4 in. long and 1½ in. wide. The flowers are deep dull purple and are produced in May in small dense clusters from the ends of the shoots. This also is a native of New Zealand.

Shrubs with Fragrant Flowers. P. pauciflorum is one of the Chinese kinds. It grows 4-6 ft. high, and carries its leaves in small clusters from the ends of the shoots. The fragrant flowers are yellowish and borne in May. P. undulatum is an Australian bush or tree up to 30-40 ft. high. It has large skimmia-like leaves, dark glossy green above and paler beneath, and bears clusters of fragrant white flowers from the ends of the shoots.

Very Fragrant Flowers. P. Tobira is one of the most attractive kinds from China and Japan. It sometimes grows 20 ft. high in its native country. The thick, dark green leathery leaves are up to 4 in. long and 1½ in. across. The flowers are borne in dense clusters from the ends of the shoots. They are white when they first open but turn yellow with age, and are very fragrant. There is a variety with variegated leaves. Both the green-leaved and variegated-leaved forms of P. Tobira are well adapted to growing in pots or tubs.

Other noteworthy kinds are P. bicolor, P. Buchananii, P. ferrugineum, P. heterophyllum and P. Ralphii.

PITYROGRAMMA—*Gold and Silver Ferns* (Pityrogram'ma). Mostly tender, evergreen Ferns, notable for a yellow or silvery dust (farina) which covers the undersides of the fronds as well as the stalks. They are chiefly natives of tropical America, Japan, Africa, and Australia, and belong to the Polypody family, Polypodiaceae. One kind, P. triangularis, is native from Alaska to California. The name Pityrogramma is derived from *pityron*, a husk, and *gramma*, writing, and alludes to the spore-bearing parts which are uncovered.

Syringing Not Required. The greenhouse kinds require a minimum winter temperature of 50-55 degrees. They are grown in well-drained pots or deep pans in a compost of equal parts of loam, peat moss and leaf mold, with a little crushed charcoal and a free sprinkling of sand. They are repotted in February or March. Water is applied freely to the soil during the summer, but throughout the winter this is only moistened when it becomes nearly dry. Extra-wet or extra-dry conditions must be avoided at all times. The fronds must not be syringed, as this washes off the farina, but damping of the floors and benches must be done to maintain atmospheric humidity. No shading is required except from strong, direct sunshine.

In humid regions, such as the Pacific Northwest, P. triangularis, the California Gold Fern, may be grown outdoors and is suitable for planting in wild gardens and rock gardens in woodland-type soil. It forms a dense tuft of foliage, the leaves being up to 7 in. long and 6 in. wide and carried on foot-long stalks. The coloring of the undersides of the leaves varies from deep golden yellow to silvery white.

Sowing Spores. These Ferns are propagated by sowing spores on a surface of finely sifted, sterilized soil in pots (see Ferns).

The chief kinds for greenhouses are P. calomelanos, silver; P. peruviana argyrophylla, silver; and P. chrysophylla (P. calomelanos variety aureo-flava), golden. The colors refer to the undersides of the fronds.

PLACEA (Pla'cea). Tender, deciduous (leaf-losing) bulb plants which belong to the Amaryllis family, Amaryllidaceae, and are found growing wild in Chile. The bulbs are 1 in. in diameter; the leaves are linear (long and narrow); the flowers, which are funnel-shaped and 1 in. in length, are produced on the top of a stalk 9 in. long. They are similar in appearance to the flowers of the Amaryllis, but they have a small corona like that of Narcissus and open in summer. The colors are yellow and purple, white and crimson, or purple and white. Placea is supposed to be the original Chilean name.

Bulbs for the Greenhouse. These plants require a minimum winter temperature of 45 degrees and the best soil compost consists of two parts of turfy loam, one part of dried cow manure, and a free sprinkling of sand. Repotting is done in August, 6-in. pots being used. These are well drained with crocks, over which a layer of rough siftings from the soil is placed. Sufficient of the soil is then filled in, so that, when it is made firm, the tips of the bulbs are 1 in. below the rim of the pot. Three bulbs are placed in each pot, and the remainder of the compost is added, the tips of the bulbs being buried just below the surface.

Summer and Winter Treatment. After potting, they are placed in a cold frame and covered with old ashes or peat moss. When well rooted, which takes from 8-12 weeks, they are taken into the greenhouse. Water is carefully applied at first. When growth becomes active, the soil is kept moist; but it must not be allowed to become waterlogged. Excessive wetness or dryness of the soil is fatal.

The atmosphere must be kept moist and the foliage syringed daily, until the plants are in flower. Less atmospheric moisture is then required, and the plants are placed in a cool, shaded position so that the flowers will remain fresh for as long as possible. When the flowers have faded the plants are exposed to full sunlight and, as the leaves wither, less water is given. After the leaves have died down, the soil is kept quite dry until the time for repotting. These bulbs are not easy to cultivate, so that the directions given above must be adhered to carefully.

Propagation is by offsets, the small bulbs which develop around the old ones being removed at potting time and planted separately in small pots.

The Chief Kinds. P. Arzae, yellow and purple; P. grandiflora, white and crimson; P. ornata, white and red.

PLAGIANTHUS (Plagianth'us). Tender, evergreen and deciduous (leaf-losing) shrubs from New Zealand and Tasmania which belong to the Mallow family, Malvaceae. The name Plagianthus is derived from *plagios,* oblique, and *anthos,* a flower, and refers to the way the flowers hang on the trees.

The plant known in gardens as P. populnea is now known as Hoheria populnea, and the one called P. Lyallii is known as Gaya Lyallii, which see.

For Mild Climates. These shrubs thrive in climates such as that of California, in ordinary, well-drained, loamy garden soil. Very light soil can be made suitable by digging in liberal quantities of well-decayed compost; heavy clay soil should be removed and replaced with loam and leaf mold, peat moss or compost.

Propagation Is by Cuttings. Well-ripened shoots are removed with a heel in September and inserted in a bed of sand or sand and peat moss in a cold frame. The frame is kept close until rooting takes place. When well rooted, the cuttings are potted separately and are gradually hardened off and planted out in their permanent positions in early fall or spring.

The chief kinds are P. betulinus, a graceful tree with slender, birchlike leaves and shoots, and white flowers in drooping clusters in August; and P. divaricatus, a shrub 4-8 ft. tall, with cream flowers in June.

PLANERA AQUATICA—*Water Elm* (Planer'a). A broad, spreading, leaf-losing (deciduous) tree that is native from southern Illinois and Missouri to Texas and Florida and is hardy to about Washington, D.C. It belongs to the Elm family, Ulmaceae. Its name honors J. J. Planer, a German botanist.

The Water Elm is infrequently cultivated. It may be propagated by seeds, layering and by grafting on the Elm. In nature it grows in swamps and presumably requires a wet or at least moist soil.

PLANE TREE. Platanus, which see.

PLANNING THE GARDEN
The First Step in Making a Beautiful Home Landscape

Careful planning of a garden as a preliminary to its actual development and construction is more important than the average beginner realizes. If, before the actual work of planting were started, more thought were given to matters of design, the kinds of plants to be used and their arrangement, much disappointment and expense would be avoided and more good gardens would grace our city, suburban and country homes.

In this field, as in many others, a little foresight is worth a great deal of hindsight; changing plantings of trees, shrubs and evergreens and altering such basic features as paths, terraces, steps and the like after they are installed are likely to prove expensive, perhaps

A well-planned small garden with flower borders surrounding a well-kept lawn.

prohibitively so. You may have to live for a long time with the kind of landscape you create at first; therefore it is very important that you take sufficient time and give adequate thought to its initial planning.

Even before planning on paper is started, the amateur who has had but little experience in garden making should take steps to familiarize himself with other gardens, with the various kinds of plants that thrive in the locality and that are offered for sale by local nurseries, and especially with the sizes and appearances of these plants after they have grown for several years and are approaching maturity. Visits to parks, botanical gardens and other public plantings and the observation of gardens in the vicinity are all immensely helpful. Unfortunately, most amateurs who landscape their own homes make their most important decisions at the time of their greatest ignorance, and only with the passing years do they come to see their mistakes. A little time spent in familiarizing

oneself with plant materials, with what others have done in the line of garden designing and with the possibilities (as well as the limitations) of the lot that is to be landscaped is time well spent.

Design. Good design is, of course, basic to a satisfactory garden development. In general, simplicity should be favored over fussiness and extravagance. Restraint in planting, in introducing ornaments, statues, gazing globes, sundials and similar objects, in constructing rock gardens and other features where they really do not fit into the landscape, in introducing twists and curves into paths unnecessarily and in using plant materials of a gaudy and colorful character, is an absolute essential for good landscaping. Originality is fine, so long as the results do not appear to be forced.

There are few places where the owner has complete control over all factors of design. The shape of the lot, its soil and exposures, the house, outcrops of rock, slopes, existing trees on the property itself or on neighboring land must all be taken into consideration. Sometimes they can be changed to better the design, sometimes the expense of changing them is prohibitive and the design must be woven around them. Often this necessary compromise ends in a more attractive place than might have been expected.

Nor does the design stay constant. One important change is the growth of trees and shrubs. These changes govern the scale of planting from year to year. Also, the growth of a tree and its increasing shade and roots often damage the appearance of nearby shrubs or less vigorous trees. On the other hand, the loss of trees by storm or disease may change the design radically. There are also the changes from season to season, a most important consideration. The design of a place is never finished. The owner can develop a watchful eye that will tell him when plants should be removed to prevent overcrowding, when the removal of a branch will improve a vista, when a little color in one place is needed to balance color in another. Whenever anything is planted, he should ask himself whether it will help or hurt the general effect

of the surrounding plants, whether it will thrive and look well in future years. In time it becomes more and more easy to find the right answer.

Simple Principles. In attempting to create a pleasing garden picture, it is helpful to understand a few of the simple underlying principles of design: unity, proportion, balance and variety. Unity gives the feeling that everything belongs together. Balance focuses attention on a center of interest. Proportion adds restfulness. Variety prevents monotony.

On the home grounds the house itself is the main center of interest. Wise landscaping enhances its good points and distracts attention from any weak ones. It should not seem to be an isolated building, but part of the whole pattern composed of house, lawn, trees, shrubs and flowers that reaches to the very edge of the property. In open country it may become part of a larger picture extending beyond the property, including, perhaps, surrounding fields, a background of hills or a distant view.

There can be no hard and fast rules for designing and developing one's own home and garden because no two places are exactly alike and because growing things are always changing

Tall trees planted near the house may compete with it for interest . . . and shut out sunlight.

in shape and size. The most important underlying reason, however, is that a garden and home reflect the personality of the owner. Before developing any concrete plans, it is wise to consider the design, color, form and lines that are most pleasing, then work toward a picture that will answer family needs and satisfy individual tastes. Family requirements affect the use of the land and its planting. Likes and dislikes, hobbies and recreations should be discussed before definite plans are made. A 60 by 120 ft. tennis court may be impossible, for example, but a quarter of that area provides ample room for badminton. Each problem has its evident limitations, from financial to topographical and climatic, so it is wise to anticipate having to make certain eliminations, certain postponements.

How to Apply the Principles of Design. If a large tree is directly in front of the house, it will compete with it for interest. If it is a little to one side, however, it will seem to frame the house and provide unity by bringing the elements of the picture together. If there is a high, heavy planting on one side and very little on the other, there is a lack of balance and proportion, and the planting will look incomplete. Too much thick, massive foliage from trees such as Copper Beeches, low-crowned Maples, thick evergreens and many shrubs tends to overpower the house, yet if all the plants are small the house will be too dominant.

Symmetry exists where the design is the same on one side as the other. But balance in landscape planting is often attained in other ways. A tall, lacy, open tree like a Honey Locust can be balanced by a smaller but denser and coarser Magnolia Soulangeana. Two small Hemlocks will balance a larger one. A large tree near one end of a house balances a heavy chimney at the other end. A small Dogwood leaning toward a pool balances a taller but more upright Dogwood on the other side. If it leans away from the pool it will detract from the picture by leading the eye away from the center of interest.

Matched evergreens at either side of the front entrance and a balanced foundation planting give symmetry to this pleasing landscaping scheme.

Low Mountain Laurels provide an effective foundation planting for this house. The picture could be improved by planting a group of low shrubs in the foreground.

Variety is achieved by the use of different types of plant material. There is variety in shape, size, texture, density, line and color. All these add interest to the planting, yet they must be combined so as to blend harmoniously.

Utility as well as beauty must be considered in the design. Lack of convenience is lack of order, and therefore poor design. The simplest solution to each problem is apt to be the most orderly and the most satisfactory.

Planning the approach to the front door, for instance, explains the necessity for order and simplicity as well as beauty. Usually it is best to let the path run straight to the house. If this cuts the lawn into long rectangles very unequal in area, then it is better to have the path run immediately beside the driveway and make a right-angle turn near the house. The front door opening onto a paved terrace can make a most attractive entrance. Such a terrace, however, should be used only when the distance between the house and street is comparatively great, otherwise the area will look too cut up.

There are the additional problems of construction, drainage and cost to consider. The width of the walk must be adequate for the length. It may have to be fitted to a slope, or have steps. The material chosen must be suitable for the type of house. And for the finishing touch, a tree may be planted near it to serve the dual purpose of shading the walk and framing the entrance. Each part of the design, from making the first plans to planting the last flower, must be treated individually, yet be considered as part of the whole pattern.

Planning by Units. The first step in the design comes in dividing the property into general units according to use. First is the entrance area. This is shared by every visitor, seen by every passer-by. Next is the service area adjoining the kitchen. It should include kitchen, garage, fuel delivery, laundry and vegetable garden. It must be easily accessible, yet screened from the more peaceful living areas, from the neighbors and from the public. Last comes the living area. This may include a terrace and adjoining bit of lawn or garden, space for games, a grill, varied vistas or special gardens. Access to each area from the other areas and from the house is important. Each unit should function conveniently and unobtrusively.

It is easy to define the various uses of the individual units. The theory behind a satisfying total effect, however, is difficult to express. There should be harmony throughout, a pleasing juxtaposition of open areas and a variety of foliage masses. House, lawns and planting should blend together so that the eye is led easily from one part of the property to the next. While the attention may be held by a beautiful window, a fine flowering tree, or a bed of bright Tulips, none of these should seem to be separate units, but highlighted parts of a satisfying whole.

On a landscape plan, open areas of pleasing shape are separated by varied lines drawn to represent walls or foliage, and it is easy to sense a coherence of units radiating from the house. Standing on the ground, however, the normal angle of vision, which is about 30 degrees, reduces appreciation of the unity of the whole to a series of small pictures, each with its own elements of composition, its simple foreground, its center of interest, background and frame. In a landscape the sides of the frame are dissimilar, perhaps the line of a terrace below, an overhanging branch above and varied plants on

Simplicity and dignity characterize this front lawn and entrance area. Hedges of Hemlock in the front, tall evergreens in the rear, and low evergreens at the front of the house provide winter foliage.

This front entrance area appears slightly cluttered because of the number of individual trees and small groups planted in the lawn area. A better effect would be obtained if these plants were grouped.

either side. Each step toward a door, through the house or across a terrace, produces a new frame for the picture ahead.

Each picture will be at its best at a particular time of day with certain shadows or reflected lights, or at a certain season. If it is satisfying at its worst season, then added color, rightly placed, enhances its appeal at more favorable seasons. So it is best to solve the skeletal winter problem first, then add summer color.

It is a good general rule to make the areas nearest the house more formal, merging into less formal areas farther away. The degrees of formality and informality should be adjusted to the character of the house and the tastes of the family.

The front lawn and entrance area should be treated simply. Good trees, good grass, well-kept flower beds have distinction, while elaboration generally produces a feeling of restlessness.

Boundary planting is an individual problem. Shutting other people out is very apt to result in shutting the owner in. Too much boundary planting makes the place look smaller. While it may be advisable to screen some unsightly objects as completely as possible, sometimes the best method of hiding telephone poles is to offer something better to look at nearby. Much depends on the size of the lot and on the attractiveness of the neighboring lots. It is often more satisfactory to accept the outlook frankly, plant a hedge or build a fence with a flower bed inside. Between this and the house may be lawn or a pattern garden. Another solution is to have enough boundary planting to act as a screen on that part of the lot where the house is nearest to neighboring houses. If there is an attractive view, planting should enhance it, not hide it.

Planting Plans

Even an inexperienced person can make a plan of his house and grounds that will be of great help in developing his planting and in clarifying his ideas for a garden so they can be worked out in detail. The use of definite measurements aids

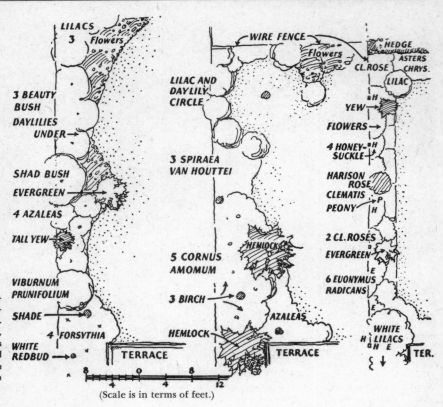

Shade, privacy and seasonal interest are provided by this planting screening a terrace (left). A more simple screen planting, with color in the sunny portions (center). Narrow plantings and succession of bloom against a fence form a pleasing screen (right).

(Scale is in terms of feet.)

in determining proper planting distances and shows whether the desired plantings are correct for the area.

For most people, the problem is to work with a house already built, and plantings already present. If it is the place where the owner has lived for many years he must try to look at familiar surroundings as if he had never seen them before. Perhaps it is best to discard all existing plantings and start over. Perhaps a new design can be worked out or an old one improved by doing away with certain trees or planting new ones, changing walks or moving shrubs to more favorable locations. The condition of old plantings in relation to neighboring yards may suggest that an entirely new type of planting is needed to meet the changed environment. There may be a garage to be screened or a garbage bin to be concealed.

Selecting the Plot. Other people are faced with the problem of buying a new lot on which a new house is to be built. Here they have the chance to decide what type of lot is best adapted to the family's needs and likes. It may be one with an open level area where children can play actively, or one with a wooded section where a wild garden can be developed. The Rose, Iris or Peony fancier will want a lot with good soil and plenty of sun. When there is a choice of lots with large trees, their kind and condition are important. Trees known to be resistant to breakage and in good condition are preferable, of course.

Lots with steep slopes are more difficult and expensive to develop and maintain than level ones, but a moderate slope up from the road gives a pleasant setting. A rocky outcrop or a brook is an invitation to the gardener who likes informality, but the one who wants a formal design had best avoid the expense that eliminating such natural features entails.

Drainage must be considered. The lot lower than its neighbors or the street may be flooded and become a recurring source of expense, and a discouragement to gardening.

If there is a plot plan available from architect

A well-planned terrace located near the house forms part of the intimate living area of a garden.

In this planting, a low, massive Boxwood at the right provides balance for the taller, looser-growing trees at the left.

Small trees, such as the Flowering Dogwood shown here, may be used effectively near many contemporary houses. The bold evergreen foliage of the Rhododendron contrasts well with the more graceful pattern of the Dogwood. The Rhododendron and the Pyracantha espaliered against the wall hold their green foliage through the winter.

Ornaments like this bird bath, even though attractive in their design, should be carefully placed and used with restraint. This is especially true in small gardens.

or surveying engineer, it will give a head start to the preparation of a planting plan. Otherwise it will be necessary to measure the lot, the house with its doors and windows, and all existing features such as walks, drive, garage, trees and flower beds. A straight line of known length and compass direction, such as the front line of the house or the street front, is taken as a base. All straight lines parallel to it are put in first, and then those at right angles. Trees can be located in relation to these more easily measured fea-

tures. The irregular lines of shrub beds and borders then can be sketched in with fair accuracy. If there are objects on nearby property to be screened, or a view to be framed, their location should be on the plan. Coordinated sheets (marked with $\frac{1}{8}$- or $\frac{1}{10}$-in. squares) are to be had at any stationery store and are useful for this basic plan. Let each square represent a square foot on the ground. Tracing paper then can be placed over the basic plan and several experiments for the general design roughly

A seat located where a pleasant view may be obtained is a useful garden feature.

In making plans for a garden a simple path system should be included. Stepping stones are adequate where moderate traffic must cross a lawn area.

worked out. In these sketches various existing features can be omitted or changed around, in addition to planning for gardens, new trees and shrubs and so forth.

In considering these preliminary sketches it is important to reckon on the expense of upkeep. If the place is to be formal, it has to be maintained in the best possible order to produce a strong effect. Clipping of hedges and grass edges takes much time. Flower beds require more

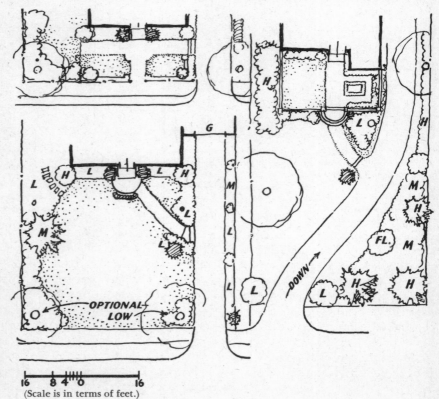

Plans for small property. (Upper left) A narrow yard for farmhouse or small home. (Lower left) A square yard. The lack of long front path permits great privacy. (Right) A deep yard with the house set well below the street. The terrace and a small garden are to the front. Key: H, high; M, medium; L, low; Fl, flowering shrub; G, garage.

(Scale is in terms of feet.)

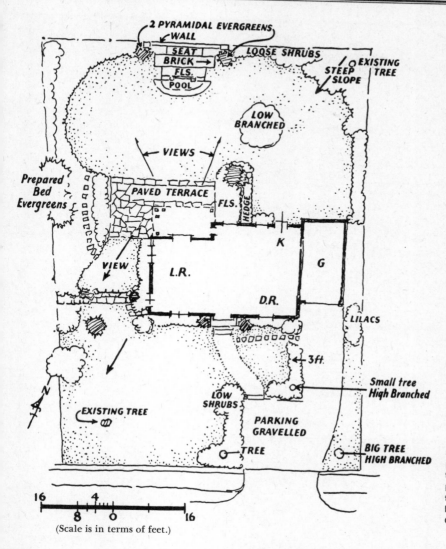

2 PYRAMIDAL EVERGREENS
WALL
SEAT
BRICK
FLS.
POOL
LOOSE SHRUBS
EXISTING TREE
STEEP SLOPE
LOW BRANCHED
VIEWS
Prepared Bed Evergreens
PAVED TERRACE
FLS.
HEDGE
K
G
VIEW
L.R.
D.R.
LILACS
3 ft.
Small tree High Branched
LOW SHRUBS
PARKING GRAVELLED
EXISTING TREE
N
TREE
BIG TREE HIGH BRANCHED

16   4
8   0   16
(Scale is in terms of feet.)

A typical property plan, with privacy in the rear, a paved terrace with view of a garden pool, and parking for guests off the road. Key: L.R.—living room; K.—kitchen; D.R.—dining room; G. garage.

attention than shrubs. A plan requiring much change in grade naturally will be more expensive to carry out than one that conforms to existing grades. Therefore it may be helpful before deciding on a certain plan to get some idea of the cost of grading from a contractor.

After the design that seems most promising has been chosen, the details can be worked out. Paths should be adequate, the main entrance at least four feet wide, the side ones at least two and a half feet. Drives must be at least eight feet wide, and ten feet is better. It takes a minimum of a 60-foot circle to turn a car, but on a small place it is often satisfactory to widen the ap-

proach to the garage so that two cars can pass or park.

Selecting Possible Plant Material. The preparation of a list of possible plant material is next to be considered. Everything on the list will not be used, but it is helpful to narrow down the choice from the tremendous number of plants that can be grown in any locality. First, possible shade trees can be listed, then small flowering trees, evergreen trees and shrubs and deciduous shrubs. Perennials and annuals may be worked out later as a separate problem, or, if the garden plan is to be simple, they may be included in this list.

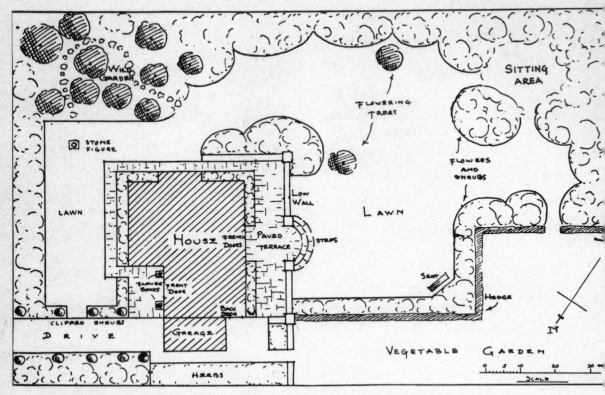

Plan for garden on a half-acre site on slightly sloping ground. Note the paved, walled terrace, from which the lawn slopes away gently, bounded and broken by ornamental trees and shrubs.

Garden plan for a long, narrow plot, with a sunken formal garden near the house.

Beside the name of each plant, its size at maturity in height and spread should be noted. Next should be added its contribution to the landscape effect. This may be bloom, fruit, the time and color of both. It may be autumn color, contrast in foliage color or texture. It may be a weeping form, or a narrow fastigiate one, or winter interest in bark, twigs and form. Each plant must be carefully considered for its suitability to the site, its soil and exposure. It should be known to be dependable in the locality. One section of the property may require plants that will thrive under very dry conditions, another those that will grow in shade. These conditions may dictate a choice of plants that otherwise would not be considered at first. A check of the list may show that there is a preponderance of interest for one season, and not enough for another. Certain eliminations and additions will strengthen the list. Even so, it is not finished. There may be further changes as the work on the plan proceeds.

With this list for easy reference, the location of plants may be drawn on the plan. In all of this, there is a weighing of the plants against each other. Perhaps just one or two of the shade trees will be chosen from a list of ten, for their

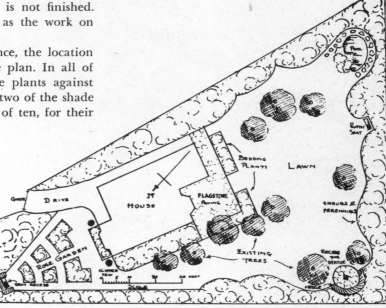

Plan for a quarter-acre garden of tri-angular shape, giving pleasant views from the main windows, with the boundaries effectively screened.

suitability to the size of the lot and its conditions, their beauty, durability and effect on the other plants to be used. So with the rest of the list there will be further eliminations.

After the shade trees have been chosen the distribution of the evergreens, which are the year-round framework, should be determined.

Often the only evergreens are those strung along the front of a house for foundation planting. This gives the house the appearance of crowding into itself without relation to the rest of the lot during the time that the deciduous plants are without their leaves. Using evergreens in groups, or alone if they are large, along the sides of the

Conditions such as this face many new property owners. Careful planning is needed to achieve satisfactory and economical land-scaping. A moderate slope rising towards the house is favorable to good planting.

Closely sheared hedges and neatly trimmed grass give formality but add to upkeep.

A typical young planting. The shade trees are placed sufficiently far from the house to allow for future growth, but some of the evergreen plants used close to the house are likely to grow too large with the passing of the years.

lot will tend to tie the whole planting together.

Placing the Plants. In deciding where to place the different plants, all their aspects must be considered so that there will be a satisfactory distribution of bloom, fruit, fall color, and winter interest. Often one plant can be used to set off another. Flowering Dogwood against Hemlock, the silver-gray foliage of the Russian Olive

The wrong choice of plant material may result in situations like this. With the passing years, Spruces that were set out as small young specimens have grown to a size completely out of scale with the house.

rising above the green of Viburnums, orange-berried Honeysuckles next to those with red berries, are examples. It is usually better to have shrubs in groups of several of a kind. The larger the place, the larger the groups should be. Repeating groups of one kind of plant material helps to give unity. However, the groups should not always give the same-sized mass. Although repetition gives unity, contrast gives interest and prevents monotony.

On this plan, planting distances must be measured out. Room must be allowed for normal

Groups of shrubs and evergreens give seclusion to this shaded lawn.

growth. There may be a skimpy look for the first few years, but that is better than many years of overcrowding later on.

The foundation planting should be simple, with two or three rather than a dozen textures and forms. All plantings should be subservient to the house. It is disastrous not to take into account the ultimate size of the plants. Too often evergreens are used that are attractive when small, but they soon smother the house and take the light from the windows.

A location of such importance as the front door demands the maximum of seasonal effect in every plant. That is the reason for the prevalence of evergreens, but they are not the only possibility. Boxwood or Yew give the darkest greens at the doorstep, but the planting on each

[9—4]

A well planned garden with lawn, terrace and perennial border

[9—4a]

Planned for summer color, this garden features Roses and annuals

[9—5]
*Simplicity of design adds dignity
to the front yard*

[9—5a]
Annuals in borders provide summer color

[9—5b]
Perennial Borders can be effective

[9—5c]
A special plot for cut flowers is useful

A corner of a flower garden in an informal setting.

side of them, instead of being evergreen, may be a colorful line of cluster Roses edged with Pansies or Petunias. Invariably there should be major emphasis at the doorway, a bit less at the corners, with a mere connecting link between, its height adjusted to the height of the windows or other architectural lines.

There can be minor accents to emphasize a side door or add interest to an expanse of wall. The play of light and shade and sparse branches seen against a wall are worth having. If there is a terrace the planting at its edge may be larger than at the house, permitting the use of colorful flowers against the house walls. With an asymmetrical house and terrace, a wider selection of plants gives a pleasant effect.

It should be remembered that every tree and shrub between the house and the street is in effect part of the foundation planting. Many a front yard would be improved by the addition of a shade or flowering tree, or a few shrubs away from the house itself. Specimen shrubs should be chosen carefully. They may be used in matched pairs to mark the entrance to a garden, or as accents.

Gardens and seclusion should be synonymous. Some are patterns of paths and flower beds, others are informal borders around an open lawn area. In either case they may include evergreen accents, clipped or unclipped, enclosing hedges or flowering shrubs for background and flowering trees to shade a bench or pool. In preparing a plan on paper it is well to remember that a garden seen from above gains interest as a pattern. Seen from eye level, however, the attention is drawn toward the planting along each side of a path or grass panel and its terminal, which may frame a vista or hold the interest with an especially steady and strong planting effect. The end of the garden may be only across the lawn from a door or bay window, but it is the place for the main flower display. Untried novelties should be relegated to the more inconspicuous sides.

This formal garden, enclosed by hedges and walls to provide seclusion, consists of a pattern of flower beds with grass paths between.

Lawns are important in landscape design. They give a simple, restful feeling in contrast to the more intricate composition of the shrub borders and flower beds that surround them. High trees do not break the sense of space that a lawn can give, but specimen shrubs or trees with low branches should be placed with care and restraint so that they do not become disturbing elements.

Where to Plant the Flower Garden. A place may have flowers in abundance without any space being set aside for a garden. Vines, beds beside the house or terrace, planting along the boundary fence, flowering trees and shrubs can accomplish this. If, however, there is to be a definite garden there are certain fundamentals to be considered. The very name garden comes from *garth,* meaning an enclosed place. Flowers, to be effective, need a background, and the smaller the space the more vitally important it is to have every plant well chosen.

Proportions are important. If the area is rectangular its lines are usually pleasing when its length is about two and a half times its width. The natural focal point is the far end, where there may be balanced plantings for a background. If there is a feature here, such as pool, sundial or bench, it should not be set too close to the background, because any impression of overcrowding disturbs the feeling of peace and restfulness that is the underlying satisfaction of any garden or planting. In choosing features it should be remembered that spiky evergreens, stepping stones of glaring materials, stodgy bolsters of shrubs, too many ornaments, are distracting and depressing.

A squarish area may be made into a circular garden or an octagon, or remain a square. The eye tends to look to the center, and any planting or feature in this center must be well chosen, and in proportion to the area. If it is too small it will give a feeling of inadequacy, if it is too

Repeated groups of Doronicums and Tulips give unity to this flower border.

large, it will create a sense of overcrowding.

Overcrowding may come from poor design or from too heavy or overgrown planting. It also comes from poorly chosen or wrongly placed garden features. Large formal gardens need large, important features, but small ones are seldom improved by the many items sold as "garden ornaments." Gazing globes, stone animals and metal birds are eye-catchers. They tend to be disturbing in a small garden and therefore inappropriate. Bird baths, pools of good propor-

Small specimen trees with low branches, such as this Flowering Crab Apple, must be carefully located so that important views are enhanced, not blocked.

tion, chairs and benches have their place, but they should be placed where they add to the picture as a whole. Some gardens are made more gay and attractive by brightly colored chairs and tables, but generally a quiet green is better than a bright yellow or red that will dominate the whole scene.

Choosing Plants for the Flower Garden. In planting flower beds and borders, first select accents and edging of plants that are attractive over a long season. Coral Bells, low Campanulas or Primroses, for example, are distinctive at all

This pergola provides a sheltered walk from flower garden to vegetable garden. It also serves to support Grape vines which in season crop abundantly.

seasons. Behind these come the higher flowers, Phlox or Iris, building up to the tall Asters and Delphiniums, some in well-spaced clumps, some in drifts, some in irregular lines. Tall perennials lose their effect in thick blocks. They should be planted sparsely. Height in the center of a square bed breaks the view and unity of design, but height against an enclosing wall or hedge has great value, for it carries through the line of the design.

Such plants as Oriental Poppies, Tulips and Bleeding Hearts, which lose their foliage soon after they bloom, should be among other foliage to hide their deficiencies, or interplanted with annuals as their leaves die down. The gardener soon learns that spring bloom tends to be in the front and fall bloom toward the back; hence low annuals among the early perennials give a fuller late-season effect.

In a small garden particularly, plants should be chosen for a long season of bloom, for interesting foliage and neat habit. Many a plant is as important out of bloom as it is in flower.

Peonies, magnificent in bloom, are also good for the early spring effect of their red stems, and the good summer green of their foliage. Baptisia, Dictamnus and Thalictrum all have good foliage. Grassy Iris and the bending leaves of Daylilies offer a fine contrast to them. The glossy green of perennial Candytuft, the fine gray of Pinks, the feathery silver of Artemisia, the reddish tinge in many low Sedums give a sense of color and movement even when they are out of bloom.

It is in flower beds that the gardener has the greatest opportunity to experiment with different combinations of color, form and texture. In addition to color contrast there are the fine, fluffy steeples of Astilbes, the big, smooth trumpets of Lilies, the spires of Delphiniums set with rosettes, the heavy round heads of Peonies, the bells of Platycodon. In striving for good growth and plenty of bloom there will be continual change in the planting. The gardener will learn how to interplant for a maximum effect. This is another way of saying that deeply planted bulbs will grow through shallow carpets of Chrysanthemums, that Violets will grow well under Lilacs, and Plantain Lilies will fill up shady corners. Knowledge of the form and color of plants as well as of their requirements is essential in making the design that thing of beauty and work of art which is a garden, and in which every gardener seeks to combine what nature offers.

PLANTAGO—*Plantain* (Planta′go). A group of temperate-region, perennial and annual herbaceous plants and subshrubs, best known perhaps because of kinds that are among the commonest weeds in lawns, waste places and elsewhere (see Plantain). A few have decorative merit and are occasionally grown in gardens. P. Psyllium is the source of Psyllium seed, which is used medicinally. Plantago belongs to the Plantain family, Plantaginaceae. The name Plantain is derived

The Rose Plantain, Plantago major rosularis.

from a Latin word that has ancient origins.

Plantagos are very easily cultivated in any well-drained soil in sunny places. They are readily raised from seeds.

Kinds that may be grown in gardens include P. argentea, foliage silvery; P. Cynops, a low, evergreen subshrub that is hardy to southern New England; P. lanceolata marginata, with white-variegated leaves; P. major rosularis, Rose Plantain, a very old garden plant that produces rosettes of green bracts in place of the usual tail-like spikes of flowers, seeds freely and reproduces itself true from seeds; P. major rubrifolia, with red-purple leaves; P. nivalis, leaves densely covered with silvery hairs, suitable for rock gardens.

PLANTAIN. This name is applied to certain kinds of the tropical genus Musa (which see), and to members of the genus Plantago, some of which occur commonly as weeds in paths and waste places and are troublesome on lawns. When small, the weeds can be destroyed by several applications of sulphate of ammonia, which should be put on the weeds in settled, dry weather in spring and early summer. The simplest way of dealing with these weeds, however, is to apply one of the modern synthetic hormone selective weed killers. See also Plantago.

PLANTAIN, FALSE. See Heliconia.

PLANTAIN LILY. See Hosta.

PLANTAIN, RATTLESNAKE. Goodyera, which see.

PLANTER. Containers which accommodate

Planters such as this are a decorative feature in home or office. They are formed with wood and furnished with metal troughs, in which potted plants are set, plunged above the rims of their pots in peat moss.

A small china planter with Sansevieria and Dracaena Godseffiana growing in it.

Ready-prepared planter mixes are sold by dealers in garden supplies. They are convenient and easy to use.

A large planter filled with Episcias and Maidenhair Fern thriving in a living room.

several indoor plants and in which the plants are arranged for effect are often called planters. Such containers may be portable troughs resembling window boxes or permanent installations of masonry or other suitable materials. Permanent planters are sometimes located so that their tops are level with the floor, in other cases they are elevated. The term planter is also frequently used for small, decorative, plant containers, made of ceramic materials, wood, metal, etc. and designed to accommodate one or more small plants and display them to advantage. These small planters are akin to dish gardens.

In most cases planters do not have holes in

A piece of driftwood hollowed out makes an effective small planter. Bromeliads grow in this one.

their bottoms or other means of drainage, but provision for this is usually made in the case of built-in, permanent planters located in the floor. Planters made of wood are usually fitted with leakproof linings of zinc, galvanized metal, aluminum or other suitable metal. Copper should not be used as a lining material because it may prove poisonous to the plants.

Planters may be filled with porous soil or one of the planter mixes which are mixtures of peat moss, perlite, vermiculite, small lumps of char-coal and similar materials and the plants set directly in the soil or in the planter mix, or plants growing in pots may be arranged in the planter without removing them from their pots and the spaces between them filled with peat moss and the top of the soil in the pots and the rims of the pots covered with the same material.

Care should be taken to put in the same planter only those kinds of plants that require the same cultural conditions. If this is done success is more certain and incongruities in appearance which may result, for example, from having Cacti growing with Ferns or Begonias, are avoided.

Maintenance of planters calls for good judgment in the matter of watering, especially with those that are not provided with drainage. An over-wet condition of the soil or other rooting medium is likely to soon bring disaster. Fertilizing plants growing in planters should be done with great restraint or not at all and only completely soluble fertilizers of types especially recommended for house plants should be used when fertilizing is deemed desirable.

Foliage should be kept free of dust by spong-

ing it occasionally when necessary with mild soapy water. A daily misting over with an atomizer spray of water benefits most plants and helps to keep those growing in planters in good condition. Faded leaves and flowers should be removed promptly.

PLANTER MIX. A term used for certain soil substitutes used in planters, window boxes and sometimes for potting plants. Planter mixes are usually mixtures of some or all of the following ingredients: peat moss, sedge peat, vermiculite, perlite and crushed charcoal.

Careful attention to planting dates is necessary to achieve fine results.

PLANTING: AN IMPORTANT GARDEN OPERATION
When and How to Plant for the Best Results

Planting is one of the most important details in the cultivation of trees, shrubs and other plants; the way in which it is carried out and the time when it is done have a considerable influence on the welfare of the plants.

The details of planting deserve far greater consideration than they usually receive from amateurs; if the work is done incorrectly it may seriously retard the development of the trees or other plants. See also Transplanting and Pricking Off.

The Best Times to Plant. Generally the best seasons to plant hardy leaf-losing (deciduous) trees, shrubs and other perennial plants are early autumn and early spring, before new growth begins. In places where winters are not severe many kinds can be planted safely in mild weather

during the winter, especially vigorous trees and shrubs. In severe climates, if planting cannot be finished before the ground freezes hard, it is wise to defer the work until early spring, except in the case of spring-flowering bulbs, such as Crocus, Narcissi and Tulips, which must be planted in fall. If special precautions are taken it is possible to move trees even when they are in full leaf. See Shade Trees.

So much depends on the weather and the character and condition of the soil that hard and fast rules cannot be laid down. Late fall and winter planting are less likely to be satisfactory on heavy, clayey soils than on porous, sandy or gravelly ones. Plants known to be slightly tender in a given locality usually give the best results if planting is done in spring.

Clumps of perennials are transplanted in fall or early spring with as much soil as possible clinging to their roots.

The root ball is placed in a hole big enough to accommodate it without crowding, and soil is pressed firm about it.

Spring planting of hardy plants should always be done as early as possible. Late spring planting as a rule yields less satisfactory results the first summer; the newly transplanted items do not have sufficient time to re-establish their root systems before hot, dry weather makes demands upon them to provide the foliage with large amounts of moisture. For a similar reason (the desirability of giving the plants time to form new roots before the ground freezes hard and all root growth ceases) fall planting should be done as soon after the first frost as possible.

Hardy evergreens may be moved with entirely satisfactory results slightly later in the spring and slightly earlier in the fall than deciduous trees, shrubs and perennials. The best time in spring to transplant them is just when their new growth is beginning or immediately previous to that; they should not be moved when their new shoots are quite large.

Fall transplanting may begin as soon as the hottest summer weather is over—in September or even in late August—and may continue until the ground freezes, but it is a mistake to transplant evergreens so late in fall that the specimens have little or no time to make new roots before hard winter weather arrives. The prompt development of new roots is especially important in the case of evergreens, because their leaves transpire (give off moisture vapor) all winter and this loss must be made good by the roots, otherwise the leaves scorch and die and portions of the bush or tree, or all of it, may be killed.

Tender plants that are set in the garden for the summer and stored indoors over winter, are planted at various times in spring according to the needs of the particular kinds, and sometimes depending upon when they are wanted to bloom. With such leafy items as Geraniums, Fuchsias, Heliotropes, Marguerites, Wax Begonias, Lantanas, Coleus and Dahlia plants that have been started early indoors, it is wise to wait until the weather is warm and settled and there is no danger of the plants receiving a severe set-back to their growth as a result of exposure to cold nights. Tender bulbs and tubers such as Gladioli, Tuberoses, tuberous Begonias and Dahlias, that have no foliage at planting time, may be set out somewhat earlier, soon after all danger of late frosts has passed.

Annuals, started indoors in pots and flats, may be planted out as soon as the weather is warm and settled enough for their kind, or planting may be delayed until the beds are cleared of spring-blooming plants such as Tulips, Pansies and Sweet Williams.

Planting a deciduous tree with bare roots. *(Top, left to right)* Hole is too deep, and roots are crowded. Hole is too shallow, and tree is not perpendicular. Proper-sized hole in relation to roots and size of tree. *(Bottom, left to right)* Tree properly staked. Tree supported by guy wires secured to "dead men."

Young vegetable plants that have been raised indoors, in a cold frame, or in a seed bed outdoors, are planted in the garden at various times according to their particular needs, and in some cases according to when harvest is wanted. With some, such as Tomatoes, Peppers and Eggplants, most usually one planting is made, and that as early as it can be done without serious danger of the young plants' suffering from exposure to excessive cold. In other cases, for instance with Broccoli, Cabbage, Cauliflower and Celery, two or more plantings may be made, the first as early as weather conditions permit and the others some weeks later to ensure a succession, or a long harvesting season.

Prepare the Ground in Advance. It is an advantage to prepare the soil at least two or three weeks in advance of planting, so that it may settle before the plants are put in. Planting in loose soil is not a good practice, for, as the soil sinks, the roots may be exposed or they may sink with the ground, and eventually be too far below the surface of the ground.

Balled and Burlapped or Bare-rooted. Perennials and other plants that are quite small are usually transplanted with little or no soil

When a small deciduous tree is to be transplanted, first dig a hole of ample size to accommodate the roots without crowding.

Improve the soil by adding decayed organic matter such as compost, peat moss, leaf mold or old manure.

Mix this organic matter thoroughly with the undersoil, break all lumps and remove large stones.

Fill around the plant with fertile, porous soil and work it well among the roots; take care not to bunch the roots, nor to twist or curl them.

Cut off any dead and damaged roots with a sharp knife or shears; be careful not to permit the roots to become dry at any time.

When the hole is about half filled, tread the soil firmly with the ball of the foot, at the same time holding the trunk of the tree to keep it upright.

Lay a stick across the hole and use this as a guide to set the tree at approximately the depth it was previously; spread the roots.

attached to their roots—they are moved bare-rooted. Exceptions are pot-grown specimens, which are set in the ground without breaking up the ball of soil in which the roots are growing. Larger perennial plants—clumps of perennials, as they are often called—are dug up and transplanted with as much soil sticking to the roots as is conveniently possible; sometimes, for convenience, the root ball is wrapped tightly in a piece of burlap.

Deciduous (leaf-losing) trees and shrubs may

After the soil is firmed, add more soil to bring the surface to grade or to form a shallow depression so that watering will be easier.

Then firm the added soil by treading as before; do this only when the soil is dry enough not to stick unpleasantly to the shoes.

be moved bare-rooted, or balled and burlapped (see Ball). When the latter plan is followed, care must be taken to lace the ball of soil in which the roots are growing securely and to make sure that the ball is not broken in handling or in transit or at the time of planting. With bare-rooted plants particular care must be exercised that the roots do not dry, even for a brief period, at any time.

Evergreens, except very small ones, should al-

ways be moved with a good ball of soil attached to their roots, never bare-rooted. In all cases great care should be taken that the roots do not dry out.

Planting from Individual Containers. Many kinds of plants are set out in the garden from individual containers. Bedding plants such as Geraniums, Lantanas, Fuchsias and Heliotropes are usually planted from pots. In California and some other parts of the West it has long been the custom for nurserymen to grow shrubs, trees and other plants in tin cans of various sizes— one gallon, five-gallon and so on.

This latter practice has spread in recent years to other parts of the country, and now in the

Finish the surface by loosening the upper inch or two with a fork. A mulch applied afterwards helps to retain moisture and promote root growth.

Prune away any unwanted shoots or branches; if staking is deemed desirable, the stake should be driven before the tree is set in the hole.

East and elsewhere many nurserymen carry a wide variety of plants in tin containers and in containers of special paper composition.

Plants grown in these containers and in pots can be set out much later than bare-rooted or balled and burlapped specimens of the same kinds; for example, it is perfectly practicable to set out Roses from containers when in bud or even bloom and, if given adequate aftercare, they will scarcely show the effect of moving.

When plants in leaf are set out from flowerpots or other containers, three important requirements must be met:

1. The soil in which the plants are growing must be moist. To ensure this, it should be soaked thoroughly a couple of hours or so before planting.

2. The plants should be removed from the containers and be set in place without breaking the ball of soil in which the roots are growing.

3. After planting, the roots must be kept uniformly moist. This means individual watering of the plants in dry weather, and at more frequent intervals than is necessary for plants that have been planted longer. Unlike well-established plants, specimens that have been recently transplanted do not have their roots down deep in the earth where they can tap supplies of

It is very important that a good mass of roots be retained even with small evergreens, and these must be protected from wind and sun so that they do not dry. To avoid delay and unnecessary exposure two men are planting here, one spreading the roots, the other filling in soil.

A slight depression is left about each plant and as soon as the soil is made firm it is watered thoroughly. Some pruning back of the top is done to compensate for the inevitable loss of some of the roots.

Evergreens must usually be transplanted with a ball of soil attached to their roots, but small specimens can be moved bare rooted. Here holes are being dug to receive bare-rooted Japanese Holly, Ilex crenata.

moisture, and thus they need this special attention.

When setting out plants from containers, it is important to make holes of ample size and to be sure that good soil is packed firmly about the root ball; loose planting permits water that is applied to run down the side of the ball rather than through it.

Austrian Pines dug with good balls of soil which have been securely wrapped in burlap are delivered at the planting site.

A few hours later, the same Pines have been planted to form a screen. For each a large hole was dug, the tree centered in it, good topsoil packed around the roots and then the tree was well watered. Each tree was securely guyed to three stakes.

Planting from Flats or Boxes. It is common practice to grow young plants that are to be set in the open garden and in window and porch boxes, in flats or shallow boxes. At planting-out time, these of necessity suffer more disturbance of their roots than plants grown individually in pots and other containers, but the added convenience of being able to grow twenty, thirty or more young plants in a single flat, instead of hav-

ing a large number of pots to care for, ofter outweighs this disadvantage.

It is important to transplant from flats befor the plants are so excessively large that they suffe from crowding and lack of nourishment. It is good idea, about two weeks before the plants ar set out, to take a knife and slice the soil in th flat into small rectangles, each containing single plant; this severs the roots and give time for new rootlets to start from the cut end before planting time, thus favoring rapid re establishment of the newly transplanted plant

In any case, the flat or box of young plant should be well watered a couple of hours befor the plants are transplanted, and every care shoul be exercised to retain a good ball of roots wit soil attached on each plant.

Condition of the Soil. It is a mistake to plan when soil is sodden, for it cannot then be broke easily into small particles, and to cover the root with lumpy, sodden soil is merely to court disap pointment. Furthermore, firming the soil b packing it (and this is a necessary procedure o good planting) seriously damages the texture o the soil, especially if it is at all clayey. If the soi is a little too wet at planting time it is a grea advantage to have some dry soil of good qualit for placing among and about the roots, for i then can be packed down firmly, without harm

In preparation for planting a balled and burlaped evergreen, hole of adequate depth and considerably wider than the roo ball is dug.

After the evergreen is placed in the hole at about the same depth as it previously grew, the burlap is removed from around the ball.

Good topsoil mixed with peat moss, humus or other organic matter is then filled in around the ball.

The soil is packed firmly about the roots with a stout piece of wood.

The saucerlike depression around the ball is then filled with water several times. After the water has soaked away it is filled with soil to grade level and a mulch is spread over the surface soil.

The Hole Must Be Large Enough. The first thing to do is to dig a hole large enough to take the roots when these are spread out, or to dig a hole considerably larger than the soil ball; to dig a small hole and cramp in the roots of a newly transplanted plant is a common cause of failure.

In planting small-sized ornamental trees, fruit trees, climbing Roses and others which are required to develop as quickly as possible, a hole 2 ft. deep and 2-3 ft. wide should be prepared; for larger specimens, proportionately larger holes should be prepared. The excavated soil should be placed at one side—the good topsoil in one heap, the less fertile undersoil in another. All very poor, infertile subsoil should be discarded and replaced with good soil. Such preparation gives the trees the opportunity of forming fresh roots freely, which they cannot do in hard, unfertile, or lumpy soil.

Deciduous trees are usually transplanted when they are dormant. This Willow is in leaf.

Special care is taken to move the trees because they are in leaf.

If the ground is poor, liberal amounts of organic matter—peat moss, compost, leaf mold or humus and, if possible, some decayed manure —should be mixed with the topsoil before it is filled in again.

Firm Planting Is Necessary. It is most necessary that trees and shrubs and other plants be planted firmly. In the case of trees and shrubs, the soil should be trodden down as it is put on the roots, or should be well packed around the ball. It is a mistake to fill in all the soil and then tread it down; with bare-rooted specimens the correct way is to cover each layer of roots and

pack the soil before the next layer of roots is covered. The roots of bare-rooted specimens should be spread out to their full extent.

When planting perennials, annuals and other small plants, the soil may be firmed with the fingers or with a stick.

It is sometimes found that the roots of bare rooted trees and shrubs are so entangled or matted together that it becomes a difficult matter to spread them out; the correct way to deal with them is to soak them in water; it will then be easier to disentangle them and spread them to their full extent.

Another detail of importance is to keep the roots moist during the time the trees and shrubs are out of the ground. When they arrive from the nursery they should be unpacked promptly and, if planting cannot be done at once, be "heeled in" by planting them temporarily, close together, in soil, in a sheltered place.

How to Revive Shriveled Plants. If Rose bushes or other small, leaf-losing shrubs and

After planting, the leafy trees are pruned by cutting out about one third of their top growth, watered and securely staked with three guy wires.

The shock of transplanting is lessened in flat-grown annuals if the soil is sliced into blocks, each containing a single plant, about two weeks before planting time.

The slicing process makes it easier to remove individual plants with good balls of soil and roots.

trees that are dormant are found to be so dry on being unpacked that the branches have begun to shrivel, they should be entirely buried in moist soil for a day or two; this has a markedly beneficial effect and, if they are not dried beyond recovery, soon restores the branches to their normal condition.

Leafy plants may be revived by watering the soil and spraying the foliage with water two or three times a day, at the same time keeping the plants out of drafts and wind, and shaded from direct sun.

Planting too deeply is a common error and is responsible for many failures and for much disappointment.

When trees and shrubs are received from a nursery there is usually a soil mark on the stem which shows how deeply they were planted, and it is safe to set them at the same depth. The uppermost roots should not be covered with more than 2 or 3 in. of soil. Planting deeply with the object of making a tree firm in the ground is wrong; if support is needed by trees to keep them upright it should be provided by stakes or guy wires.

Planting too deeply can also bring poor results with herbaceous perennial plants. Peonies are a good example of herbaceous perennials that suffer markedly from being planted at too

Young annuals, vegetables, etc., should be planted in holes large enough to hold their roots without crowding. The soil should be made firm about the roots.

great a depth; the buds on the crowns of Peony plants should not be more than 2 in. under the soil surface. Most other herbaceous perennials should be set not deeper than this, and some, such as Bearded Iris, are planted even more shallowly.

Bulbs, too, may be harmed by being set too deeply, although in most cases inexperienced gardeners plant them too shallowly. Some kinds, notably Madonna Lilies, fail to thrive if they are

It is important to plant bulbs at the right depths and at the right times. These Grape Hyacinths are being set out in fall. The flowering plant is Sternbergia lutea.

set deeply; in the case of Madonna Lilies the tips of the bulbs should not be more than 2 in. below the surface. In no case should bulbs be set so deep that they are encased in a clay subsoil or other infertile substratum or are in water-logged soil. Where unfavorable underground conditions exist, these should be corrected before the bulbs are planted, or it may be possible to avoid them by setting the bulbs at the minimum depths suitable for their kinds.

Annuals and biennials that are transplanted from pots, flats, cold frames and nursery beds should usually be set very slightly deeper than they have previously been, at such a depth that their surface roots are covered with not more than 1 in. of new soil.

Planting too shallowly can also be responsible for inferior results. If the surface roots of trees, shrubs, herbaceous perennials and annuals are exposed to sun and winds instead of being protected from drying by a shallow layer of moist soil over them, the plants are bound to suffer severely.

The kind of plants that are most commonly planted too shallowly are the majority of bulbs. It is true that a few kinds must be set near the surface, but, with most bulbs, beginners and inexperienced gardeners make the mistake of not planting them deeply enough. This is particularly likely to be the case with those kinds which produce roots from the portions of their stems that are underground, as is the case with

many Lilies. Bulbs planted too shallowly are likely to make weakly growth, to split into many smaller bulbs and to produce fewer flowers than those planted at a more reasonable depth. The exact depth to plant varies greatly according to kind and to a lesser degree according to the character of the soil; on light, sandy soils deeper planting than on heavy, clayey ones should be the rule.

Finishing the Job. Whenever a planting job is done it is important to complete it in a workman-like manner. The surface should be made even, all debris, such as burlap, string, pruning and the like, picked up and taken away, all foot marks removed and the surface slightly loosened with a cultivator, rake or other appropriate tool.

When trees and shrubs, including evergreens are planted in spring, it is a good plan to form a ridge of soil around each so that a saucer-shaped depression that will hold water is left above the roots. This makes soaking the soil on subsequent occasions an easier task. Ordinarily it is not necessary to form saucers around plants set out in fall, but under some circumstances it may be desirable then, too. If there is any danger that a newly planted tree may be loosened by wind or blown over it should be staked securely. See Staking.

Judicious pruning at planting time, by reducing the above-ground portions of the plant, will compensate for the inevitable damage that is done to the roots in any planting operation.

Unless the soil is moist at planting time and adequate rain falls shortly after the planting is finished, it will be necessary to water leafy plants in, to settle the soil about their roots and to make sure that they do not suffer from lack of availability of moisture. This watering should be thorough, sufficient water being given to make sure that the soil is saturated to the depth the roots go. Plants that are without leaves at planting time, such as dormant deciduous trees, shrubs, Roses, herbaceous perennials and bulbs, need not be watered in, following planting, even though the soil be moderately dry.

Trees and shrubs, especially evergreens or other kinds that are in leaf when they are transplanted, benefit tremendously if the surface of the ground about them is mulched with compost

[9–6]

This garden is planned to produce the maximum show of flowers from a small area

[9—7]
Aluminum Plant
(Pilea Cadierei)

[9—7b]
Polygonum campanulatum

[9—7c]
False Dragonhead
(Physostegia virginiana)

[9—7a]
Portulaca

A neat ridge of soil should be firmed around each newly planted tree to provide a saucer to make watering easier. Note that the trunk of this newly planted tree (center) has been wrapped in burlap to prevent danger from sunscald and that three stakes have been driven around the tree.

A few feet above the ground the trunk is secured to the three stakes by wires that pass through short pieces of hose where they encircle the tree.

well-rotted manure, leaf mold, peat moss or other suitable material following planting. This conserves moisture and tends to promote a reasonably even soil temperature that is favorable to the development of roots.

It is common practice to wrap the trunks of newly moved deciduous trees with burlap or with a type of paper that is made especially for the purpose, to eliminate danger from sunscald and consequent splitting of the bark. Such protection is left in place for a full season after planting. Another practice sometimes followed is to spray the above-ground portions of plants in leaf with latex or plastic sprays, of kinds especially made for the purpose and obtainable from dealers in garden supplies. These sprays temporarily seal the pores (stomata) of the leaves and so materially reduce moisture loss by transpiration.

Evergreens set out in exposed, windy locations may be assisted to re-establish themselves by erecting a screen of burlap or by sticking evergreen branches in the ground about them to provide shade and windbreak for some weeks or months.

Aftercare. Following planting, care must be taken that the newly moved plants do not suffer from lack of moisture. Daily sprinkling of the soil should be avoided; instead, the soil should be inspected at weekly intervals and, if it seems to be approaching dryness at a depth of 3 or 4 in., it should be soaked to a depth of 8-9 in. or more and then left unwatered until it again approaches a similar stage of dryness. This type of care should extend for at least one full growing season in the case of trees and shrubs, including evergreens; for a lesser period in the case of plants that re-establish themselves more quickly.

Temporary shading is often helpful to newly transplanted plants that possess foliage at the time they are moved; this shading is especially necessary if the roots have been much disturbed or if the weather is such that it makes for rapid transpiration (loss of moisture vapor) from the leaves. Whenever possible, experienced gardeners choose times for transplanting leafy plants when the transpiration rate is low—periods of dull weather when atmospheric humidity is high and there is no wind which might cause rapid drying. But this cannot always be done; often planting must be performed under conditions other than ideal. Then it is that shading the newly set-out plants with burlap, slat screens, branches of evergreens or other suitable devices is advantageous. The shade may be left in place for two or three days to two or three weeks or more, until the plants seem to have recovered from the shock of transplanting and are able to stand, without shade, without wilting.

Spraying newly transplanted plants lightly with water at frequent intervals, two or three times a day say, also helps to check transpiration and is helpful in encouraging the plants to re-establish themselves and get over the shock of having been moved. Such sprinklings must not be confused with watering. The function of the sprinklings is not to soak the soil (indeed, care should be taken not to do this; at most, the soil surface should be just moistened), but to wet all leaves, both their upper and lower surfaces, and all trunks and stems. This periodic spraying, like shading, should be kept up until the plants have recovered considerably from the shock of transplanting.

PLANTLET. A little plant. Sometimes the term is used to describe tiny seedlings, but more frequently it refers to small plants that form or the leaves or other parts of larger plants, as i the case with certain Kalanchoës and Tolmei Menziesii.

PLASHING. A term used in the renovatior of Hawthorn and other hedges. It consists o cutting back the side growths of overgrown anc old hedges, partly cutting through the mair stems, laying them in the line of the hedge anc pegging them into position by means of stake driven into the ground vertically.

When the work is carried out in a correc manner the old branches live and strong youn, shoots appear from below where the cuts wer« made. By this means a hedge that has becom« very thin at the bottom can be transformed, ir the course of a year or two, into a really stron, and vigorous hedge again.

In a smaller way, plashing can also be usec for filling gaps in hedges; a branch or two partl cut through and pegged into a gap will soor strengthen the weak place. This method is partic ularly useful where, owing to the large numbe of roots, it is not possible to insert a young plant.

PLATANUS—*Plane Tree* (Plat'anus). Leaf losing (deciduous) trees of large size that ar« natives of North America, southeastern Europ« and Asia Minor. The eastern American Plan« Tree, P. occidentalis, is also called Buttonwooc and sometimes Sycamore, although this latte name traditionally belongs to Ficus Sycamorus

Platanus is the only genus of the family Platan aceae. The name is the old Greek one for th« tree. It was probably derived from *platys,* broad in allusion to the large leaves.

Trees Which Shed Their Bark. The Plan« trees are peculiar because of the way in which they shed their bark. Some bark shedding is con stantly taking place, but every few years mor« than usual is thrown off, and sections 2 or ! feet long and 12 in. or more wide may fall fre quently during the summer, revealing large area of the young, yellowish or greenish bark beneath This natural bark shedding may be one reasor why some of the Planes are such good tow trees, for a good deal of the dirt accumulated or the trees is thrown off with the bark.

Another peculiarity of the Plane trees is the

Plantlets developing along the edge of a leaf of Kalanchoë Daigremontiana.

The London Plane, Platanus acerifolia.

The Buttonwood, Platanus occidentalis, a native of eastern North America, is one of the most noble of trees. Its bark scales off the trunk and major branches, exposing large light yellow patches.

microscope, look like minute stems of Bamboo.

The leaves of Plane trees are like those of the Sycamore Maple in shape, but are larger and glossier. They differ in that the base of each leaf forms a definite cap which fits closely over the young buds. When a leaf falls, the hollow that has fitted over the bud is clearly seen.

Trees Which Need Plenty of Space. Plane trees form magnificent specimens where they have space to develop. They naturally form large trunks, with shapely wide-spreading heads, and this should be remembered at planting time. Close spacing should be avoided when trees are intended for ornamental purposes. They should never be less than 60 ft. apart—80 ft. would be better.

When the trees are planted along the sides of streets, wide spacing results in less pruning being required; but it is rarely as a street tree that the Plane is seen at its best. Magnificent specimens may be seen where they can grow without the constant cropping of the branches that is often so necessary when Planes are used as street trees.

How to Prune Plane Trees. Young Plane trees need pruning. Those in nurseries should have their side branches shortened once or twice during summer, and now and then a lower branch should be removed. When planted in permanent

These London Plane Trees growing in New Jersey have been severely pruned back periodically for a great many years.

manner in which the tiny flowers are congregated into dense round heads at the ends of stringlike stalks, and the way in which the fruits mature in round ball-like masses. These heads of fruits persist throughout winter, and break up in spring. The seeds are covered with jointed hairs which, when closely observed under a places, trees may be 8-10 ft. high with a clear leading shoot, and one third of the lower part should be clear of branches. After permanent planting, attention to pruning must still be given, the object being to keep the leading shoot clear of rivals, to regulate the development of side branches, and to remove the lower branches as may be necessary.

The object in view should be to produce a tree with the lower part of its trunk free from branches, the trunk running well up into the crown, supporting a shapely head of sturdy branches. Such a tree is able to withstand storms much better than a tree that has been allowed to grow with two or more main stems starting a few feet from the ground. Plane trees, especially the London Plane, stand repeated severe pruning extremely well. If necessary, they can be restrained to any convenient size or shape by cutting them hard back every year or two. This treatment is often necessary in city gardens.

Propagation can be carried out by seeds or by cuttings of ripened shoots, 12 in. long, inserted in a cold frame or border out of doors in autumn or by layers pegged down in spring, the layers being shoots a year old from "stool" plants. They may also be propagated by air layering. Young plants grow very rapidly, and they may be 8-10 ft. high and sturdy trees at the end of the third year.

Plane trees thrive in any ordinary soil but prefer one that is fairly rich and not too dry.

The London Plane is Platanus acerifolia, presumably a hybrid between P. orientalis and P. occidentalis. The origin of this very widely grown and useful tree is unknown. When given suitable conditions, it grows over 100 ft. high with a stout, erect trunk at least 12-15 ft. in girth, with a very wide-spreading, but shapely head of branches. The lobed leaves are 6-10 in. across, according to the age and vigor of the tree. The balls of fruits are borne 2-6 together at intervals on pendulous stalks. The London Plane withstands the dust of cities better than most other trees.

The Buttonwood or Plane Tree, P. occidentalis, a native of eastern North America, is one of our most noble leaf-losing (deciduous) trees. It forms a wide-spreading tree, 100-150 ft. tall and also develops a tree trunk of great girth.

Less easy to transplant than the London Plane, the Buttonwood also takes less kindly to city conditions, although it is a good tree for country towns where the atmosphere is not much polluted. The fruit clusters or balls are nearly always solitary, occasionally in pairs (those of the London Plane are nearly always in twos and sometimes more).

The Oriental Plane, P. orientalis, is a very large tree, native to southeastern Europe and Asia Minor, where it sometimes exceeds 100 ft. in height and produces a trunk up to 20 ft. in diameter. The leaves are divided into finer segments than those of the London Plane, but among seedling trees the leafage is very variable. The Oriental Plane is scarcely known in the United States, and trees offered under this name by nurserymen are almost always London Planes.

P. cuneata, from the Himalayas, is often regarded as a form of P. orientalis. It appears to be a smaller, slower-growing tree with smaller leaves.

Other Kinds. P. racemosa and P. Wrightii are two kinds from California, Mexico, etc., that are less hardy than the others mentioned and are suitable for planting in mild climates only.

Economic Uses. The wood of the Plane trees is of good quality, very prettily marked when sawed radially, and useful for furniture and other purposes. The wood of Plane trees, when cut radially, is sometimes called Lacewood because of its pretty marking.

PLATYCERIUM—*Staghorn Fern* (Platycerium). Tender Ferns which are found wild in tropical Africa, Malaya, tropical Asia, Madagascar, Java and Australia. They are quite distinct in appearance from all other Ferns and have two kinds of fronds, barren and fertile. The fertile (spore-bearing) fronds are from 18 in. to 3 ft. in length, flat, narrow at the base, and spreading out to a great width at the tips, where they are deeply divided and bear a striking resemblance to the horns of the stag or elk. These fronds are pendulous and produce the spores in large, irregular patches.

At the base of the fertile fronds the barren fronds are produced; these are thin, almost round, heart-shaped at the base, green when

The remarkable Staghorn Fern, Platycerium bifurcatum (alcicorne).

young, but brown and papery when they mature.

The name Platycerium is derived from *platys,* broad, and *keras,* a horn and refers to the shape of the fronds.

Ferns Which Grow on Trees. As these Ferns are epiphytal (grow on the branches and trunks of trees), the barren fronds serve the dual purpose of supporting them and collecting food material. They lie flat against the branches, completely encircling the smaller ones and so hold the plant in position; dead leaves and other organic material collect behind them and provide the Ferns with food. The thin, threadlike roots also adhere closely to the branches of the supporting trees and obtain their moisture from the water which trickles down the trunks. Small green buds are formed at intervals, on the roots; eventually they expand and develop into new plants.

Ferns for the Hothouse and Cool Greenhouse. The majority of these Ferns require a minimum winter temperature of 55 degrees, but one kind,

P. bifurcatum (alcicorne), a native of Australia, can be grown in a greenhouse with a minimum temperature of 45 degrees. They need a light, porous, moisture-holding compost. The most suitable mixture consists of equal parts of orchid peat (osmunda fiber) and finely chopped sphagnum moss. To this should be added a small portion of crushed charcoal, which prevents the compost from becoming sour, and some half-decayed oak leaves.

Various Methods of Cultivation. There are various methods of growing these Ferns. In a greenhouse where suitable positions are available, large slabs of cork bark are fixed to the wall to form pockets; the special compost is then inserted behind the cork, and the plants, placed on the surface of the compost, are held in position by wooden pegs.

They are also sometimes grown on pieces of tree trunk, which are supported in an upright position, either by being fixed in the soil in the floor of the greenhouse or in large flowerpots. The plants are held in position by a little of the compost placed behind the barren or clasping fronds. They are at first fixed to the trunk with an encircling band of thin wire, but later they attach themselves and become self-supporting.

May Be Grown as Pot Plants. A slab of cork bark, or a piece of tree branch, preferably Cedar, Cypress, Redwood or some other long-lasting kind, the length of which is twice the depth of the pot, is placed upright in the pot. The pot is nearly filled with crocks, which provide adequate drainage and also hold the bark or branch in position. The plant is then fixed to the bark or branch in the way previously described. The barren fronds eventually envelop the support and hide it completely from view.

The soil compost must be kept moist throughout the year. During the summer months water is applied copiously, but for the remainder of the year it is only given when the soil is approaching dryness.

The Ferns should not be disturbed after they have been fixed to the support; a top-dressing of fresh compost annually, in spring, is sufficient to keep them growing vigorously. They are shaded from strong sunlight and a moist atmosphere is maintained by damping the floor and benches whenever they show a sign of dryness.

Propagation. All kinds, except P. grande, produce from their bases small rooted Ferns which may be detached and planted in a pan filled with sifted soil compost. The detached plantlets are held in position on the surface of the soil by pegging them in place with pieces of wire bent to hairpin shape or by wooden pegs. The soil is kept moist and, when the plants are large enough, they are fixed in their permanent positions in the manner already described.

These Ferns may also be raised from spores but this method is rarely adopted (except for P. grande, the kind which does not produce small plants from the roots), as it is a much slower process. The spores must be fully ripe before they are sown. To test them for ripeness when the spores are brown a frond is gathered and placed in a paper bag, which is hung in a well-ventilated position for a few days. The spores which are found at the bottom of the bag are sufficiently ripe for sowing. A deep pan or pot is nearly filled with crocks, over which a layer of rough peat or moss is placed. The remainder of the space is filled with peat moss and finely chopped sphagnum moss.

The spores are sprinkled on the surface and the compost is kept moist by standing the pot in a saucer of water. Development is very slow, but when the young Ferns are large enough to handle they are lifted carefully and set 2 in. apart in deep pans filled with similar compost, where they are kept moist until they are large enough to fix in their permanent positions.

The Chief Kinds. For the cool greenhouse: P. bifurcatum (alcicorne), 2-3 ft. For the hothouse: P. grande, 4-6 ft.; P. Willinckii, 2-3 ft.; and P. Stemaria (aethiopicum), 2-3 ft. The measurements refer to the fronds.

PLATYCLINIS. Dendrochilum, which see.

PLATYCODON   GRANDIFLORUM—Balloonflower (Platyco'don). A hardy herbaceous perennial which belongs to the Bellflower family, Campanulaceae. It is a native of China and Japan. The name Platycodon is derived from platys, broad, and kodon, a bell, and refers to the form of the flowers.

For Flower Border or Rock Garden. This attractive plant grows 12-18 in. high and bears

Platycodon grand-
iflorum, the Bal-
loon Flower.

somewhat saucer-shaped, or broadly companu-
late, blue flowers in July and August. (The
popular name of Balloon Flower is derived from
the somewhat balloon-shaped flower buds.) Platycodon flourishes in ordinary well-cultivated garden soil in a sunny or only slightly shady position, and dislikes being disturbed. It is suitable
for planting towards the front of the herbaceous
border or in the rock garden. Planting is preferably carried out in October or in early spring.

Raising Seedlings. As Platycodon flourishes
best when left undisturbed from year to year,
seedlings should be raised if an increased stock

A group of the
clear blue Platyco-
don grandiflorum
Mariesii flowering
freely in a semi-
shady border.

is required. Seeds are sown in a flat of sifted
sandy soil placed in a slightly heated greenhouse,
or in a cold frame in April. The flat of seeds
must be kept moist and shaded.

When the seedlings are an inch or so high
they should be potted separately in 3-in pots,
filled with sandy, loamy soil, and grown in a cold
frame. As soon as they are well rooted in the
pots, the seedlings are planted out of doors where
they are to grow. Platycodon can also be propagated by division in spring.

The flowers of the typical kind, Platycodon
grandiflorum, are blue; there is a white variety,
album. The variety Mariesii is more dwarf, with
larger, deep blue flowers.

PLATYLOBIUM—*Flat Pea* (Platylo'bium). A
small group of evergreen flowering shrubs, natives of Australia, which belong to the Pea family, Leguminosae. They are not in general cultivation, but are suitable for the cool greenhouse
and for outdoor cultivation in California and
similar mild climates. They grow from 12 in.
to 4 ft. in height, have small, opposite triangular
leaves, in the axils of which the yellow, pea-
shaped flowers are produced in summer. The
calyx has two large upper lobes which unite to
form a hood; the seed pods are flat and winged.
The name Platylobium is derived from *platys,*
broad, and *lobos,* a pod, and refers to the flat
seed pods.

Flowering Shrubs for a Cool Greenhouse. They
require very little heat, sufficient only in winter
to keep the temperature above freezing point.
The best compost consists of equal parts of loam,
peat and sand.

Repotting is done after the plants have finished
flowering. The shoots are slightly shortened, and
syringed frequently to assist them to break into
growth; the plants are then repotted in slightly
larger well-drained pots. Potting is done firmly,
and the shoots are again syringed frequently to
assist the roots in penetrating the new compost; no water is applied to the soil until it becomes moderately dry, and then it is kept moist
through the summer.

From July to September the plants are placed
out of doors on a bed of ashes in a sunny position to ripen the shoots for flower production.
They are taken into the greenhouse before frost

and the soil is only moistened during winter when it becomes fairly dry. When growth becomes active in spring, more water is given and the soil is kept moist until the plants have finished flowering.

Propagation is by seeds and cuttings. Seeds are sown in pots of sandy soil in spring.

Cuttings of short firm side shoots are inserted in a greenhouse or close cold frame in July and August.

The chief kinds are P. obtusangulum, 12 in., yellow and red, May; P. formosum, 4 ft., yellow, July.

PLATYSTEMON CALIFORNICUS—*Cream-cups* (Platystem'on). An attractive annual, a native of California, belonging to the Poppy family, Papaveraceae. The word Platystemon is derived from *platys*, broad, and *stemon*, stamen.

This plant is far less often grown in gardens than many other hardy annuals, but it is well worth a place in a sunny border, in light, well-drained soil. It is not likely to flourish on heavy, clayey ground, though this can be made suitable by mixing in peat moss, leaf mold, thoroughly decayed manure and sand.

For a Sunny Border. Platystemon does well in full sun but it does not thrive in excessively hot and humid weather. It reaches a height of about 12 in., has attractive grayish-green leaves, and comparatively large, saucer-shaped flowers of light yellow or sulphur-yellow color. Although

The hardy annual Platystemon californicus.

the individual blooms are not long-lived, they continue to open for some weeks if the faded ones are picked off.

The seeds should be sown thinly, out of doors where the plants are to bloom, early in spring. The seedlings should be thinned to 4 or 5 in apart.

For the Greenhouse. From seeds sown in September attractive plants in 4-in. pots may be had in bloom in the cool, sunny greenhouse in late winter and spring. A night temperature of 45-50 degrees is suitable.

PLATYTHECA GALIOIDES (Platythe'ca). A dwarf, tender shrub of Australia, belonging to the family Tremandraceae. It is a heathlike plant with slender stems and grows about 18 in in height. The leaves are linear (long and narrow) and ¾ in. long, and are produced in whorls of nine or ten. The light purple flowers which are rotate (wheel-shaped), five-petaled, and one inch in diameter, are produced in the axils of the leaves in summer. The name Platytheca is derived from *platys*, broad, and *theke*, a cell, and refers to the broad anther cells.

A Free-flowering Greenhouse Shrub. When grown in the greenhouse, this shrub requires a minimum winter temperature of 45 degrees and the best soil compost consists of four parts of fibrous peat and one part of sand.

Repotting is done after flowering. The shoots are shortened by one half, and are frequently syringed to assist new shoots to form. When these are ¼ in. in length, the plants are taken out of the pots and the crocks removed from the roots with minimum disturbance of the roots. The ball of soil is not broken, but some of the main roots are loosened so that they may enter the new compost more readily. The pots are well drained with crocks, and these are covered with rough leaves. When potting, the soil must be made very firm.

Summer and Winter Treatment. No water is applied to the soil until it becomes moderately dry, then it is well moistened. This system of watering is continued until the plants are well rooted, and for the remainder of the summer the soil is kept moist. During the winter much less water is required, but the soil must not be allowed to remain dry for long periods, nor must it become waterlogged, as these conditions are fatal.

Very little syringing and shading are required. Immediately after the plants have been repotted, and until they become established, the stems are lightly sprayed daily, and the plants are shaded from strong sunlight. Afterwards, they are exposed to full light, and the greenhouse is ventilated freely in favorable weather throughout the year.

Propagation Is by Cuttings. Firm side shoots are removed with a "heel" in spring and inserted in pots of fine sandy peat, in a greenhouse propagating case. When sufficient roots are formed, the cuttings are potted separately in 2-in. pots, and subsequently in larger pots. To obtain bushy plants, the tips of the main shoots are pinched out and the subsequent side branches are treated similarly.

PLEACH. A method of training trees by interweaving their branches and by pruning them appropriately so that they form continuous narrow walls or hedges of greenery.

PLECTRANTHUS (Plectran'thus). A considerable group of tropical and subtropical perennial herbaceous plants, subshrubs and shrubs that are widely dispersed over the warmer parts of the Old World, Australia and the Pacific islands. Those cultivated are grown chiefly in greenhouses and one or two as window-garden plants. Plectranthus belongs in the Mint family, Labiatae. The name comes from *plectron,* a spur, and *anthos,* a flower, and refers to the swollen base of the flower tube.

Cultivation. These plants thrive in a greenhouse where a minimum winter temperature of 55 degrees is maintained. They need a moist atmosphere and light shade from strong summer sunshine. The soil should be rich with organic matter, rather coarse and well drained. From spring to fall the plants should be watered generously, but during the winter months the soil should be kept in a dryer condition.

Well-established plants that have filled their pots with healthy roots benefit from regular applications of dilute liquid fertilizers. Occasional

This path at Williamsburg, Virginia, is covered with a continuous arch of pleached trees.

pinching of the shoots during the early part of the growing season is usually necessary to ensure desirable bushy plants.

Propagation is readily effected by seeds sown in spring in pots or pans of light soil rich in humus, and by cuttings made in spring and placed in a close propagating case in a greenhouse or under approximately similar conditions in a window garden. The young plants should be potted, as soon as they have made roots about an inch long, in small pots in a sandy soil well mixed with peat moss or leaf mold.

Chief Kinds. P. chiradzulensis, 8 ft., flowers bright blue, winter; P. fruticosus, shrub, 3-4 ft., blue, summer; P. Oertendahlii, 6-8 in., white, summer-fall.

PLEIOBLASTUS (Pleioblast'us). A group of Bamboos closely related to Arundinaria and requiring the same cultural general care. See Bamboo. They belong to the Grass family, Gramineae. The name is derived from *pleios,* many, and *blastos,* a shoot or sprout. These plants are natives of the Orient and most are tender in the North, although a few may be expected to live as far north as New York City in sheltered locations. Among the hardiest are P. distichus, P. pumilus, P. variegatus, P. viridi-striatus and its variety vagans.

Kinds. P. Chino (Arundinaria Maximowiczii), 6 ft., leaves green, mottled yellow; P. distichus (Bambusa disticha), 2-2½ ft., leaves bright green; P. Hindsii (Arundinaria Hindsii), 12 ft., leaves glaucous beneath; P. humilis (Arundinaria humilis), 3 ft., leaves pale green; P. pumilus (Arundinaria pumila), 2 ft., stems with waxy covering; P. variegatus (Arundinaria variegata), 3 ft., leaves green and white striped; P. viridi-striatus (Arundinaria auricoma), 4 ft., leaves striped green and yellow. P. viridi-striatus variety vagans grows 2 ft. tall, has green leaves and spreads to form large clumps.

PLEIOGYNIUM SOLANDRI — *Burdekin Plum* (Pleiogyn'ium). An Australian evergreen tree that is planted in California and Florida. It attains a height of 40-60 ft. and produces plumlike fruits that are used for preserves. Pleiogynium belongs to the botanical family Anacardiaceae, the Cashew family. Its name is derived from *pleios,* many, and *gyne,* woman,

but the application of the etymology is unclear.

The Burdekin Plum is propagated by seeds. It seems to thrive on a variety of soils.

PLEIONE—*Indian Crocus* (Ple'ione). These Orchids grow wild chiefly in northern India, but they are also found in other parts and in Tibet, Burma and Ceylon. All are epiphytal or semi-terrestrial, many growing wild on banks and tree trunks. They are sometimes included in Coelogyne by botanists, but they have long been known as Pleione. They differ from Coelogyne in their habit of growth and need different treatment.

Most of these Orchids are deciduous (leaf-losing), and from small fleshy pseudobulbs which are of annual duration only. The leaves are plicate (folded lengthwise like a fan) and are on the top of flask-shaped pseudobulbs, from the bases of which arise the flowering stems. Most kinds bloom in winter.

Pleiones produce comparatively large flowers most of which are some shade of pink, but some are white with bright red blotches.

Pleione is named after Pleione, the mother of the mythological Pleiades. These plants belong to the family Orchidaceae.

Winter-flowering Orchids. A greenhouse in which the winter temperature does not fall below 50 degrees is needed for the cultivation of these Orchids; in summer it will, of course, be considerably warmer, though tropical heat is not needed. Shading should be placed in position early in the year but removed in early autumn.

Best When Repotted Every Year. Repotting should be done soon after the flowers fade (with some kinds, in December). The flower pans should be well drained; the compost consists of two parts of osmunda fiber, two parts of loam fiber, one part of sphagnum moss and a little sand and leaf mold. The compost should be moist and the bulbs placed about 2 in. apart, five or more in a pan. The compost may be rather higher in the center than at the sides of the flower pans. The bulbs should be watered very little until growth is active. As growth advances more warmth is necessary.

After the bulbs are fully developed, water is seldom required until growth begins again. A shelf near the glass throughout the year is the best place for them except when they are in flower; then they are placed on the greenhouse benches.

The Chief Kinds. P. praecox has rose-purple flowers, those of the horticultural variety Wallichiana being slightly larger and of darker coloring; P. maculata has white sepals and petals, the lip marked with crimson; P. lagenaria has light rose-lilac sepals and petals, the lip marked with crimson and purple.

PLEIOSPILOS (Pleiospi'los). Dwarf succulents belonging to the family Aizoaceae, and embraced by the great group of plants broadly classed as Mesembryanthemums. The name is from *pleios,* full, and *spilos,* spot, and refers to the conspicuous spots on the leaves.

These succulents, which thrive under conditions similar to those recommended for Mesembryanthemum, produce their thick, dull green, almost stone-like leaves in pairs, between which the comparatively large, stemless daisy-like flowers are produced in early autumn. The plants

Pleiospilos Nelii.

Pleiospilos simulans.

need a distinct rest when the new leaves are fully grown.

Cultivated kinds include P. Bolusii, with short stems, short, broad leaves, and golden-yellow flowers; P. Nelii, similar to P. Bolusii but more compact; P. nobilis, thick, narrow, gray-green leaves with small, raised dots, yellow flowers; and P. simulans, large fleshy triangular leaves and large yellow flowers.

PLEROMA—*Brazilian Spiderflower.* Tibouchina, which see.

PLEURISY ROOT. Asclepias tuberosa, which see.

PLEUROTHALLIS (Pleurothall'is). Free-flowering Orchids which are found wild in the West Indies and Central America. They are epiphytal (grow on trees) and evergreen; the place of pseudobulbs is taken by slender stems which bear a single leathery leaf. The flowers are usually in many-flowered spikes from the junction of stem and leaf, often three together. The flowers are pale in color and small, the sepals often almost concealing the smaller petals and lip. The plants bloom at various periods of the year. The name is derived from *pleuron,* a side vein, and *thallo,* to bloom, and refers to the inflorescence. Pleurothallis belongs to the family Orchidaceae.

Orchids for a Warm Greenhouse. Nearly all these Orchids grow wild at considerable altitudes; they require a greenhouse in which the night temperature is as near 60 degrees as possible throughout the year. Light shading must be given through the spring, summer and early autumn, and the plants must be watered liberally in warm weather and, when necessary, in winter.

A suitable compost consists of three parts of osmunda fiber, two parts of sphagnum moss and one part of leaf mold; drainage should be free. Repotting is done in late winter or early spring, just as the new growths are seen, and plants which are large enough may then be divided if an increased number is required. Some of the smaller sorts can be grown on pieces of wood or small flower pans suspended in the greenhouse.

The Chief Kinds. P. Birchenallii bears flowers with purplish-red sepals and whitish petals in spring and summer; P. Roezlii has large port-wine-colored flowers in February and March; P. gelida bears erect spikes of yellowish flowers; P. astrophora has very small starry flowers, deep purple and white.

PLICATE. A botanical term meaning pleated, or folded in the manner of a fan, or somewhat resembling that condition in general appearance.

PLUG. A small piece of grass turf cut from established turf areas and used for planting new lawns. Only a few grasses, such as Zoysia, are commonly propagated in this way and the method is more common in the South than in the North.

PLUM: MOST VERSATILE OF TREE FRUITS
A Guide to the Culture of Many Different Kinds for All Regions

The Common, or European Plum is thought to have originated in southwestern Europe or the Caucasian region of western Asia. It came to North America with the earliest colonists and is now valued as a home garden fruit and is the basis of the important Plum and Prune industry of the Pacific coast and the plum-growing regions near the Great Lakes. The Japanese Plum, although of Chinese origin, was introduced from Japan in 1870. The Damson Plum came from the region around Damascus in Asia Minor. America has several native Plum species, but none are of major importance, although they furnish varieties for regions where the imported species fail.

The Plum is the most widely distributed tree

Japanese Plum variety Shiro.

The Stanley Plum is a favorite for eating as a fresh fruit.

fruit in the United States and Canada. There are varieties suitable for cultivation in every state.

The commercial Plum industry is mostly located in California, Oregon, Washington and Idaho, in which states Prunes are grown extensively. The fruit-growing regions near the Great Lakes in Michigan, Ohio, New York and Ontario are suitable for Plums, but production there is small in comparison with that of the Pacific coast.

Plums of the European type vary considerably in hardiness, but on the average are about as hardy as the Baldwin Apple. The Japanese varieties vary more, some being less hardy than Peaches, others hardier than the European varieties. The native Plums in various species and varieties range widely in their climate tolerance: some withstand the harsh winters of the prairie provinces of Canada, while others can tolerate the climate of the hot, humid Gulf Coast States. The Damson Plums are very hardy.

Site and Soil

The best sites for Plum orchards are near large bodies of water, which prevent the temperatures from going too low on still, cold nights in the winter, or on frosty nights when the trees are blooming. The cold water in the spring tends to delay blooming until danger of frost is past; this is a desirable feature, as Plums are early-blooming and easily injured by frost while in bloom.

Sloping sites provide air drainage and circulation, and temperatures on a slope are much safer than in a low spot surrounded by higher land. Good air circulation also reduces losses from brown rot, a fungus disease that is more serious where moisture remains long on the foliage (see Pests and Diseases). The Japanese varieties are better on a north-facing slope, which tends to delay their early blooming.

Plums are thought to do better on clay loams rather than the lighter soil types which are preferred for Peaches. The lighter soils, if not too light, may be used if they are reasonably fertile, in good physical condition and well supplied with moisture. Whatever the soil, good drainage is important; Plums are susceptible to injury from a high water table, as are most other fruits. They are, however, more tolerant of excessive moisture than Peaches and Cherries.

Propagation

Plum trees are usually propagated by budding on the Myrobalan Plum (Prunus cerasifera) rootstock. This stock is more tolerant of poor soil aeration than other Plum rootstocks, and most varieties of the European Plum do well on it. Moreover, it is a cheap, easily propagated stock; trees from nurseries are usually on Myrobalan roots. Marianna, a selected clone of Myrobalan Plum which grows readily from cuttings, is occasionally used, and it is thought to be nematode-resistant.

Peach rootstocks are sometimes used for Plums to be grown on the lighter soils; the Japanese Plums grow as well on Peach as on Myrobalan Plum. In the past, the St. Julien rootstock, a strain of the Damson Plum, has been used in North America, and it is still considered a satisfactory Plum rootstock in Europe.

In the upper Mississippi valley the Myrobalan rootstock is not hardy, and seedlings of Prunus americana, a native American Plum, are used for the varieties of native and hybrid Plums grown in that region.

The Sand Cherry, Prunus Besseyi, has been used to a limited extent as a dwarfing stock for Plums, but trees on this rootstock should be used only in garden plantings.

Pollination

Plum varieties differ in their pollination requirements; some are fully self-sterile, others are self-fertile (for definitions of these terms, see the article under each). Among the self-fertile varieties of European Plums are Reine Claude, Italian Prune, Stanley, Agen, California Blue and Yellow Egg. Since there are apparently one or more clones of some Plum varieties and some are listed as self-fertile by one investigator and self-sterile by another, it is well to plant more than one variety to insure cross-pollination. The Japanese and American varieties should not be used to pollinate varieties of the European type.

The Damson varieties, Shropshire and French, are self-fertile.

A few Japanese varieties—Beauty, Methley, Climax and Santa Rosa—are partially self-fertile, but the others are self-sterile, and more than one variety should be planted to be certain of adequate cross-pollination. The European varieties do not pollinate the Japanese ones.

Self-sterility is common among the native American Plum species and cross-pollination should be provided for all varieties. The Japanese-American hybrids are all self-sterile and many have poor pollen, so that they are not suitable pollenizers for each other.

Some of the Japanese-American hybrids, however, have good pollen, and are known to be good pollenizers of other Japanese-American Plums. Kaga and South Dakota 27, both desirable varieties, are among these. Surprise, a native Plum variety, is also a good pollenizer for the Japanese-American hybrid Plums.

Compass is a suitable pollenizer for the Sand Cherry-Plum hybrids.

Planting

The trees may be planted at any time during the winter on the West Coast and in the fall in the milder parts of the East. Elsewhere spring planting is safer. The spacing varies somewhat according to the fertility of the soil and the vigor of the variety. The usual spacing is 20 by 20 ft., but as much as 25 by 25 ft. is some-times better. Either one- or two-year-old trees may be used.

Preparation of the soil and planting the trees are the same as for the Apple, which see.

Soil Management

Plum trees are much more tolerant of grass sod than Peach trees are, and in general the soil may be managed as for Apple trees. The principal requirement of the method of managing the soil is to maintain good tree vigor and productiveness. This may be done in various ways.

Cultivation until midsummer, followed by a cover crop, is effective, but it leaves the soil subject to erosion in spring and early summer and, as the orchard grows older, cover crop growth becomes weak. Where erosion is a problem the maintenance of a grass sod which is discouraged at intervals by using a disc harrow is a suitable method of handling the soil. The sod is not completely eliminated at any time. Some cover always remains as a protection against erosion, yet it does not offer much competition for moisture and nutrients at critical times.

Mulching is also a satisfactory method of handling the soil, and a hay mulch may be expected to supply much, if not all, of the nutrient requirements of the trees. Mulching is especially satisfactory for home orchards.

Nitrogen is most likely to be the best element for the orchardist to supply to the soil. Phosphorus is usually present in abundant supply for Plum trees, and need not be added unless required for the cover crop. Trees from 1 to 3 years old should receive up to one-half pound of nitrate of soda after the first year, and from ½ to 2 pounds from the third to the fifth years; older trees should receive from 2 to 4 pounds, depending on tree vigor. Other materials to supply equivalent amounts of nitrogen may be substituted. Tree vigor, as shown by new shoot growth, color and size of foliage and size of crop should be the guiding factor in determining fertilizer applications rather than hard and fast rules as to number of pounds per tree.

Potash deficiency occasionally shows up in Italian Prune trees. The leaves appear nearly normal in the spring, but by midsummer a slight curling of the midrib appears and this is followed by the death of the marginal leaf-blade tissue. Usually only the outer foliage on the tree is affected.

This condition may be corrected with heavy applications of manure and potash fertilizers. Response is sometimes delayed a year or two. It is likely that heavy mulching with hay in connection with the potash applications might be effective in reducing the effects of potash deficiency.

Pruning

Plum trees vary greatly in growth habit, from upright to spreading. The European varieties are mostly upright, especially when young, the Damsons are very upright, while the Japanese varieties vary from upright to the very spreading habit of Burbank.

The modified leader type of tree is preferred. The head is formed at planting time by selecting 3 or 4 well-spaced branches and removing the others. During the first few years pruning should be very light and corrective in nature to promote the development of a structurally strong tree without bad crotches. The center should not be allowed to become too dense, as this reduces the effectiveness of the sprays needed to control brown rot.

Bearing Plum trees are pruned lightly, mostly by thinning throughout the tree. Large water sprouts (sappy, upright-growing shoots) are cut out. Heavy pruning tends to dwarf the tree and delay bearing, and should be avoided. The Japanese varieties require heavier pruning than the European varieties.

Pruning on the Pacific coast should be much heavier than in the East, as the hot, dry summers favor heavier crops than can grow to large size with the moisture available. The smaller fruiting branches are thinned out. The shoots of the previous season's growth are thinned out or headed back to stimulate the vigorous growth that produces satisfactory crops of large Plums in the climate of the West Coast.

In the colder parts of the country pruning should be delayed until the severe cold of winter is definitely past.

Thinning the Fruit

Many varieties of Plums tend to overbear. If the crop is not reduced drastically by thinning, the fruit will be small and of poor quality. Tree vigor is reduced and limb breakage is excessive. Brown rot disease damage is reduced if the fruits are thinned so that they do not touch each other.

The Japanese varieties, especially Abundance and Burbank, need drastic thinning or they will bear heavy crops of undersized fruit. Pruning to a certain extent is a thinning operation, but fruit-thinning is needed as well. The excess Plums are removed so that those left will be 2-3 in. apart, and will not touch each other when mature. Thinning reduces losses from brown rot disease and limb breakage. The Prunes and the Damsons are not thinned.

Thinning is done after the June drop, at which time the trees naturally shed some of their young fruits.

Harvesting

Plums are of poor quality unless they become nearly ripe on the tree. For home use they should ripen fully before they are picked. Fruit size, sugar content and dessert quality increase markedly if picking is delayed until the fruit is nearly ripe.

The more mature the fruit is, the more carefully it must be handled; but ripe fruit, if carefully handled, has much greater consumer appeal than the immature low-quality produce so often seen on the market.

The ripe fruit should be stored at 32 degrees F., if it is to be held before it is used. Less mature fruit should be held at a higher temperature.

Varieties

The Plum varieties cultivated in North America are derived from several species and they exhibit great diversity in color, flavor, texture and form. The trees, too, vary greatly in their ability to thrive under the diverse climatic conditions.

Common or European Plum (Prunus domestica). Varieties of this kind are most important and the commercial Plum industry of the world is based upon them. These varieties have been grouped by pomologists according to their fruit characters. The important groups are:

Prune Group: These are oblong or ovoid, purplish Plums which have a high sugar content and which dry without fermenting at the pit and produce a rich, sweet-flavored Prune (dried fruit).

Agen has very sweet, small reddish-purple fruit and is very productive.

Imperial Epineuse has the largest fruit of any Prune variety. The fruits are dark red, very sweet and of high quality and are suitable for eating fresh, drying, and canning.

Stanley is used chiefly as a fresh fruit. It is hardy and productive. Its fruit is of medium size, dark purple and of good quality.

Green Gage or Reine Claude Group: The fruits of the varieties of this group of Plums are yellowish-green or golden, sweet, very rich and of the highest quality. The following are the important varieties: Reine Claude (of medium size and ripening late in the season), Golden Transparent Gage, Jefferson, Washington and Imperial Gage.

Yellow Egg Group: The varieties in this group are few in number but distinct in appearance. Their fruits are of large size, long oval in shape, with a more or less distinct neck, and have yellow flesh. The skins of the fruits are yellow or purple. Yellow Egg and Golden Drop are the principal varieties.

The Lombard Group: Varieties in this group produce red, purple or blue-colored, medium- to large-sized fruits, and include Lombard, which is heavy-yielding and has red fruits of comparatively poor quality; Pond, which has large red fruits, also of poor quality; and Albion, California Blue, Pacific, Grand Duke and President, which have blue or blue-purple fruits.

The Damson Group: These small, purple, tart-flavored Plums are derived from P. domestica variety institia. They are borne very profusely on small, hardy trees. They are prized for culinary purposes, as they make an excellent jam and Plum butter. Shropshire and French Damson are the best varieties. The Mirabelle Plums are yellow, sweet Damson Plums, little grown in this country, but esteemed in France. American Mirabelle is a sweet, high-quality Mirabelle of American origin. It makes an excellent sweet preserve.

Japanese Plums. The Japanese varieties are red- or yellow-fruited, and are pointed at the apex. The trees vary greatly in hardiness, from Kelsey, which is less hardy than the Peach, to Burbank and Abundance, which are hardier than the European Plums.

Burbank and Abundance are commonly planted in dooryards in the East, but are not grown much commercially. Japanese varieties grown in California include Beauty (very early), Formosa, Gaviota, Kelsey, Santa Rosa and Wickson. Shiro, yellow, is grown in Ontario.

Native American Plums. These are of several species, and are of value chiefly for their suitability for climates too harsh for varieties of the European and Japanese species. They are grown for home use, but rarely for market.

P. americana is native east of the Rocky Mountains and is especially suited to the upper Mississippi valley and Canada because of its unusual winter hardiness. DeSoto and Hawkeye are two varieties of this species.

P. nigra is even hardier than P. americana. It is native to eastern Canada. Cheney is the leading variety.

P. hortulana grows farther south in the Mississippi valley than P. americana and is suitable for jelly and jams. Wayland, Golden Beauty and Miner are varieties of this species.

P. Munsoniana is the Wild Goose Plum which is planted in the southern part of the Mississippi valley because of its heat tolerance.

P. Besseyi, the Sand Cherry, is a native of the Great Plains, where its hardiness and ability to thrive under dry land conditions have made it useful to the natives of that region. It has been sold extensively by eastern nurseries, but it is wholly unsuitable for eastern conditions because of its low quality and the susceptibility of the fruit and twigs to brown rot disease. Hybrids of the Sand Cherry and other Plum species have been produced at the South Dakota Agricultural Experiment Station, and some of these are being grown in that area. Among these are Compass, Oka, Opata and Sapa.

Japanese-American Hybrids. These are hybrids between varieties of P. salicina and P. americana which have been developed at the South Dakota and Minnesota Agricultural Experiment Stations. They are replacing the selections of the native species in the upper Mississippi valley and are useful in other regions too cold for the European Plums. They are mostly red-fruited, large, and of fairly good quality, although not equal to the best varieties of the European Plum.

Superior, Underwood and Monitor are three of the best of this group. Others are Ember, Redcoat, Fiebing, Red Glow, Pipestone, Kahinta and Waneta. Kaga and Surprise should be included in a planting of these types as pollenizers, or the crops may be light.

Flowering or Ornamental Plums are dealt with under Prunus, which see.

PLUMBAGO—_Leadwort_ (Plumba'go). Leaf-losing flowering shrubs suitable for cultivation in a greenhouse in the North and outdoors in the far South. Only two kinds are commonly grown, Plumbago capensis from South Africa, and Plumbago indica (rosea), which is found wild in India. The plant known as Plumbago Larpentiae is Ceratostigma, which see. They belong to the family Plumbaginaceae. The name Plumbago is derived from _plumbum,_ lead, and has reference to the use of the plant for medicinal purposes.

A Blue-flowered Shrub. The favorite kind is Plumbago capensis, a shrub which is suitable for cultivation in tubs or large pots in a greenhouse in which a winter temperature of from 45-50 degrees is maintained. It will also flourish out of doors in a sunny position, in mild climates such as those of Florida and California. In a greenhouse it will reach a height of 8 ft. or more; it bears clusters of beautiful pale blue flowers, in summer principally, though it usually continues to bloom more or less throughout the autumn months.

The long shoots may be trained on a trellis or other suitable support. Another way of managing this Plumbago is to train the shoots on a balloon-shaped or flat trellis fixed in the pot or

The pale blue free-flowering Plumbago capensis.

tub. A white-flowered variety, P. capensis alba, is also grown.

Planting in Beds. The most vigorous growth is assured by planting the Plumbago in a prepared bed of soil on the floor of the greenhouse. A hole 18 in. deep and 2-3 ft. across should be dug and the soil removed to make room for the prepared compost. A 6-in. layer of stones or broken brick is put in the bottom for drainage, and the remaining space is filled with a soil mixture of fibrous loam, to which decayed manure, leaf mold or peat moss and sand, forming about one third of the mixture, have been added. If these ingredients are well mixed and trodden moderately firm, they will provide good growing conditions for the roots.

Planting is best done in early fall or in spring. When planting is finished the newly set plants should be watered well. Following this, and until new roots have penetrated the new soil, watering should be done rather cautiously; the soil should be allowed to become nearly dry before any water is given, then it should be thoroughly soaked and allowed to get nearly dry again.

How to Prune. The branches will remain more or less dormant until February or March, and must then be pruned. If the plant is to be trained on a trellis against the wall of the greenhouse the shoots should be shortened by one third, or even by one half if they are weakly; they should be spread out as nearly horizontally as possible so that the base of the trellis shall be well covered with shoots. The flowers are produced by the fresh summer growths.

In subsequent years, when the framework of branches has developed, pruning consists of shortening the side shoots to within three or four buds of the base of the past summer's growth. This work should be done in February or March. Until the plant has covered its allotted space, the main branches will also have to be shortened each spring to ensure the development of fresh shoots, which will eventually provide further branches.

When cultivated in pots or tubs, this Plumbago needs similar treatment. The pot or tub must be drained by a layer of pieces of brick or crocks, and a soil compost similar to that already recommended should be used. When potting is finished a space of an inch or more should be left for watering. The uppermost roots should be covered with an inch or so of soil.

Plants grown in pots will not make such vigorous growth as others in a bed of soil. They must be pruned each spring by shortening the side shoots to within two or three buds of the base of the past summer's growth, and old or worn-out shoots should be cut out if there are

A flowering shoot of the rose-colored Plumbago indica, an attractive shrub for the greenhouse, blooming in winter and spring.

young ones that are available to replace them.

Outdoor Culture. When grown outdoors in climates where it is hardy, Plumbago capensis needs essentially the same culture as greenhouse-grown specimens. In climates where it is not winter-hardy, plants from 5-in. or larger pots may be planted in outdoor beds to provide summer bloom and may be stored over winter in a cool greenhouse, sunroom or similar place.

Plumbago indica (rosea), which bears rose-colored flowers in winter and spring, needs a higher temperature than P. capensis. It should be grown in the way described, either in a prepared bed of soil, or in pots or tubs, in a greenhouse having a winter temperature of 55-60 degrees. It is a good plant for Christmas bloom.

Propagation. Both kinds are propagated by cuttings. These are made from the new shoots and inserted in pots of sandy soil in spring or early summer. The pots are placed in a propagating case for a few weeks and kept moist, and shaded from bright sunshine. P. indica can also be easily increased by root cuttings.

PLUM, CHERRY. See Prunus cerasifera.

PLUM, DATE. Diospyros Lotus, which see.

PLUME GRASS. Erianthus, which see.

PLUME POPPY. See Macleaya.

PLUMERIA—*Frangipani* (Plumer'ia; Plu'meria). Tender evergreen flowering shrubs from tropical America which belong to the Periwinkle family, Apocynaceae. They form sturdy, branching shrubs, 20 ft. in height, and are clothed with lance-shaped leaves, 6-12 in. in length. The lateral veins run parallel to one another and are joined to veins near the margins of the leaves. The flowers, which are produced in terminal clusters, are tubular, with five spreading petal tips, white, yellow, pink or red, waxy in texture, 2-3 in. across and fragrant. The name Plumeria commemorates C. Plumier, a French botanist of the seventeenth century.

Flowering Shrubs for a Greenhouse. These plants may be grown in large pots or tubs. They require a minimum winter temperature of 55 degrees and a soil compost of two parts of loam, one part peat and a free admixture of sand. Plants in large pots or tubs are kept flowering freely and in vigorous health by top-dressing them with fresh compost in spring.

Pruning is done as soon as the flowers have faded, the side shoots being cut back to three or four buds.

The branches are syringed twice daily until the flowers expand; syringing is discontinued until they have faded, and resumed for the remainder of the summer. The soil must be kept moist from March to September, but for the remainder of the year watering is done only when the soil becomes quite dry.

Outdoor Culture. Plumerias are favorite decorative plants in most tropical and subtropical countries. In the United States they are cultivated outdoors in southern California and in southern Florida. They grow well in a wide variety of soils and thrive near the sea.

Propagation by Cuttings. Firm side shoots, 3-6 in. long, are taken off in March or April. The lower leaves are removed and a cut is made just below the bottom joint. The cuttings are inserted in sand or sand and peat moss in a propagating case with a minimum temperature of 70 degrees. The case is kept close except for a few minutes each day, when it is raised and the moisture wiped from the underside of the glass. When roots are formed, more air is given and the cuttings are potted individually in small pots and eventually placed on the greenhouse benches.

The young plants are subsequently potted in 5-in. pots, and finally in 7-in. pots, from which they are set in the large pots or tubs.

The Chief Kinds. P. rubra (Frangipani), 10-20 ft., very fragrant, rose, with yellow eye, and its varieties: acutifolia, white, yellow eye; lutea, yellow; and tricolor, white, rose and yellow, are most popular. P. alba has fragrant white flowers and grows 20 ft. high. P. emarginata forms a small tree and has white flowers.

PLUM, FLOWERING OR ORNAMENTAL. See Prunus.

PLUM, HOG. See Spondias.

PLUM, MARMALADE. Achras Zapota, which see.

PLUM, MYROBALAN. Another name for the Cherry Plum, Prunus cerasifera. See Prunus.

PLUM, NATAL. Carissa grandiflora, which see.

PLUM YEW. See Cephalotaxus.

PLUNGE. This term is used by gardeners to describe the sinking of pots, or other containers in which plants are growing, in beds of ashes, sand, sand and peat moss, soil or similar material. Plants may be plunged outdoors, in cold frames or in greenhouses.

In most cases plants are plunged so that the rims of their pots are level with or slightly above the surface of the bed in which they are set. However, when potted hardy bulbs such as Narcissi, Hyacinths and Tulips are plunged outdoors to make roots in preparation for being forced, the pots are completely covered to a depth of 6-8 in.

The advantages of plunging are twofold. It prevents the soil in the pots from drying out as rapidly as it would if the pots were merely standing on the ground or greenhouse bench. Also, it keeps the roots at a reasonably even temperature, cooler in summer and warmer in winter than would be the case if they were not plunged.

When plunging in soil, it is advisable to place two or three inches of cinders or gravel beneath each pot as well as a piece of slate or flat stone immediately under the hole in the bottom of the pot. These precautions ensure good drainage and prevent earthworms from invading the pots.

If plants are plunged for a long period it is a

Plunging containers, in which herbaceous perennials are planted, in a bed of ashes.

good plan to lift them occasionally and replace them after making sure that roots are not finding their way through drainage holes in the pots and becoming well established in the substratum.

POA (Po'a). A large genus of hardy Grasses, which are found wild in most temperate regions, including North America, Siberia, the Himalayas and Europe. A few only have any horticultural value. They belong to the family Gramineae. One or two kinds are used in lawn making, and one, a variegated kind, is sometimes grown in pots in the greenhouse or planted as an edging to borders out of doors. The name Poa is the ancient Greek name for grass.

Grasses for lawns. The Wood Meadow Grass (Poa nemoralis) is used in mixtures of lawn grasses for sowing in shaded positions and under leaf-losing (deciduous) trees. Poa trivialis, the Rough-stalked Meadow Grass, is also suitable for sowing in shady places or moist positions. Poa pratensis, Kentucky Bluegrass, is one of the most important lawn grasses. It requires a well-drained soil and is chiefly used in grass mixtures for open sunny positions.

A Grass with Colored Leaves. Poa trivialis albo-vittata forms dense tufts of foliage 6 in. in height. The leaves are green and white. Small tufts may be planted in fall or in spring as an edging to flower beds or borders. It flourishes in ordinary garden soil and requires a sunny position. When they become overgrown, the clumps are lifted, divided, and replanted in autumn or spring. This is the only method of propagation.

As a Pot Plant. This variegated Grass is suitable for growing in a cool greenhouse as a pot plant in a compost of two parts loam or good garden soil and one part of leaf mold, with a sprinkling of sand. Potting is done in March or April, when small tufts are set in well-drained 3-in. pots. They are watered carefully until well rooted, then repotted in 5-in. pots. When they are established the soil is kept moist throughout the summer. During the winter the soil is only moistened when it becomes quite dry.

POCKET. This term is often used to describe a small planting area, in a rock garden, that is more or less completely bounded by rocks. Such pockets may vary in size from a few square inches to a few square feet. The soil in them should be prepared to suit the particular kinds of plant that are to be grown—peaty for those that need a soil of that character; mixed with chippings of limestone for lime-lovers; and so on. Rock-garden pockets, unlike pockets in clothing, should be without bottoms. They should be well drained and the prepared soil mixture should be of considerable depth, for most plants, 9-12 in. should be the minimum, although some, such as Sedums, Sempervivums and Thymes, will thrive in much less soil.

PODALYRIA (Podaly'ria). A group of South African evergreen shrubs, a few of which are grown in California and similar mild climates. They belong to the Pea family, Leguminosae. The genus is named after Podalyrius, the son of Aesculapius.

These plants succeed best in a well-drained, sandy, peaty soil that is somewhat acid in reaction. They need a sunny situation and are propagated by cuttings made from half-ripened shoots in summer and by seeds sown in light, sandy soil in spring.

Kinds. P. calyptrata, 6 ft., flowers pale rose; P. sericea, 6 ft., silvery, flowers pale rose.

PODOCARPUS (Podocar'pus). Evergreen trees and shrubs, some of which produce valuable timber, widely distributed in the Southern Hemisphere, in South Africa, Australia, New Zealand and South America; they are also found in India, Ceylon, Malaya, China, Japan and the Philippine Islands.

Numerous kinds are known. They vary a good deal in general appearance and in foliage. Some have long narrow leaves, in others the leaves are short and broad, or small and fine, rather like those of the Swamp Cypress or the Yew.

Evergreens for Mild Climates. These handsome trees and shrubs are not hardy in the North. In the far South and in California many kinds thrive, and they are extremely useful for landscaping purposes. They grow best in a well-drained, loamy soil.

In Podocarpus male and female flowers are usually borne on different trees, and the female flowers are peculiar because one scale in the flower is sterile. This fuses with the upper part of the stalk and develops as a fleshy, brightly colored receptacle on which the usually single seed is produced. The receptacle is edible, as is the aril which surrounds the seed of the Yew.

Podocarpus is most closely related to Cephalotaxus and Torreya among our garden conifers; it belongs to the family Taxaceae. The name is taken from the Greek *podos*, a foot, and *karpos*, a fruit, and alludes to the fleshy rootstalk or receptacle on which the seed is borne. This receptacle is more prominent in some kinds than in others.

Raising Seedlings. Whenever they can be procured, seeds should be used for purposes of propagation, for, as a rule, seedling plants are longer-lived than those raised in other ways. Sow the seeds as soon as possible after they are ripe, in pots or flats of sandy soil in a warm greenhouse. A suitable compost consists of equal parts of loam, peat and sand.

Taking Cuttings. Cuttings can be rooted in a warm propagating case or, in the case of P. alpina and P. andina, they may be rooted in a cold frame. If the trees form branches low down, the young ones are sometimes layered.

For its best development Podocarpus requires clear atmospheric conditions, a moderately moist climate, and well-drained but moist soil that is fairly free from lime. As a rule, these plants are most tender in their early years; once they have attained a height of several feet they withstand cold better than when they are very small. No regular pruning is necessary, but what little is required to shape the plants is done during summer.

A Good Hedge Shrub. Podocarpus andina is a yewlike bush or tree with leaves about the size of the Yew, but of a lighter and more cheerful shade of green. This forms a handsome tree and it is also excellent when used as a hedge shrub, for it withstands clipping as well as does the Yew.

Cultivation in Greenhouse or Conservatory. Several kinds are useful for growing in tubs or pots in a frostproof greenhouse. They require well-drained pots or tubs and a compost of two parts of fibrous loam and one part of peat with a sprinkling of sand. They must not be placed in too large pots or tubs at first, but should be fed liberally when the pots are well filled with

roots. On no account should they be allowed to become very dry at the roots.

Well-grown plants in pots or tubs are excellent for house decoration. Some form tall, narrow heads, and are very useful for placing in corners of high rooms or using as a background for floral displays and for standing in patios and on terraces in summer.

The Hardiest Kinds. P. andina (Prumnopitys elegans) is a native of the Andes of southern Chile, where it forms a yewlike tree 40-50 feet high. It is one of the hardiest.

P. alpina is a dense bush, 1-12 ft. high, with slender, straggling branches, covered with small, narrow leaves 1/4-1/2 in. long. It is a mountain shrub from Tasmania, where it is of value in protecting mountainsides from erosion. It is probably the hardiest kind. It lives outdoors at Washington, D. C. and perhaps further north.

P. macrophylla, of China and Japan, is moderately hardy. It is very variable in a wild state and may be a shrub a few feet high, or a small tree 25-30 ft. high; the thick, leathery leaves are 5-7 in. long and 1/2 in. wide. There are several named varieties: angustifolia, with small leaves; Maki, of erect habit and very dense foliage; and luteo-variegata and albo-variegata, with yellow and white variegated leaves respectively. This kind and its varieties are favorites for cultivating in tubs indoors.

P. Nagi is an entirely different-looking plant, for its leaves are short and broad, 1 1/2-2 in. long, and 3/4-1 in. wide. It is wild in one form or another in China, Japan and Formosa, and at its best forms a tree 60-80 ft. high. There are several named varieties, such as angustifolia, with smaller leaves than the type; rotundifolia, with rounded leaves; and variegata, with variegated leaves.

P. nubigena from the mountains of Chile grows as a tree or large bush with rather light green, leathery, sharp-pointed leaves 1-1 3/4 in. long and 1/4 in. wide. They are marked with two bluish bands on their undersides. This kind is moderately hardy.

P. saligna is a very beautiful and moderately hardy tree from Chile, where it grows 50-70 ft. high. It bears dark green leaves, 2-5 in. or more long, and about 1/4 in. wide; the length of the leaves varies a good deal on young and old plants.

Less Hardy Kinds. P. elongata, a native of southern and tropical Africa, forms a splendid tree up to 70 ft. tall, with narrow, thin, pointed leaves 3 in. or more long. It is adaptable for planting outdoors in mild climates only. In its young stage it is much valued as a tub plant because of its attractive habit of growth and its bright green coloring; it is much grown in California.

P. ferruginea, the Miro of New Zealand, is a large tree, 50-90 ft. high in its native land. It can be grown only in warm climates or in greenhouses. The same may be said of the spiny-leaved P. Totara and of P. Hallii. Both are from New Zealand. P. Hallii is the hardier of the two.

A few other kinds suitable for cultivation in mild climates and in tubs in greenhouses are P. falcata, the Oteniqua Yellow Wood, from South Africa; P. elata, the Brown Pine of New South Wales and Queensland; P. coriacea, from Central America; P. gracilior, from Abyssinia, Uganda and Kenya; and P. neriifolia, from India, China and New Guinea.

Economic Uses. The timber of several kinds is valuable. The wood of some is known as Yellow Wood or Podo. As the first name implies, the wood is often yellowish in color; sometimes, however, it is brown or reddish. It is easy to work, durable, finishes with a good surface, takes paint and polish well, and is procurable, in the native countries of the various kinds, in large sizes free from knots.

PODOLEPIS (Podo'lepis; Podole'pis). Hardy, tender, annual and perennial flowering plants, from Australia, which belong to the Daisy family, Compositae. There are but three or four kinds in cultivation, and they vary in height from 12 in. to 2 ft. They have thin, wiry stems and narrow leaves which clasp the stems at the base. The daisy-like flowers are terminal or axillary (in the axils of the leaves), half an inch in diameter, and composed of strap-shaped outer florets and tubular florets in the center. Surrounding these is the involucre which is composed of numerous small, overlapping bracts. The flowers, which are produced in summer, are yellow, pink, lilac, purple or white. The name

The pink-flowered Podolepis aristata is an attractive annual.

Podolepis is derived from *podos*, a foot, and *lepis*, a scale, and refers to the scaly involucres.

Sowing. A sunny position and light, well-drained soil are required. The seeds are sown in April in irregular patches in the positions in which the plants are to grow. When 2 in. high, they are thinned out to 4 in. apart. Very little attention is required, with the exception of keeping the soil free from weeds and stirring the surface with a hoe or cultivator.

Cultivation in Pots. A compost of two parts of sandy loam, one part of leaf mold and a little sand is required. Seeds are sown in April in the pots in which the plants are to flower in summer. Five-inch pots are well drained with crocks, and these are covered with a layer of leaves. The remainder of the space is then filled with the prepared compost, which is made firm and moistened. The seeds are sown thinly on the surface and covered with fine soil.

The seed pots are placed in a greenhouse having a night temperature of 55 degrees and covered with panes of glass. The moisture is wiped from the underside of the glass each day to prevent the condensed moisture from dropping on to the germinating seeds and setting up decay.

When the seedlings appear above the surface, the glass is removed and they are exposed to full light. The seedlings are thinned to 2 in. apart, and when 3 in. high are removed to a greenhouse or frame. Up to this stage the soil is only moistened when it becomes quite dry, but for the remainder of the time, and until the flowers have faded, the soil must be kept moist. When the plants come into flower the stems are supported by an encircling band of fine string or raffia.

The chief kinds are P. acuminata, 12 in., yellow; P. aristata, 12 in., pink; and P. gracilis, 3 ft., purple, lilac and white.

PODOPHYLLUM—*May Apple* (Podophyl′lum). A small group of hardy herbaceous flowering plants from the Himalayas and North America, which belong to the family Podophyllaceae. They grow 12-15 in. high, and have large, deeply lobed leaves on long, thick fleshy stalks, which rise straight up from the soil. As the leaves push up through the soil in spring, they are folded back like a closed umbrella, but as soon as they get clear of the ground they spread out horizontally and eventually expand to 8 in. in diameter.

These plants bear waxy white, cup-shaped, six-petaled flowers in May. They are followed by large, egg-shaped, fleshy fruits. The name Podophyllum is derived from *podos,* a foot, and *phyllon,* a leaf, and refers to the fancied resemblance of the leaves to a duck's foot. A drug known as podophyllin is made from the rhizomes.

For Semishaded, Moist Positions. These plants require a moist, semishaded position, and are therefore usually grown in woodlands or in shaded borders or in rock gardens. The soil is prepared by digging it deeply and incorporating generous amounts of leaf mold, peat moss or good compost. Planting is done in April, when the crowns are set just below the surface. They should not be disturbed for several years, as they flower best when firmly established.

Propagation is by lifting the clumps and dividing them into a number of separate plants in April.

The chief kinds are P. emodi, 12 in., white, with red fruits, May; and P. peltatum, with yellowish fruits, 12 in., white, May. P. emodi is a native of the Himalayas; P. peltatum, a native of North America, from Quebec to Florida and Texas.

PODRANEA (Podran′ea). Two South African shrubs closely related to Pandorea and belonging to the Bignonia family, Bignoniaceae. The name is an anagram of Pandorea. These plants need the same cultural care as Pandorea, which see.

The kinds are P. Brycei, flowers light pink with crimson netting, and P. Ricasoliana, flowers pale pink striped red.

POET'S NARCISSUS. Narcissus poeticus, which see.

POGONIA (Pogon′ia). Terrestrial orchids of North America and eastern Asia, one of which is well worth growing in bog gardens and wild gardens. Pogonia belongs in the Orchid family, Orchidaceae. The name is from *pogon,* a beard, and refers to the bearded lip of the flower.

Pogonia ophioglossoides, sometimes called Snakemouth, occurs naturally in open bogs from Newfoundland to Minnesota and southwards to Florida and Texas. It blooms from May to July, the earlier dates being for the more southern parts of its range. This orchid grows to a height of 20 in. or so. The solitary, fragrant flowers

The flowers of the May Apple, Podophyllum peltatum, are followed by egg-shaped yellow fruits. This plant is a native of eastern North America.

of the Snakemouth are pale purple in color.

Specimens obtained from dealers in native plants may be set in acid bog soil in early spring.

POINCIANA (Poincia'na). Tropical evergreen flowering trees and shrubs which grow wild in Mexico, Central and South America and in other tropical countries. They belong to the Pea family, Leguminosae. They are very conspicuous and ornamental, and have bipinnate, acacia-like foliage. The flowers, which are yellow or red, and produced in racemes, are very showy, and each has five petals, which are narrow at their bases and spread out into a rounded por-

One of the most brilliant of tropical shrubs is the Barbados Pride, Poinciana pulcherrima. In the far South and southern California it may be grown outdoors. It also is an attractive greenhouse plant.

tion at the ends. They have ten conspicuous stamens and the seed pods are long and flat, sometimes exceeding 18 in. in length. The name Poinciana commemorates M. de Poinci, a patron of botany and once governor of the Antilles. The tree known as the Royal Poinciana (Poinciana regia) is now named Delonix regia.

When cultivated in a greenhouse, Poinciana requires a minimum winter temperature of 55 degrees. The best soil compost consists of equal parts of peat, loam and leaf mold, with sand added freely. Repotting is done in March. The pots are well drained with crocks, which are covered with the rough siftings from the compost. The plants are taken from their old pots and, after the crocks and loose soil have been removed from the roots, are set in the new pots and the soil is made firm. The soil is not watered

until it becomes moderately dry, and then it is thoroughly saturated.

This method of watering is continued until the plants are well rooted, when the compost is kept moist during the remainder of the summer. For the rest of the time, the soil is only moistened when it becomes quite dry.

From the time of repotting, up to the end of the summer, the atmosphere must be kept moist by damping the floor and greenhouse benches, and the foliage is syringed, except when the plants are in flower. Throughout the winter months less atmospheric moisture is needed.

Pruning consists of slightly shortening the shoots after flowering.

Outdoor Cultivation. In the far South and in California, Poincianas are grown outdoors, as they are in many tropical and subtropical regions. They thrive without difficulty in a variety of soils and appreciate a sunny location. Young plants are usually set out from pots when they are a foot or two tall.

Propagation is by cuttings, or by seeds. The cuttings are taken off in summer. Short side shoots are detached with a heel, the leaves from the lower half of the shoots are trimmed off and the heel is pared smooth. The shoots are inserted in a propagating case with a bottom heat of 75-80 degrees.

The case is kept close but ventilation is given daily for a few minutes, and the moisture is wiped from the underside of the glass. When roots are formed the plants are potted separately in 3-in. pots, in the compost recommended above, and subsequently transferred to larger pots.

Seeds are sown in pots of light soil in spring. To facilitate germination the seeds should first be soaked in tepid water for 48 hours.

A pane of glass is laid over the seed pot and it is plunged in a bottom-heated propagating case. As soon as the seedlings appear above the surface, the glass is removed and the seedlings are exposed to the light. When 2 in. high, they are potted singly in small pots and, later on, into larger ones.

The chief kinds are P. pulcherrima (Barbados Pride, Barbados Flower Fence, Dwarf Poinciana), 10 ft., orange or yellow and red, or yellow in variety flava; **P. Gilliesii**, 10-20 ft., yellow and red; and **P. Conzattii**, a small tree, yellow-red to red.

POINSETTIA. Euphorbia pulcherrima, which see.

POISON BULB. Crinum asiaticum, which see.

POISON IVY. Rhus radicans, a native of North America, including Mexico and the West Indies, is a very variable species. It occurs as a tall vine that clings to its supports by means of rootlets produced along its stems and quickly covers walks, fences and tree trunks; as a dense ground-cover plant; and as a more or less erect non-climbing shrub. Each leaf is composed of three distinct leaflets which vary in shape from roughly oval to almost round; often they are elliptic or rhombic. Their tips are more or less pointed. Their edges (margins) may be entire (not toothed or lobed) or distinctly lobed or toothed. The leaf surface may be glossy or dull.

Rhus radicans is most commonly called Poison Ivy but it is also sometimes known as Poison Oak, although this latter name belongs more properly to R. Toxicodendron and R. diversiloba (see Poison Oak, below).

A Poisonous Pest. Poison Ivy is a serious pest because of its aggressive, spreading character and because, upon contact with it, or with objects that have been against it, many people develop a distressing and painful dermatitis, a skin eruption or irritation commonly called ivy poisoning. This condition is caused by a non-volatile, gummy substance contained in the sap of the roots, stems, leaves and unripened fruits.

The sap must come into contact with the skin to produce ivy poisoning. It is quite possible, however, for a person to develop the poisoning without actually touching a Poison Ivy plant. Handling dogs and other animals that have run where the plant abounds is a common cause of infection; other recorded cases have been traced to handling shoes and clothing worn by people who have been in contact with Poison Ivy plants, and it is believed that large particles that drift in smoke from a fire in which Poison Ivy plants are burned may cause the dermatitis, although the smoke itself does not do this.

The degree of sensitivity to the poisonous principle of this plant varies greatly with individuals. An irritative type of dermatitis that follows massive exposure sensitizes the victim so that for the rest of his or her life he or she will be poisoned by the slightest contact with the poisonous sap. Even individuals who have long considered themselves immune can be poisoned by extensive exposure and thus be made sensitive to lesser contacts later.

Treatment of Ivy Poisoning. No satisfactory

The Poison Ivy, Rhus radicans.

method of preventing dermatitis following exposure is known. In serious cases medical attention should be secured. In lesser cases various soothing lotions and other preparations sold by druggists for the purpose of relieving itching and causing the blisters to dry are helpful. Special injections given by a physician before exposure, with the object of producing immunity or partial immunity for some weeks or months, seem to produce favorable results with some people.

Eradicating Poison Ivy. Weed killers of types that affect all vegetation and sterilize the soil so that nothing grows in it for several weeks or months will kill Poison Ivy but are not always practical to use. Here belong sodium chlorate, arsenical weed killers and borax. A method that is usually more practical and is very effective is to spray the foliage when the plants are in full leaf with ammonium sulfamate (sold under the trade name of Ammate). This kills the entire plant, including the roots, but does not sterilize the soil to other vegetation. It will, however, harm and kill other plants if sprayed upon them.

POISON OAK. Rhus diversiloba and R. Toxicodendron are most properly known by the common name of Poison Oak. R. radicans (see Poison Ivy, above) is also sometimes called Poison Oak. R. diversiloba is a shrub or sometimes a vine climbing to about 8 ft. high. It is native from British Columbia to California. R. Toxicodendron is a low shrub, native from New Jersey to Tennessee and southern Missouri and southwards to Mississippi and Florida. Both species cause distressing skin afflictions exactly as does Poison Ivy (which see, above). Treatment of the poisoning and eradication of the plants are the same as for Poison Ivy. See also Rhus.

POISON SUMAC. Rhus vernix, a shrub or small tree that inhabits swamps and occurs from Maine to Minnesota and southwards to Florida and Louisiana. It causes most people to suffer from a distressing skin affliction if they come in contact with it. For treatment and for eradication of this plant, see Poison Ivy, above.

POKER PLANT. Kniphofia, which see.

POKEWEED. See Phytolacca.

POLEMONIUM — *Jacob's-Ladder* (Polemo'-nium). Hardy herbaceous perennial plants which grow wild chiefly in North America; they belong to the family Polemoniaceae. The name is an old Greek one, of which the origin i obscure.

These plants are suitable for the perennia border or rock garden; they have attractive deeply cut leaves, and most of them have blue flowers, which open in spring or summer. They thrive in ordinary well-cultivated garden soil and may be planted in autumn or spring.

These perennials are easily raised from seed which may be sown in a cold frame or out of doors in a prepared seed bed in spring. The seedlings make quick progress; those raised under glass should be planted in a nursery bor der as soon as they are 2 in. or so high. Wher well developed, they are planted where they will bloom the following year. Seedlings raised out of doors should be transplanted 6 in. apar before they become crowded.

Division in spring or early fall also provide a ready means of increase.

Jacob's-Ladder. The common perennial borde kind is Polemonium caeruleum, Jacob's-Ladde or Greek Valerian, which reaches a height o 18-25 in. and bears blue flowers in June; the variety alba has white flowers. The variety hi malayanum is more vigorous and will reach height of 2½ or even 3 ft. There is usually little trouble in maintaining a supply of these kinds when they have become established in garden, for they increase quickly by seedling which spring up from self-sown seeds. These are often so numerous that many have to be de stroyed. Those that are wanted should be lifted and transplanted when 2 or 3 in. high.

The plants will thrive in a sunny or a shady place; they are very attractive.

Rock-Garden or Ground-Cover Plants. Pole monium confertum, 8-10 in., is a useful blue flowered kind for this purpose; it flourishes in well-drained soil. Others suitable for the rock garden and for planting as ground covers are P. reptans, 6-8 in., blue, and P. Richardsonii, 6-8 in., blue (variety album has white flowers, vari ety pulchellum smaller violet to white flowers) P. flavum, 2-3 ft., has yellow flowers, and those of P. carneum, 18 in., are rose-pink. The last named is an exceedingly handsome plant.

The blue-flowered perennial Jacob's-Ladder, Polemonium caeruleum.

They will also thrive on a shady border, and there the plants last longer in bloom than they do in a hot, sunny place.

POLIANTHES—*Tuberose* (Polianth'es). Tender, tuberous-rooted plants from Mexico which belong to the Amaryllis family, Amaryllidaceae. The name Polianthes is probably derived from *polios*, white, and *anthos*, a flower, and refers to the characteristic whiteness of the blooms.

The principal kind, P. tuberosa, Tuberose, has tuberous roots, and forms a basal cluster of lanceolate (lance-shaped) leaves, 12-18 in. in

length. It produces a flower spike, at the top of which are a number of pure white, fragrant, tubular flowers, 1½-2½ in. in length. The double form, known as "The Pearl," is the most popular kind.

How to Force the Tuberose. Flowers of Tuberose may be had from April to June by forcing the bulbs in a greenhouse where a tropical temperature is maintained. Five- or six-inch pots are used; the former will accommodate one bulb and the latter three bulbs.

The best potting compost consists of two parts

of fibrous loam, and one part of equal proportions of well-decayed manure and sand. The pots are well drained with crocks, and these are covered with the rough siftings from the compost or with leaves. Sufficient of the compost is then put in, and made firm, so that when the bulbs are placed in position their tips are level with the rims of the pots. The remainder of the compost is added and made firm, leaving sufficient space for watering.

After potting, the bulbs are placed in a cold greenhouse to form a vigorous root system. Well-rooted plants can be forced into flower by placing the pots in a temperature of 70-80 degrees in a shaded position, until growth becomes active, when they should be set in a well-lighted position in the hothouse, where a temperature of 70-75 degrees is maintained.

After the bulbs are potted, no water is given until the soil becomes quite dry. The soil should then be moistened, and when the plants are growing freely it must be kept moist. When the flowering spikes are forming, weak liquid fertilizer should be given twice a week. When in flower, the plants are placed in a cool greenhouse or conservatory, where the blooms last much longer, or they may be used for cutting.

After flowering, the bulbs are discarded, as they are of no further use.

Growing the Tuberose Out of Doors. In summer the Tuberose can be grown out of doors. A warm, sunny border is required and the soil must be light and well drained. Heavy clay soil should be improved by mixing with it generous amounts of sand and organic matter such as compost, humus, leaf mold or peat moss. Planting should be delayed until the weather is settled and warm and all danger of frost is well past.

The bulbs are spaced about 6 in. apart and are covered with 3 in. of soil. They may either be planted directly outdoors or may be started indoors in pots 6-8 weeks before it is time to transfer them to the garden. The bulbs are dug before frost and are stored over winter in a temperature of 60 degrees in a dry place.

Propagation. Tuberoses are increased by means of offsets (small bulbs which develop from the sides of older bulbs), which are removed at planting time. The offsets should be planted 2 in deep and 3 in. apart in a nursery bed; they will not bloom the first year.

POLLARDING. A term used to describe a method of tree cultivation practiced in Europe more rarely in North America. The heads of young trees are cut off at a height of several feet above the ground, often 6-12 ft. New growth appear from adventitious buds which, in the course of a few years, form long, straight, pole like shoots. When these shoots have attained the requisite diameter for the purpose in view, the are cut down to within a bud or two of the base and another crop of shoots is begun. The number of years required for the rotation varies in different kinds of trees, and the purpose for which the small wood is required. Willows are often pollarded, and Limes, Beeches, Hornbeam and other trees also may be grown in the same way.

The most common example of pollarding in North America is the annual pruning that is usually done to Catalpa bignonioides nana when it is grown as a grafted plant of C bignonioides.

The famous old Beech trees at Burnham Beeches in England were pollarded in early life, but were afterwards allowed to develop as large trees. That accounts for the short, bulky trunks, each carrying a number of heavy, more or less erect branches.

Pollarding is really a modification of the coppice system of cultivation, the difference being that pollarded trees are allowed to develop a definite length of clear trunk, whereas coppice is cut back close to the ground at regular intervals.

POLLEN. The dustlike substance on the anthers of a flower are pollen grains, containing the male gametes. These must unite with the female gametes, by transference of the pollen to the stigma of the flower, before fertile seeds can usually be produced.

POLLINATION. The transfer of pollen from the stamens to the stigma of the flower to ensure fertilization of the ovules to produce seeds.

POLYANTHA ROSE. A name given to a group of garden Roses presumably derived, in part, from Rosa multiflora nana. See Rose.

POLYANTHUS NARCISSUS. The bunch-flowered or Tazetta Narcissus. Its varieties form one of the chief groups in which Narcissi are classified. See Narcissus.

POLYANTHUS PRIMROSE. See Primula.

POLYCYCNIS (Polycyc'nis). Orchids which are remarkable for the number and curious shape of the flowers. They are found wild in Central America. They are evergreen and epiphytal (growing on trees), with comparatively small clustered pseudobulbs bearing one or two rather large plicate (folded) leaves.

The arching, many-flowered stems are produced from the base of the bulbs, usually in early summer. The flowers are 1-2 in. across, with rather narrow spreading segments. The feature of each flower is the long, slender curved column.

The name Polycycnis, alluding to the curved column, is from *poly*, many, and *kyknos*, a swan. Polycycnis belongs to the family Orchidaceae.

Orchids for a Hothouse. A greenhouse having a tropical temperature in summer and one of 55-60 degrees in winter is required. A moist atmosphere must be maintained and water should be given freely in summer, but only occasionally in winter. Shading is necessary throughout the spring and summer, but exposure to light is beneficial in the autumn.

The compost should consist of three parts of osmunda fiber and one part of sphagnum moss with an addition of finely broken crocks. Flower pans or pots may be used, but Orchid baskets have an advantage: they allow the old compost to be removed and replenished without undue root disturbance. The compost should never be allowed to become stale or sodden.

Repotting, if necessary, must be carefully done either early in spring or as soon as the young growths appear.

The chief kind is P. gratiosa, which bears forty to fifty flowers on arching spikes; they are white, flushed with reddish lilac.

POLYGALA—*Milkwort* (Polyg'ala). A large group of plants belonging to the family Polygalaceae, which contains some two hundred kinds of greenhouse or hardy annual or perennial herbs, shrubs and subshrubs, very widely distributed in the temperate and warmer regions of the world.

The name Polygala is the old Greek name used by Dioscorides, and is derived from *polys,* much, and *gala* milk; it refers to the plant's supposed virtue as a promoter of milk. Although many of the Milkworts are extremely beautiful plants, only a very few are in cultivation, and of these most are hardy.

Hardy Kinds. Polygala Chamaebuxus, Bastard Box, is a charming subshrub, widely distributed in the Alps. It grows about 9-12 in. high with wiry stems, glossy, boxlike leaves and pretty pea-shaped yellow flowers, which change to bronze as they age. There is also a variety of this plant in which the flowers are pink and yellow. The plant rambles underground, spreading by means of its underground shoots.

Bastard Box may be increased either by simple division of the roots or by soft cuttings taken in spring and rooted in sand in a cold frame.

This extremely pretty little shrub is invaluable on the outskirts of the rock garden, especially as a ground cover under and between larger shrubs and small trees. Its fine evergreen foliage is attractive all the year round, and an admirable setting for the pretty flowers. Unfortunately it is not very easy to grow where summers are hot and humid. It is hardy to southern New England.

Polygala paucifolia (Fringed Polygala), a native of eastern North America, is a dwarf-growing woodland plant. This pretty plant is suitable for a cool corner in light, peaty soil or loam and leaf mold in the wild garden. It grows 6-7 in. high and the flowers are purplish-pink. It is also known as Flowering Wintergreen.

Polygala Senega (Seneca Snakeroot) is another hardy North American Milkwort, flowering in May and June. It is a taller plant than P. paucifolia, and is suitable for the wild garden in partial shade or sun. Its flowers are white or greenish.

Polygala Vayrediae, from the Spanish Sierras, is closely related to P. Chamaebuxus, being a dwarf, evergreen subshrub. The leaves, however, are narrow and the flowers bright pink and gold. It is a choice rock garden plant, propagated, like P. Chamaebuxus, by division of the roots or cuttings.

An interesting annual kind is P. lutea which is

a native of wet places in eastern North America. It grows 1 ft. tall, has orange-colored flowers and is suitable for the bog garden.

Tender Kinds. Several kinds of Polygala are suitable only for cultivation in mild climates, such as that of California, or under glass. They may be grown in a greenhouse in which a temperature of 40-45 degrees can be maintained in the winter. During the summer the conditions of the average greenhouse are suitable, or the plants may be plunged in their pots in a bed of sand or ashes outdoors.

The best potting compost for these plants is a mixture of half peat and half loam with sand added freely. When repotting becomes necessary, it should be done in late February or March. At that time the old plants are pruned by shortening the shoots as may be necessary to ensure shapely specimens; as soon as they have started into fresh growth, repotting should be done. The pots must be well drained.

Summer and Winter Management. During the summer months it is essential that the soil be kept moist while the plants are in full growth, but if it becomes sodden by overwatering they will fail. The safe rule is to give water only when the soil is moderately dry, and then to fill the pots to the rims.

During the autumn months the supply of water to the roots must be lessened gradually, and in winter the soil is only moistened occasionally to prevent its being very dry.

Propagation is by means of cuttings made from short side shoots in March; these are prepared by removing the lowest leaves and cutting the shoots beneath a joint or node. The cuttings are inserted under a hand light in the greenhouse in a bed of peat moss and sand.

The chief kinds suitable for the greenhouse and for outdoor cultivation in mild climates are P. myrtifolia variety grandiflora, purplish; P. virgata, purplish or pink; and P. Dalmaisiana, purple-red.

POLYGONATUM—*Solomon's-Seal* (Polygo'-natum; Polygona'tum). Hardy herbaceous perennial plants which are found wild in various parts of Europe and in North America chiefly. They belong to the Lily family, Liliaceae. Polygonatum is derived from *poly*, many, and *gonu*,

a knee joint. The name alludes to the jointed rhizomes of the plants.

A favorite kind is the common Solomon's-Seal, Polygonatum multiflorum; this reaches a height of about 3 ft., has arching, leafy stems and in May bears drooping, white green-flushed flowers on the lower side of the upper parts of the leafy shoots. It is a graceful and charming plant, invaluable for cutting for indoor decoration, and for planting on a shady border.

This Solomon's-Seal is very lovely if grouped in open spaces among trees, towards the front of the shrubbery, or in any informal part of the garden. It is not suitable for the herbaceous border, for it is vigorous and leafy and its rhizome or root-stock spreads quickly. It should not be planted near choice plants or where space is restricted, or it may soon become a nuisance.

It thrives in ordinary soil and should be planted or transplanted while the roots are dormant, preferably in early fall. If planting is deferred until spring the display of bloom the first year is likely to be disappointing.

Propagation is a very simple matter. It is necessary merely to dig up portions of the rootstock or rather to sever them with a spade and replant them where they are to remain. This plant may also be raised from seeds.

Good Pot Plant. Solomon's-Seal makes an admirable pot plant for the cool greenhouse or window garden. Portions of the rootstock should be potted in October in 6-in. or 7-in. pots, using loamy soil, and placed under glass; the soil should

Solomons Seal, Polygonatum multiflorum, thrives in shady locations.

be kept moderately moist during the winter months by watering when it is fairly dry. Plants grown in a sunny greenhouse will bloom several weeks in advance of those out of doors.

Solomon's-Seal may also be forced into bloom in a cool greenhouse; after they are potted in October the roots should be kept in a cold frame for a month and then placed under glass. The soil must be kept thoroughly moist when fresh growth has begun.

Native American Kinds. The native American Polygonatums are sometimes cultivated and are good plants for wild gardens and for planting in shaded places where the soil is moderately moist. They are propagated in the ways recommended above for the common P. multiflorum. Of chief interest among the American kinds are the following: P. pubescens (sometimes wrongly named P. biflorum), the Small Solomon's-Seal, which grows wild throughout eastern North America and attains a height of 1-3 ft.; P. biflorum, which grows to 4 ft. high and occurs from Connecticut to Florida and the Mississippi valley; P. commutatum, the Great Solomon's-Seal, which grows 2-8 ft. high and occurs natively throughout eastern and central North America. All these kinds have greenish flowers.

Other Kinds. P. japonicum, from Japan, is a handsome kind with white flowers tipped green, and is 1-2 ft. high; P. officinale, a native of Europe and northern Asia, has white flowers and grows about 1 ft. high; P. roseum, from Siberia, has pink flowers and is 2-3 ft. high; P. verticillatum, a native of Asia and Asia Minor, grows 2-4 ft. high and has greenish flowers.

POLYGONUM—*Knotweed* (Polyg'onum). Annual or perennial herbs or subshrubs widely distributed in many parts of the world, several kinds being prominent weeds. Some kinds are low-growing, insignificant plants, others send up straight annual stems to a height of 8-12 ft. or more, and branch and flower freely. Others are luxuriant vines with soft, woody branches which climb to a considerable height. Some are very attractive flowering plants and are grown in borders and in the rock garden.

Certain of the more vigorous perennials are liable to become a nuisance in gardens if not kept definitely under control, for they root

Polygonum campanulatum grows best in moist ground and bears pale pink flowers in summer.

deeply and every piece of root is capable of producing a new plant. The stems are peculiar by reason of the swollen joints.

Polygonum belongs to the family Polygonaceae, and the name is taken from the Greek, *poly,* many, and *gonu,* a knee joint, and refers to the swollen-jointed stems.

Propagation. There is little difficulty in raising the Polygonums from seed sown out of doors, or in a frame in spring. The perennial kinds are easily increased by division of the clumps in spring. The climbing P. Aubertii and P. baldschuanicum can be propagated by short cuttings, 4 in. long, taken with a slight heel of old wood in July–August and inserted in a frame, or

Polygonum Reynoutria is a Japanese kind that grows about 18 in. high. It is a vigorous plant and may be used as a ground cover where it is not likely to invade less vigorously growing plants.

The Chinese Fleece Vine, Polygonum Aubertii, clothing a fence and in full bloom.

Polygonum capitatum is a low-growing kind. It bears a profusion of small pink cloverlike flower heads.

by cuttings of ripened wood, 10-12 in. long, inserted out of doors in fall.

The Polygonums thrive in ordinary garden soil, but the majority are too coarse for the herbaceous border and should be relegated to the wild garden. P. baldschuanicum and P. Aubertii should be pruned in winter or early spring in order to keep them under control. When grown on the walls of buildings there is a very definite tendency for the shoots to spread over the roof and dislodge shingles or tiles. The herbaceous kinds should be cut down to the ground line in autumn.

The wild kinds are common on cultivated land, particularly in moist places, and on cultivated land that has been allowed to go uncropped or has been neglected for a season. Some of them grow very rapidly and produce large crops of seed. As flowering and seed ripening may go on for several weeks, the young plants should never be allowed to mature, for once an area of ground becomes littered with seeds it is difficult to get it clean again. P. aviculare, commonly called Knotgrass or Knotweed, is very common and flowers from spring to fall.

A Good Annual. A useful annual kind that is well suited for growing towards the rear of the border and in other places where a tall summer-blooming plant is required is P. orientale. This native of Asia and Australia is called Prince's-Feather (a common name that is also applied to Amaranthus hybridus hypochondriacus); it is naturalized in eastern North America. P. orientale comes freely from seeds sown outdoors in spring in any reasonably good soil. It prefers a sunny location. The plants should be spaced 18-24 in. apart. They are freely branched, attain a height of about 6 ft. and bloom freely through summer and fall. The bright pink flowers are borne in branching spikes.

For Rock Garden or Flower Border. P. affine is a very decorative plant from the Himalayas. It forms a compact plant 9 in. high and produces dense short spikes of pink flowers in summer. P. amplexicaule is a dwarf plant, from the Himalayas, producing slender spikes of red flowers in summer. Both thrive in well-drained soil and are suitable for the rock garden, or front of the herbaceous border. They grow best where summers are not excessively hot and winters not extraordinarily cold.

Favorite Climbing Plants. P. baldschuanicum, a native of Bokhara, is an excellent decorative kind. It is a vigorous climber suitable for planting to cover walls, trellises and even trees. Its soft, woody branches grow very rapidly, and in summer heads of delicate pink flowers appear which are succeeded by decorative fruits. This plant should only be grown where there is plenty of room, otherwise it may give trouble. It looks well when allowed to grow over an old tree.

P. Aubertii, known as the China Fleece Vine and the Silver-Lace Vine, is similar but has white flowers. It is a native of western China and Tibet.

P. Bistorta, a widely distributed plant in the Northern Hemisphere, grows 6-12 in. high and

Planting

[9—8]
*Balled and burlapped Blue Spruce
and container grown Japanese Maple*

[9—8a]
Fertilizing in preparation for planting

[9—8b]
Planting Sweet Williams

[9—8c]
Planting Gladiolus corms

[9—9]
Frangipani
(Plumeria rubra)

forms a dense mass; the showy red flowers are in dense slender spikes in summer. This is a very conspicuous plant in alpine meadows, making a red covering in July, and is suitable for moist places, which are especially favored by the variety superbum.

P. capitatum is a prostrate plant from the Himalayas. It has heart-shaped leaves 2 in. long and 1¼ in. wide, mainly green with a broad brownish zone about the middle and a reddish midrib and margin. The flowers are a pretty shade of pink, and are produced during summer in small, round heads on short, slender stalks. This plant's proper place is the rock garden, where it thrives in ordinary well-drained soil.

Other Vigorous Kinds. P. cuspidatum, a Japanese kind sometimes called Mexican Bamboo, is a handsome plant but it spreads so rapidly that it is safe to plant only in the rare place where it can be rigidly confined. Unless controlled, it can become a pernicious weed.

P. campanulatum, 3 ft., bears terminal clusters of pink flowers in summer and is excellent for moist positions.

P. molle, from the Himalayas, grows 4 ft. high and has large terminal heads of flowers which are pink in the bud and cream-colored when expanded.

P. sachalinense, from the Island of Sakhalin, is a white flowered vigorous kind which forms annual branches at least 12 ft. high, bearing handsome leaves up to 12 in. long and 8 in. wide. It is very imposing in a large wild garden.

P. Reynoutria, a newcomer from Japan, 18 in., bears white flowers and bright red fruits. It has merit as a ground cover.

POLYPODIUM—*Polypody Fern* (Polypod'-ium). Hothouse, cool greenhouse and hardy evergreen and leaf-losing (deciduous) Ferns, Polypodiums are found wild in many parts of the world, including tropical, semitropical and temperate zones.

The fronds vary from a few inches to 6 ft. in length, and are either simple (undivided), pinnate (feathery—once divided), or bipinnate (twice divided). A characteristic feature is the naked sori; the indusium (spore case covering) is absent. The name Polypodium is derived from

The Common Polypody, a native of northern Europe, Asia and western North America. It occurs in many distinct varieties.

poly, many, and *pous,* a foot, and refers to the branching rhizomes.

Treatment of Hothouse and Greenhouse Kinds. The hothouse kinds require a minimum winter temperature of 55 degrees and the cool greenhouse kinds one of 45 degrees. The best compost consists of equal parts of loam, peat, leaf mold and sand, with a small quantity of crushed charcoal added.

Repotting is done in February, March or April, or as soon as new growth commences. The plants are removed from their pots and the roots examined; those with a well-developed and healthy system of roots are repotted in large pots; those which have not filled the pots with roots are slipped back in the same pots and not repotted until later in the season, or until the following spring.

If the soil has turned sour, owing to defective drainage, and the roots have decayed, the Ferns must be given special treatment. Every particle of soil is washed from the roots in a pail of tepid water and the roots are cut back to live portions. The plants are then repotted in pots just large enough to hold the roots without cramping them.

Repotting. Well-rooted plants are prepared for repotting by removing the crocks and all loose soil from their roots. The new pots are well drained with crocks, which are covered with rough siftings from the compost or with coarse leaves. As the new compost is filled in, it is made firm by pressing it with the fingers.

After potting, the soil is not watered until it is

moderately dry, for there should be sufficient moisture in it for the immediate needs of the Ferns. It is then given a thorough soaking, and it is advisable to continue with this method of watering until the plants are well rooted.

During the remainder of the summer the soil must be kept moist. When growth has finished, at the end of the summer, the water supply is lessened, and during winter the soil is only moistened when it becomes moderately dry.

The deciduous (leaf-losing) kinds are only watered occasionally during the winter, sufficient being given to prevent the rootstocks from shriveling.

A moist atmosphere must be maintained at all times of the year, by damping the walls, floor and benches, but less humid conditions are required in the winter, especially in very cold weather.

Ferns for Hanging Baskets. Several kinds are suitable for growing in hanging baskets, especially P. subauriculatum. The baskets are lined with moss and filled with the potting compost. The Ferns are then planted and the baskets are suspended from the roof and watered as recommended for pot plants.

The best method of moistening the compost is to immerse the basket in a pail of water. Very large baskets should be suspended by a wire or chain running through a pulley wheel so that they are easily lowered into the water.

Treatment of Hardy Kinds. These require a shaded or semishaded position, and are suitable for planting in the rock garden and wild garden, in shaded borders, in sheltered nooks in the shrubbery, or in specially prepared beds. The best soil consists of equal parts of loam (or good garden soil) and leaf mold.

Planting is done in fall or spring and the soil is kept moist by watering in dry weather. A layer of leaf mold, applied in March or April, is beneficial, for it helps to conserve the moisture.

The fronds of the deciduous kinds must not be removed until spring, as they serve as a protection for the crowns.

How Spores Are Sown. Most kinds are raised by sowing spores as soon as they are ripe. A frond is gathered and placed in a paper bag, which is hung in a room or shed for 24 hours.

Those spores which are found in the bottom of the bag are fit for sowing.

Small pots are prepared by half-filling them with crocks which are covered with the rough siftings from the compost. The remainder of the space is then filled with finely sifted compost, which is moistened by immersing the pot in a pail of water. The spores are sown thinly on the surface; a pinch of spores held between the thumb and forefinger is sufficient for a 5-in. pot.

No surface watering is given after the spores are sown. The soil is kept moist by standing the pot in a saucer of water, and a pane of glass is laid over the top.

As soon as the young Ferns are large enough to handle they are pricked out in little clusters, 1 in. apart, in deep seed pans, filled with finely sifted compost. The soil is moistened and a pane of glass laid over them for a few days until they are established. When large enough to be potted separately, they are set in 2-in. pots and subsequently in larger pots.

The hothouse kinds are raised in a greenhouse where the night temperature is 65-70 degrees, the cool greenhouse kinds in 50-60 degrees and the hardy kinds outdoors or in a cool greenhouse or cold frame.

Propagation can also be effected by division, the crested and tessellated varieties being principally increased in this way. Those grown in a greenhouse are divided at potting time. They are taken out of their pots, the crocks and soil removed from the roots, and are separated into a number of pieces, each containing a portion of the crown or rhizome, together with roots, and one or more fronds.

Each divided portion is repotted in a pot just large enough to hold the roots comfortably. The hardy kinds are treated in the same way in April and the divisions are planted at once in their permanent positions.

The Chief Kinds. The chief kinds for each purpose are listed below, with an indication of the average length of their fronds.

For the hothouse: P. albido-squamatum, 2 ft.; P. loriceum, 18 in.; P. pectinatum, 2 ft.; P. quercifolium, Oak-leaved Fern, 3 ft.; and P. verrucosum, 3 ft.

For the cool greenhouse: P. aureum, 4 ft.; P.

aureum Mandaianum, with bluish silver, wavy leaves; P. Billardieri, 18 in.; P. pustulatum, 3 ft.; P. subauriculatum, 3 ft.; P. subauriculatum Knightiae, with long, hanging fronds.

Hardy kinds: P. vulgare, 12 in., and its varieties bifidum, cristatum, elegantissimum, hesperium, occidentale, and trichomanoides; P. polypodioides, 6-8 in.

POLYPODY. Polypodium, which see.

POLYPTERIS HOOKERIANA (Poly'pteris). A plant that is native from Nebraska to Mexico and is sometimes cultivated as a flower-garden annual. Its name is derived from *polys,* many, and *pteron,* a wing, and refers to the hairs that are attached to the seeds. Polypteris is a member of the Daisy family, Compositae.

Polypteris Hookeriana blooms for a long period in summer and fall. Its flowers, which re-

Polypteris Hookeriana, a native of North America, bears pink flowers and has a long blooming season.

semble those of Scabious, are rose-pink and decidedly attractive. They are excellent for cutting and are especially suitable for table decoration.

The plant itself is rather loose in growth and attains a height of 2-4 ft. Its foliage is rough-hairy, its stems somewhat sticky.

The culture of this plant presents no difficulties. Seeds may be sown outdoors in a sunny place, in fertile, well-drained soil in spring, and the plants thinned to stand about 1 ft. apart; or the plants may be raised from seeds sown earlier indoors and then be set out in the garden after all danger of frost has passed.

POLYSCIAS (Poly'scias). Tropical evergreen shrubs and trees which are cultivated for their ornamental foliage, and were previously included in the genus Panax. They are found wild in New Zealand, tropical Asia and the Pacific islands and belong to the Aralia family, Araliaceae. They have deeply divided, aralia-like leaves, which are green or green and white. The small clusters of whitish flowers are inconspicuous. The name is from *polys,* many, and *skius,* shade, from their leafiness.

Details of Cultivation. These plants are grown outdoors in the far South, where they succeed without difficulty in any fairly good soil in part shade or full sun. When grown indoors, they require a minimum winter temperature of 55 degrees. The best soil compost consists of equal parts of loam, peat and leaf mold, with a sprinkling of sand and charcoal added. Although they grow up to 20 ft. in height, young plants in small pots, 5-6 in. in diameter, are the most decorative.

Large plants are potted annually in February or March. They are taken out of their pots, the crocks and loose soil are removed from the roots, and the plants are then transferred to larger pots. After potting, they are shaded from sunlight and the atmosphere is maintained in a moist condition by frequently damping the floor and benches.

Until the plants are well rooted, the compost is only moistened when it becomes quite dry, after which it is kept moist throughout the summer. Much less water is required in the winter, sufficient only being given to prevent the leaves from shriveling.

Propagation is by stem or root cuttings, or by suckers or air-layering. To obtain stem cuttings or shoots, the top of the old plant is cut off in early spring. This causes a number of shoots to form. When they are 4 in. in length, the shoots are taken off and the lower leaves removed; they are then inserted in a propagating case with a bottom heat of 70-75 degrees.

Pieces of old roots cut into 1-in. lengths may also be used to produce new plants. They are inserted in pots of sandy soil, with their tops level with the surface. It is not necessary to place them in a closed case as they have no leaves. Suckers, or shoots, which rise up through the soil, may also be detached with a few roots, potted, and treated as rooted cuttings. Air-layering, which see, may be done in spring.

The Chief Kinds. P. Balfouriana, leaves edged

or spotted white; P. Guilfoylei, leaves margined white. In P. Guilfoylei variety Victoriae the leaves are finely divided.

POLYSTACHYA (Polystach'ya). Small-growing but free-flowering Orchids which, although found wild chiefly in Africa, are also represented in tropical America and Asia. All are epiphytal (grow on trees), with small, evergreen clustered, somewhat conical pseudobulbs, with usually short terminal spikes of flowers, which have smaller petals than sepals. Many of the flowers are of uniform coloring and open principally in summer. The name polystachya means many-spiked and is from *poly,* many, and *stachys,* a spike. Polystachya belongs to the family Orchidaceae.

These Orchids are grown in a greenhouse with a tropical atmosphere in the summer, and a winter temperature of 55-60 degrees. They must not be overwatered, but the compost should not be allowed to get too dry. Flower pans are preferable to pots, owing to the small size and shallow roots of the plants. Shading must be afforded from spring to fall.

Some of the smaller kinds do well if attached to pieces of wood and suspended. The compost should consist of two parts Osmunda fiber, two parts of sphagnum moss, and a few decayed oak or beech leaves. Free drainage is essential. Repotting should be done as fresh growths are seen.

The Showiest Kinds. P. Pobeguinii, from French Guinea, is distinct from all the others, as the flowers are crimson throughout and borne in numbers on slender arching stems, 8-12 in. long. P. paniculata, from Uganda, has leafy stems which terminate in an erect branched panicle, thickly set with small orange-red flowers. P. affinis (bracteosa), from Sierra Leone, has drooping panicles of brownish-yellow flowers. P. luteola, from tropical America and tropical Asia, has greenish-yellow flowers. P. laxiflorus has erect, branching spikes bearing many small, creamy-white and greenish flowers.

POLYSTICHUM—*Holly Fern, Shield Fern* (Polys'tichum). Tender and hardy evergreen Ferns which are found wild in many parts of the world, especially in tropical Asia, tropical America, South Africa, Japan, Europe and North America. The fronds of these Ferns vary in length from 12 in. to 3 ft. They are mostly bipinnate (twice divided). The rachis (frond stalk) is mostly covered with fine brown hairs or scales and the undersides of the fronds bear dotlike sori (spore clusters) which are covered with peltate (umbrella-shaped) indusia (spore-case coverings). The name Polystichum is derived from *poly,* many, and *stichos,* row, and refers to the fact that the sori are arranged in rows. Polystichum belongs to the family Polypodiaceae.

Treatment of Hardy Kinds. These require a shaded position. They flourish, and are shown to best advantage, in woodland gardens and in rock gardens. (They are attractive when associated with rocks.) They are of easy culture, thriving in somewhat acid, woodland soil that is fairly moist. They need shade from strong sun.

Greenhouse Kinds. These kinds need a minimum winter temperature of 50-55 degrees. The best soil for them consists of equal parts of loam, peat moss and leaf mold with a free admixture of sand.

Repotting is done in February or March. The plants are taken out of their pots and the crocks, as well as any loose soil, are removed from the roots with a pointed stick. The pots into which the plants are to be placed must be clean. If they are new they should be soaked in water and allowed to dry before use. They must be well drained with crocks, which should be covered with the rough siftings from the soil or with leaves to prevent the potting soil from washing down and clogging the drainage.

The soil compost must contain the correct amount of moisture. To test it, squeeze a handful. If moisture exudes, the soil is too wet. If, when the hand is opened, the soil trickles out, it indicates lack of moisture. When a handful of soil is squeezed and the hand opened, the soil should just hold together, but fall apart at the lightest touch. When potting, the compost should be pressed moderately firm with the fingers, not rammed with a potting stick.

Summer and Winter Management. Care must be taken to avoid overwatering these Ferns, especially before their pots are well filled with roots. Throughout the summer, the soil must be kept moist, and for the remainder of the year water is applied only when the soil approaches dryness; then enough water is given to thoroughly saturate the entire mass of soil. The atmosphere is kept constantly moist by damping the floor and the benches between the pots, but the fronds (leaves) must not be syringed. The Ferns should be shaded from direct, strong sunlight except during the winter months.

How Spores Are Sown. Most of these Ferns are raised by sowing spores as soon as they are ripe. (See Ferns.)

Propagation by Division. Many kinds can be propagated by division. Those which are growing in a bed out of doors are lifted in March or April and separated into a number of pieces, each containing a portion of rhizome with roots and fronds attached. The divided portions are then replanted in their permanent positions.

The greenhouse kinds are removed from their pots in February or March, and divided as advised for the hardy sorts. The divisions are set in separate small pots and treated as advised for when you repot. P. aculeatum proliferum produces small plantlets on its fronds, and these may be used for purposes of propagation.

The Chief Kinds. *For the greenhouse:* P. adiantiforme (capense), 3 ft.; P. aristatum (East Indian Holly Fern) and its variety variegatum, 1½ ft.; P. tsus-simense, 2 ft.; P. viviparum, 1½ ft.

Hardy kinds: P. acrostichoides (Christmas Fern), 12-20 in.; P. aculeatum, 3 ft., and its varieties angulare, cristatum, grandiceps, proliferum, imbricatum and plumosum; P. Braunii (Shield Fern), 2 ft.; P. Lonchitis (Mountain Holly Fern), 18 in.; and P. munitum (Giant Holly Fern), 3½ ft.

Polystichum is so closely related to Aspidium that great confusion exists in their classification. Some botanists include Polystichum in the genus Aspidium; others keep them apart.

POMADERRIS (Pomader'ris). Evergreen shrubs suitable for cultivation in a greenhouse in which a minimum winter temperature of 45 degrees is maintained, and outdoors in California and in the South. They belong to the family Rhamnaceae and are found wild in New Zealand and in the southern parts of Australia. The name is derived from *poma,* a lid, and

derrhis, skin, and refers to the skinlike covering of the fruit.

These shrubs reach a height of 3-20 ft. and bear bunches of small flowers in spring or summer. When grown in pots they are cultivated in a compost of half peat and half loam with sand added freely.

During the summer months the greenhouse in which they are grown must be ventilated freely and the soil in the pots kept moist. Free drainage is essential, for, while it is necessary that the roots should not suffer from dryness, it is just as important that the soil should not become sour. In winter far less water is needed, though even then the soil must be kept reasonably moist.

Propagation Is by Cuttings, about 3 in. long, made from side shoots taken from the old plants in summer, and inserted in a bed of sand or sandy peat in a propagating case in the greenhouse. The cuttings must be shaded from sunshine and kept moderately moist.

Some of the chief kinds are P. apetala, greenish; P. betulina, yellow; and P. elliptica, yellow.

POMEGRANATE. See Punica Granatum.

POMELO OR GRAPEFRUIT. Citrus paradisi. See Citrus.

POMPON. This term is used to describe certain small, tight, button-like heads of flowers. It is usually only applied when other varieties of the same kind of flower bear larger and less compact and stylized heads of bloom. The term is also applied to the varieties that produce flower heads of this type; thus we have pompon Chrysanthemums, pompon Dahlias and pompon Zinnias.

PONCIRUS TRIFOLIATA—*Trifoliate Orange* (Ponci'rus). This hardy, leaf-losing (deciduous) shrub, sometimes named Aegle sepiaria, is a native of Japan and China. It grows about 10 ft. high, has smooth, green stems with sharp spines, and glossy, three-lobed leaves. In May it bears white, fragrant flowers which are followed by small orange-like fruits. It belongs to the Rue family, Rutaceae. The name is from *poncire,* a Citrus. The plant is hardy outdoors in sheltered locations as far north as New York City.

Needs a Sunny Place. Young plants are planted in autumn or spring in deep, well-drained, loamy soil. A sunny position should be chosen to insure the production of flowers and fruits. In mild climates it may be planted to form a hedge. No pruning is required, except to shorten extra-vigorous shoots, in June, to preserve the symmetry of the bush.

This shrub is used as a stock on which to graft various Citrus fruits to improve their hardiness, and it has been used in hybridizing. The hybrids are called Citranges and are valued as ornamentals; their fruits can be used for making acid, cooling drinks. Three of the most important of these hybrids are those named Coleman, Morton and Rusk. (See also Hybrid Citrus, under Citrus.)

When to Take Cuttings. Propagation is effected in August by inserting cuttings, made from firm, half-woody shoots, in a cold frame or greenhouse. Seeds may be sown in a greenhouse —temperature 50 degrees—in spring.

POND. The construction of ornamental ponds in gardens is dealt with under the heading of Water Gardens.

POND APPLE. See Annona.

POND CYPRESS. See Taxodium ascendens.

POND LILY. Nymphaea, which see.

PONDWEED. Potamogeton, which see.

PONDWEED, CAPE. See Aponogeton.

PONTEDERIA—*Pickerelweed* (Pontede'ria). Hardy aquatic perennial flowering plants, natives of North America, which belong to the family Pontederiaceae. P. cordata has a creeping rhizome and long-stalked, heart-shaped leaves and bears a raceme (loose spike) of blue, funnel-shaped flowers in summer. The name Pontederia commemorates G. Pontedera, an Italian botanist of the seventeenth century.

For Shallow Ponds. The rhizomes are planted in early fall or early spring in ornamental pools or ponds or by streamsides where the water does not exceed 12 in. in depth. They are set in the mud at the bottom of the pool, and should not be disturbed for many years, or until it is necessary to increase them or clean out the pool.

Propagation is by lifting and dividing the rhizomes in autumn or spring.

The principal kind is P. cordata, 2-4 ft., violet-blue, summer. Its variety angustifolia, sometimes called P. montevidiensis, has narrower leaves.

POOL. See Water Gardens.

POOR-MAN'S-WEATHERGLASS. Anagallis arvensis, which see.

POPINAC. Acacia Farnesiana, which see.

POPINAC, WHITE. Leucaena glauca, which see.

POPLAR. See Populus.

POPLAR, TULIP. Liriodendron Tulipifera, which see.

POPPY. See Papaver.

POPPY, BLUE. See Meconopsis.

POPPY, CALIFORNIA. Eschscholzia californica, which see.

POPPY, CELANDINE. Stylophorum, which see.

POPPY, HORNED. Glaucium, which see.

POPPY, ICELAND. Papaver nudicaule, which see.

POPPY MALLOW. Callirhoë, which see.

POPPY, MATILIJA. Romneya, which see.

POPPY, MEXICAN TULIP. Hunnemannia, which see.

POPPY, PLUME. Macleaya cordata, which see.

POPPY, PRICKLY. Argemone, which see.

POPPY, TREE. Dendromecon, which see.

POPPY, WATER. Hydrocleys nymphoides, which see.

POPPYWORT. Meconopsis, which see.

POPULUS: POPLAR, ASPEN AND COTTONWOOD
Quick-growing Trees for Ornament and Shelter

Populus. (Pop'ulus). Leaf-losing trees, often of very large size, this group is widely distributed in Europe, Asia and North America; a few kinds are wild in other regions, one being a native of tropical Africa. It is almost impossible to suggest how many kinds or species there may be, for some that have been described as species are un-doubtedly hybrids.

Where two or three kinds grow together, they often hybridize freely, and numerous seedlings appear when a suitable seedbed occurs in the vicinity of the parent trees. Seedlings may even appear at a long distance from large trees, for the seeds are easily carried by wind.

As many Poplars are much alike in foliage, and the leaves on a single tree may vary a good deal in size and shape, their correct identification from twigs is very difficult. A further difficulty arises from the fact that male and female flowers are borne on different trees, and as propagation is frequently by cuttings, trees of one sex only may be known in the gardens of a particular country.

The seeds are small and often sparingly produced in the fruits among a mass of cottony fiber. As they lose their vitality very quickly, they should be sown as soon as ripe.

Attractive in Bloom. Some of the Poplars are very attractive when in flower, particularly the male forms; and in some instances the young leaves are reddish and conspicuous. The chief tints in their autumn coloring are yellow and gold, with reddish tinges in those of the Aspens. Populus belongs to the Willow family, Salicaceae; the name is the ancient Latin name of the Poplar.

Propagating Poplars by Cuttings. Although it is possible to increase Poplars by seeds sown as soon as ripe, it is often difficult to keep them true to type, owing to the possibility of cross-fertilization, so that seeds are rarely relied on. It is more usual to insert cuttings of well-ripened, one-year-old wood, 9-12 in. long, during autumn in moist soil out of doors. The cuttings should be set 3 in. apart in the rows, for long shoots may be expected to grow during the first summer. It is wise to keep the young trees to single shoots. Populus alba and the Aspen group may also be increased from suckers.

Planting. Poplars should be set out in permanent positions by the time they are 3 or 4 years old; they may be planted in autumn, winter or spring. They require moist, loamy soil and are not suitable for soils containing much iron. When the ground is inclined to waterlogging,

mounds 1½-2 ft. high may be built on which to plant the trees. Many kinds withstand a good deal of exposure and thrive near the sea.

Good Shelter Trees. Poplars are also well adapted for shelter belts and endure severe pruning. In the dry plains of the Middle West and West the Poplars, commonly called Cottonwoods, are the most valuable of shade trees. For this purpose it is advisable to plant only male specimens, because the great amount of cottony material produced with the seeds blows about and litters lawns, gardens and other places.

Some of the Poplars are excellent trees for planting in moist places either as isolated specimens or in small groups; and some, such as the Carolina Poplar, are popular as street trees. They should, however, not be planted without proper consideration, for all have invasive roots that travel far in search of moisture and may clog drains and sewers. Their branches are mostly brittle and liable to storm damage.

How to Prune. During the early years all unwanted branches should be gradually removed from the lower part of the trunk.

The objective then should be to produce a

It is usually unwise to plant Poplars as near to a house as this row of young Lombardy Poplars. The roots of Poplars are likely to clog drains or sewers to which they gain access.

reasonably long length of trunk free from branches, the single trunk being carried well into the head of the tree. The head should be of uniform shape, made up of strong branches. This pruning may be carried out during summer, and all wounds should be protected by painting them with tree-wound paint.

Quick Growers. Poplars are among the quickest growing of all hardy trees, and they are valuable for planting in places where a fast-growing tree is required to block out an ugly view. Trees have been known to attain a height of 50 ft. in 15 years. They are good trees for planting along the sides of roads, and several kinds form excellent street trees in seaside towns. The White Poplar (Populus alba) succeeds on sand dunes, where its suckers help to bind the sand.

The Aspens. Several kinds of Poplar form a small group known as Aspens. Mature trees usually have rounded leaves with much-indented margins; juvenile trees, which are easily raised from suckers, have leaves of varying shape and size. Even on the calmest days the leaves quiver and are rarely still. This characteristic has given rise to various legends but is due to the fact that the leafstalks are flattened, not rounded as in other Poplars; the weight of the leaf blade favors constant agitation.

Populus alba pyramidalis is sometimes called Populus Bolleana.

The Aspen, Populus tremula, a graceful tree the leaves of which quiver almost continuously. Catkins, leaves and bark are shown.

The European Aspen, Populus tremula, is found wild in northern Europe and northeastern Asia, extending into very cold regions. It forms an interesting tree, but is better adapted for the colder than the warmer parts of North America. The variety pendula has weeping branches, and Davidiana is a Chinese form with smaller leaves than the typical kind. P. tremuloides, the Quaking Aspen, is the North American counterpart of P. tremula: the male form is the more decorative, for its purplish catkins are very conspicuous in spring.

The Parasol Poplar. The variety pendula of P. tremuloides, known as "Parasol de St. Julien," is a very attractive male tree with weeping branches. P. grandidentata, the Large-toothed Aspen of North America, has larger leaves than those trees previously mentioned.

The White Poplars, of which Populus alba, sometimes called Abele, is the type, are decorative trees by reason of the bark of the young shoots, and the undersides of the leaves being covered by a dense silvery felt. Populus alba forms a large tree, up to 80-90 ft. high, with a widely spreading head, and reproduces itself by suckers. These latter may become so abundant as to be a nuisance. There are several well-marked varieties of Populus alba, such as nivea, with very white shoots and leaves; pyramidalis, with a habit of growth like that of the Lombardy Poplar; globosa, with a rounded head, and pendula with weeping branches. P. alba is widely distributed in Europe and in Asia, north of the Himalayas. P. tomentosa is an allied tree from China.

The Gray Poplar. P. canescens, the Gray Poplar, is a large tree rather like P. alba with gray bark. It is sometimes said to be a natural hybrid between P. alba and P. tremula.

The Black Poplar, P. nigra, forms a large tree with a wide-spreading head. It is a native of Europe and Asia and attains a height of 90 ft. Several distinct varieties of this tree are known.

The Lombardy Poplar. One of the best-known of all Poplars is P. nigra variety italica (pyramidalis), commonly called the Lombardy Poplar. This is a conspicuous tree by reason of its stiff, erect branches and narrow habit of growth. Until quite recent years, male plants

Populus canadensis serotina forms a large tree up to 100 ft. tall. Leaf and bark are shown.

only were known, but there is a female tree at Kew Gardens in England from which fertile seed was obtained by hand pollination, and numerous seedling trees have been raised.

The Birch-leaved Poplar. A very striking variety of P. nigra is betulifolia; it has smaller leaves than the type, hairy shoots and a burred trunk. Two other varieties of stiff, erect habit of growth, rather like that of the Lombardy Poplar, are thevestina and plantierensis; they are varieties of P. nigra.

The Carolina Poplar, P. canadensis, is considered to be a hybrid, probably between P. nigra and P. deltoides. It is known only as a male tree. It grows rapidly and attains an eventual height of 60-90 ft. It was originally discovered in a French nursery in 1750. A number of similar hybrids or forms are distinguished by variety names. These include: P. canadensis variety serotina, with wide-spreading and ascending branches; variety Eugenei, of narrow pyramidal growth; variety marilandica, similar to variety

The Lombardy Poplar, Populus nigra variety italica, is erect and narrow in outline.

serotina but branches more distant and not generally ascending (this is the kind often planted as Carolina Poplar); variety erecta, a narrow, erect-growing kind, and variety regenerata, which produces its foliage earlier in spring than variety serotina.

A Golden-leaved Poplar. A very good golden-leaved tree is P. canadensis aurea. It grows very fast, and the leaves retain much of their golden color throughout the summer, although it is best when the leaves first develop.

The Balsam Poplars are favorites by reason of the fragrant, balsamic odor of their buds and leaves. P. Tacamahaca, the Balsam Poplar or Tacamahac, is a native of the northernmost United States and Canada. This kind grows to a height of 90 ft. It was at one time known as P. balsamifera, but that name, according to the rules of botanical nomenclature, belongs to an entirely different kind.

P. trichocarpa is the Western Balsam Poplar. It occurs as a native from Alaska to southern California and under good conditions attains a height of 180 ft.

The Cottonwoods are so called because of the abundant cottony material that accompanies the seeds. Most important of the Cottonwoods is P. deltoides, which is native from Quebec to Flor-

The Cottonwood, Populus deltoides, a native of the eastern United States, is a popular shade tree in the central states.

ida and Texas. This is a tree of noble appearance. It is much planted in the central states as a shade tree.

Very similar to P. deltoides is the Great Plains Cottonwood, P. Sargentii. Like its relative, it favors moist soils. It occurs natively from Iowa, Manitoba and Kansas westward to the Rocky Mountains.

Some Newer Asiatic Poplars. P. Wilsonii is a distinct, large-leaved Poplar from China; it was introduced in 1907. Another very striking Poplar, introduced from China in 1900, is P. lasiocarpa. In this the leaves may be 10 in. long and 6-8 in. wide, with red stalks and midribs. In China it grows 40-60 ft. high. Other new kinds are P. szechuanica and P. koreana.

There are very many other kinds of hardy Poplars, but the selection mentioned above will be sufficient for most people.

Economic Importance of Poplar Wood. The wood of many of the Poplars is of considerable commercial value. It is much used as a source of wood pulp and for the manufacture of matchsticks, matchboxes, fruit and flower baskets, as well as for other purposes. Larger wood of other kinds is used for the bottoms of carts and wheelbarrows, glass rolling, etc. The wood is very useful for brake blocks, as it does not fire quickly when subjected to friction.

PORANA (Pora'na). A small group of Old World tropical twining plants, one of which, P. paniculata, is grown in gardens in Florida and in other warm parts of the country. Porana belongs to the Morning Glory family, Convolvulaceae. Its name is a native East Indian one.

Porana paniculata is sometimes called White Corallita, but, as the name Corallita more properly belongs to Antigonon, which occurs in both pink- and white-flowered kinds, it seems best not to apply it to Porana.

This Porana attains a height of 30 ft. and blooms profusely. It grows without difficulty in a variety of soils. It is readily propagated by seeds and by cuttings of side shoots taken in summer and inserted in a close propagating case.

PORTLANDIA (Portland'ia). Tropical, evergreen, flowering shrubs from the American tropics, including Mexico and the West Indies. They belong to the same family as the Bouvardia, biaceae. These evergreen shrubs, which grow to 10 ft. in height, have oval, pointed, op-ite, leathery leaves, 2 in. in length. The flow-are funnel-shaped at the base and spread out the tip into five lobes; they are 2-3 in. in gth, scarlet or white, and some are sweetly ated. The name Portlandia commemorates Duchess of Portland, a great patron of botany. lowering Shrubs. Portlandias are suitable for wing outdoors in frost-free, warm countries y. When grown in a greenhouse, they require vinter temperature of 55 degrees; the best ting compost consists of equal parts of fibrous m, leaf mold and peat, with sand freely led. Repotting is done after the plants have shed flowering. They are lightly pruned into pe as soon as the flowers have faded, and are quently syringed to accelerate the develop-nt of the dormant buds.

When the new shoots are half an inch in gth, repotting is done. The plants are care-ly knocked out of their pots, and the crocks l any soil which is not full of roots are re-ved with a pointed stick. The new pots, ich should be two sizes larger, are prepared by cing crocks in the bottom and covering them h rough siftings from the compost or with igh leaves. The plants are placed in the rmest part of the greenhouse and are fre-ently syringed to encourage root action.

Overwatering after potting often results in the cay of the roots. Well-established plants are ot moist at the roots during the summer, but the approach of autumn less water is given, d during winter and early spring the compost only moistened when it becomes moderately y.

The greenhouse is kept moist at all seasons of e year by damping the floor and benches. uch less damping is required in winter, when e temperature is considerably lower.

Except when the plants are in flower, the iage is syringed twice a day in summer and ce a day in winter, except in very cold weather. he plants are shaded from sunlight until the w shoots are fully formed in late summer, nen they are exposed to full light to ripen them r flower production.

Propagation Is by Cuttings; shoots 2 in. in

length are taken off in early summer. The leaves are removed from the lower part of the stem and a cut is made just below the bottom node.

The shoots are inserted in a propagating case with a bottom heat of 75 degrees. The case is kept closed except for a few minutes each morn-ing, when it is lifted to change the air, and the glass is wiped dry on the underside.

This practice is continued until roots are formed. More air is then gradually admitted. When the foliage is sufficiently hardened, the cuttings are potted. After they have recovered from the shock of potting, they are placed on the greenhouse benches.

The chief kinds are P. grandiflora, 10 ft., white; P. platantha, 3 ft., white; and P. coccinea, 3 ft., scarlet. All bloom in summer.

PORTUGAL BROOM. See Cytisus albus.

PORTUGAL LAUREL. See Prunus lusitan-ica.

PORTULACA—*Purslane, Sun Plant* (Portula'-ca). A small genus of the Purslane family, Portulacaceae, widely spread throughout the world. Only two sorts are of real horticultural importance. The name Portulaca is an old Latin name used by Pliny, who, however, spelt it Portilaca.

Portulaca grandiflora is a brilliant and popu-lar dwarf annual of prostrate habit, native to Brazil. The trailing stems, 4 or 5 in. in length, are furnished with somewhat fleshy cylindrical leaves, and carry at their tips several large flow-ers of great brilliance and beauty. Each is about 1 in. in diameter and of exquisite satin texture; the range of colors is extremely varied and bril-liant—yellow, purple, scarlet, pink, etc. Both single- and double-flowered forms are available.

P. grandiflora is a true sun lover and is only really a success in sunny locations. Seeds should be sown in spring in the open where the plants are to flower. Sow thinly and cover the seeds thinly. Plants from seeds sown thus make sturdier specimens and are in every way more satisfactory than those raised indoors and planted out. If the seedlings come up too thickly they may be thinned to stand 3 in. apart.

Portulaca oleracea, the Common Purslane, is a hardy annual, some 6 in. high. It is a native of southern Europe and is one of the most "pesky"

The double-flowered Portulaca grandiflora bears a profusion of gay-colored flowers.

of garden weeds. A variety of this plant, P. oleracea variety sativa, is sometimes grown in the vegetable garden. The young, succulent, fleshy shoots are used in salads, while the older shoots are used as a potherb and for pickling.

PORTULACARIA AFRA (Portulacar'ia). A South African succulent shrub that is grown outdoors in California and in similar climates, and as a greenhouse and window-garden plant. It attains an ultimate height of 12-20 ft., but is an attractive foliage plant even when quite small. Its flowers are pale pink and are arranged in small clusters.

Portulacaria belongs to the botanical family Portulacaceae, the Purslane family. The name is an adaptation of Portulaca, which is the name of a nearly related group of plants. In its native country Portulacaria afra is esteemed as food by both wild and domestic animals.

This succulent thrives without difficulty under the care recommended for Cacti (which see). It is very easily increased by means of cuttings

Portulacaria afra has an interesting branching habit and grows well as a house plant where the atmosphere is dry.

taken at any time of the year, spring or summer preferred.

POSOQUERIA (Posoquer'ia). Tropical, evergreen flowering shrubs, from tropical America, which belong to the Madder family, Rubiaceae. They form bushy shrubs up to 6 ft. in height, have oval to oblong, coriaceous (leathery) leaves and produce terminal clusters of drooping, narrow, tubular, white flowers in summer. The name Posoqueria is a native name applied to P. longiflora in Guiana.

Cultivation. These shrubs may be grown outdoors in southern Florida. They may also be cultivated in greenhouses. When so grown they require a minimum winter temperature of 55 degrees and a soil compost of equal parts of loam, peat, leaf mold and coarse sand. Repotting is done in February or March. They are first pruned into shape and placed in the warmest part of the hothouse; the stems are syringed several times a day until the dormant shoots break into growth. They are then taken out of their pots, the crocks and loose soil are removed from the roots, and the plants are repotted in slightly larger pots, which are well-drained with crocks.

The soil is not watered until it becomes moderately dry, as it should contain sufficient moisture for the immediate needs of the plants. It is then thoroughly moistened and the same treatment afforded until the roots have freely entered the new soil. During the remainder of the summer the soil is kept moist, but, when growth is becoming less active in the autumn, the water supply is gradually reduced. During the winter, the compost is only moistened when it becomes moderately dry.

The atmosphere must be kept moist throughout the year by damping the floor and benches as soon as these become dry, although damping is done less frequently during the winter, when the temperature is much lower and the moisture does not evaporate so quickly.

From March to September the foliage is syringed twice a day (except when the plants are in flower); for the remainder of the year syringing once a day is sufficient. The plants are shaded from strong sunlight from April to September; for the remainder of the year no shading is required.

When to Take Cuttings. Propagation is by cuttings; shoots 2-3 in. long are removed in March or April. They are rooted in a propagating case having a bottom heat of 70-75 degrees. To prevent the leaves from wilting, the case is kept close, but each morning the top is raised for a few minutes and the moisture wiped from the underside of the glass.

After two or three weeks of this treatment, roots will form and the propagating case is ventilated more freely. After a few days the rooted cuttings are potted separately in 3-in. pots and subsequently in large ones. To induce a bushy habit of growth, the leading shoot is pinched back to three or four buds and the resultant side shoots are similarly treated.

The chief kinds are P. longiflora, 6 ft., white; P. latifolia, 20 ft., white; and P. formosa, 12 ft., white. All flower in late summer.

POST OAK. Quercus stellata, which see.

POT. Standard pots or flowerpots are made of unglazed earthenware in various sizes. Normally their heights equal their diameters and their tops are broader than their bases. A wide rim runs around the top of each pot which permits stacking them inside of each other without

A group of standard flowerpots of various sizes.

Ornamental pots, such as this, are sometimes used for terrace plants.

danger of sticking and consequent breakage. In the bottom of each pot are one or more drainage holes. In addition to standard pots special types, with drainage holes in their sides as well as bottoms, are made especially for Orchid as well as other fancy types, including glazed ones. Containers similar to pots but proportionately shallower are called pans. See Pan.

POTAMOGETON — *Pondweed* (Potamoge′-ton). Aquatic perennial weeds of slight horti-cultural value. Numerous kinds are found in the ponds, lakes, rivers and canals of North America. They are mostly submerged plants with slender, closely jointed stems and small, semi transparent leaves. Some kinds have floating leaves. The small green flowers, which are in the form of a spike, are inconspicuous.

Sometimes the submerged kinds, especially P. densus, with crinkled green leaves, and P. cris-pus, with reddish leaves, are planted in aquar iums for their ornamental effect.

Potamogeton belongs to the family Potamoge-tonaceae. The name is derived from *potamos,* river, and *geiton,* neighbor, and refers to the plants being found in rivers.

POTASH. The normal plant requires for its healthy growth a number of minerals absorbed from the soil through the roots. If one of these necessary minerals is lacking, or inadequate, or if the balance of the different minerals is wrong, the plant will not grow so well, and may fall a prey to fungal and bacterial diseases much more readily than a normal plant.

The most important substance from this point of view is potash. Certain plants are especially sensitive to a shortage of potash: for example, Peas, Beans, Potato, Tomato, Apple, Pear, Raspberry, Gooseberry, Plum and most other fruits. All plants, even if less definitely respon-sive, will be more healthy if adequately supplied with potash.

Many soils are deficient in potash, and other soils not actually deficient may have an excess of some other constituent such as phosphates. Both these types require potash dressings, and it is safe to apply these frequently and in considerable quantity without danger of applying excess. As a general rule, it is better to repeat small doses frequently than to give a large dressing all at once. See Fertilizers.

POTATO: MOST USEFUL OF VEGETABLES
A Guide to Its Culture as a Garden Crop

The Potato is widely cultivated in temperate regions, and its stem tubers, which grow underground, are a popular food. A tender, herbaceous perennial. The plant comes from South America where it was highly valued by the Indians. Its botanical name is Solanum tuberosum; it belongs to the family Solanaceae.

Planting Potatoes.

Potatoes can be cultivated in many different kinds of soil, but the finest crops are dug from well-drained loamy land. They may be planted on the same site year after year with good results, if the ground is maintained in a fertile condition by liming, manuring and so on. In a garden of moderate size, however, it is wise to include the Potatoes in any system of rotation of crops which may be practiced so that they shall have a change of soil periodically.

Preparing the Ground. The ideal way to prepare heavy, clayey land for Potato cultivation is to plow or dig it in autumn; it is left in a rough condition throughout the winter months. When the ground dries in spring the soil will break into small particles—in other words, it will be friable when harrowed or forked over. Exposure to rain, frost and wind does immense good to land of this type.

If this plan cannot be followed, it is the custom of some gardeners who have to plant Potatoes on clayey land to plant as they dig. The tubers, set in a furrow, are covered by soil as the digging proceeds. This method is advantageous because once the site is planted it is not trodden on again until late spring or early summer, when the first earthing-up or weeding is done, and by that time the surface will have dried.

Light or well-drained loamy soil should be plowed or dug in spring, manure or compost being buried in the furrow or trench as the work proceeds.

Digging a heavy crop of Potatoes.

It is not necessary or desirable to manure land heavily for Potato cultivation in the garden. A moderate dressing of decayed manure or compost, put on the land and mixed with it, and supplemented by several applications of a suitable complete fertilizer, will ensure satisfactory results.

Sprouting. The preparation of the sets or planting tubers, commonly called "seed potatoes," is a matter of great importance because it has a considerable effect on the yield. It has been found that if Potato tubers already possessing a few sprouts are planted, a heavier crop will result than if dormant or unsprouted tubers are used.

Tubers required for planting in spring should be chosen carefully; those weighing about 2 oz., or the size of a small hen's egg, are considered to be the most suitable. Larger tubers may, however, be used; they can be cut into pieces, each part to include a few sprouts, at planting time. To produce sprouts the tubers are set on end in shallow boxes, or specially made trays having short wooden legs which allow of their being placed on top of each other to save space. This is done 2-4 weeks before planting time.

What is called the "rose" end of the tuber, that which possesses the greater number of "eyes" or buds, is placed uppermost. The boxes or trays must be in a light, fairly warm place; there the tubers start into growth and by planting time will possess several short, sturdy sprouts. It is necessary that the tubers be fully open to the light or the sprouts will be weak and "drawn."

Sprouting before planting them is strongly to be recommended for all types, but it is especially necessary in the cultivation of early varieties; Potatoes treated in this way will start into growth sooner than dormant tubers.

Reducing the Number of Sprouts. Before the tubers are planted the question of the number of sprouts to be left on each one must be decided.

If only one sprout is left on each tuber, the crop will consist of a limited number of large Potatoes; if two sprouts are left there will be a large number of large Potatoes, and others of good size; if three sprouts are left there will be a certain number of small tubers, although most of them will be large or fair-sized. If all the sprouts are left on, or if dormant tubers are planted, the number of small Potatoes will be still greater.

For general garden cultivation the best practice is to leave two or three sprouts on each of the tubers.

There is no doubt as to the advantages of sprouting the tubers before planting, and limiting the number of sprouts. This ensures early development and a minimum of small Potatoes, and thus prevents waste of crop.

Potatoes as a Cleaning Crop. Those who are faced with the problem of making a new garden on land which has not been cultivated previously or which has been out of cultivation for many years, and bringing the soil into good condition for sowing or planting, will find it an excellent plan to crop it with Potatoes for the first year. There is no better cleaning crop for new land.

The site should be plowed or dug in spring to get rid of tree roots and as many perennial weeds as possible. The Potatoes are planted in spring. During the summer months the practices of weeding, hoeing and earthing-up will help very considerably to cultivate the land, break down lumpy soil and get rid of coarse weeds. By the end of the summer, or early autumn, the ground will be in first-rate condition for sowing or planting after the crop of Potatoes has been lifted.

It is most important to have the site thoroughly prepared where it is intended to make a new lawn by sowing Grass seeds, and Potato cultivation is ideal preparation. Early September is a suitable time to sow the Grass seeds, and if a crop of early Potatoes is grown they will be off the ground by the end of August, thus allowing time for the final leveling and seedbed preparation. The Potato tops, or vines, should be burnt on the site, together with any other garden rubbish which has to be destroyed; this practice helps to get rid of weed seeds and seedling weeds and thus saves labor later.

There are two chief types or classes of Potato —the Early, and the Maincrop or Late; numerous varieties of each type are available.

The First Plantings. The earliest crops of Potatoes are produced from plantings of Early

[9—10a]
Cinquefoil
(Potentilla fruticosa variety)

[9—10c]
Primula obconica

[9—11]
Removing plant from pot

[9—11a]
Transferring it to a larger, well-drained conta

[9—11b]
Filling new soil around roots

[9—11c]
Packing soil with potting stick

varieties made as soon in spring as soil and weather conditions allow. This will normally be 1-2 weeks before the average date of the last killing frost in the locality but in sheltered locations (such as on a south-facing slope protected from cold winds by a windbreak or hedge) on sandy soils they may be planted 3-4 weeks before the average date of the last killing frost. This latter date varies considerably, of course, according to geographical locality. Gardeners not familiar with it, as it applies to their own gardens, may obtain information from the County Agricultural Agent of the county in which they live or may be guided as to when to plant by the practices of local experts.

On heavy (clayey) soils planting can not be done quite as early as on light (sandy) ones. Under no circumstances should planting be done until the soil is in a workable, crumbly condition; planting in wet, sticky soil is sure to bring disappointing results.

As soon as young shoots from the Potatoes show through the surface of the ground and are 2-3 in. tall, soil should be drawn (hilled) up to them with a hoe or plow so that all except the very tips of the shoots is covered; this serves as a protection against cold.

Tubers (sets) of Early Potatoes are planted 4 in. deep and 12-15 in. apart in rows spaced 18-24 in. apart. It is a great advantage to place a layer of compost or decayed manure in the furrows before planting. The tubers root freely into either of these materials, and vigorous growth is thus promoted.

Early Potatoes may be dug as soon as the tubers of the new crop are large enough to use. This can be ascertained by lifting a plant or two as a trial, and will usually be within 10-12 weeks from the time of planting.

Plants need not be all lifted at once; the better plan for the home gardener is to dig his Early Potatoes as he needs them for table use, and thus to extend the harvest over a period of several weeks. It must be remembered that the Potato plants have not completed their season's growth when the first ones are lifted at the end of 10 or 12 weeks; if the plants are left in the ground the tubers will increase in size and number (and thus give a heavier crop) for some

time after these Potatoes have been removed.

Early varieties of Potatoes will have completed their growth and matured by July or August, according to locality, by which time Maincrop varieties will be available for digging for immediate table use. Early varieties should be all lifted when maturity is reached, which is evidenced by the tops' dying down naturally.

It cannot be said that Potatoes need a great deal of attention during the summer months; the two details of chief importance are weeding and earthing-up. As soon as the tops show through the soil, the ground between the rows should be forked over shallowly, the soil being broken down into small particles. Later on, it should be hoed frequently to keep down weeds. The work of earthing-up will then be a comparatively simple matter for the soil will be friable and easily moved. Earthing-up when the soil is hard and lumpy is a laborious task and it cannot be carried out satisfactorily.

Fertilizers for Potatoes. Before the soil is earthed up fertilizer should be applied alongside the plants. Specially compounded mixtures made for the purpose are sold by seedsmen and horticultural stores and will be found beneficial. Or the following mixture will be found satisfactory: superphosphate, five parts, and sulphate of ammonia, two parts, the mixture being applied at the rate of 3 oz. per yard run of row.

Earthing-up is done by drawing up the soil on each side of the row so that it supports the Potato stems and leaves only a few inches of

Soil may be earthed up around Potatoes with a draw hoe. The simplest way is to do one side at a time, drawing the soil up into a moderately steep ridge.

vine or growth exposed. It should not be completed on one occasion. The first earthing-up is done when the Potato tops are about 6 in. high and the second about four weeks later. The purpose of earthing-up is to support the stems of the plants and to protect the tubers and help their development.

A second planting of early Potatoes may be made 2-3 weeks after the earliest kinds. The tubers are set 5 in. deep, and 15 in. apart, in rows 24 in. from each other. They should be treated in the way already explained so far as the details of sprouting the tubers, planting, the use of fertilizers and earthing-up are concerned.

Late or Maincrop Potatoes. These are planted in about 6 weeks after the first earlies; they provide the chief supply during the winter and early spring months and will be ready to be lifted in September. The tubers are set 5 in. deep and 18 in. apart in rows, 2-2½ ft. from each other. It is a mistake to crowd them, for that prevents the soil from being properly cultivated between the rows. The other details of management—sprouting the tubers, planting, the application of fertilizers and earthing-up—are carried out in the way already described. In the home garden it is usually best to concentrate on early crops; late potatoes need a good deal of care with spraying.

Lifting Potatoes. There is no advantage in leaving Potatoes in the ground after the leaves have turned yellow; it is, in fact, unwise to do so, for there they are exposed to risk of damage by soil pests of various kinds.

After they have been dug, the Potatoes should be left on the ground for two or three hours if the weather is fine, so that the skins may harden before they are stored. If the weather is wet it is a good plan to spread them out under cover of a shed or other suitable place.

Storing Potatoes. The Potatoes must not be exposed to the light for more than a few hours or they will begin to turn green and will thus be rendered unfit for use in the kitchen. When dry, they may be stored in sacks or boxes, in any cool, dark, frostproof place. Only sound Potatoes should be stored in bulk; if diseased ones are put away with sound ones, the latter may also be spoiled. A winter storage temperature of 35-40 degrees is desirable for best results.

There are a large number of varieties of Potato. These will be found described in seedsmen's catalogues. It is wise to consult your State Agricultural Experiment Station or your County Agricultural Agent regarding varieties specially recommended for particular soils and localities.

POTATO, AIR. Dioscorea bulbifera, which see.

POTATO BEAN. Apios americana, which see.

POTATO ONION. A variety of Onion that is propagated by natural division of the bulb. See Onion.

POTATO, SWEET. See Sweet Potato.

POTATO VINE. Solanum jasminoides, which see.

POTENTILLA — *Cinquefoil* (Potentil'la). Mostly hardy, perennial plants and shrubs which are found wild in many parts of the world; some are natives of the northern part of America, others of the European mountains and of northern Asia. They grow 6 in. to 2 or 3 ft. high, and have leaves and flowers which are similar in shape to those of the Strawberry, though the flowers exhibit a wide range of color.

Some of the kinds are valuable plants for the perennial border, others for the rock garden and some for the shrub border. Potentilla belongs to the Rose family, Rosaceae. The name is derived from *potens,* powerful, and alludes to the medicinal properties the plants were thought to possess.

The hardy herbaceous perennial kinds of

Flowering shoot of the yellow shrubby Cinquefoil named Potentilla fruticosa.

Potentilla nevadensis, a native of Spain, is a prostrate kind that bears small yellow flowers freely during late spring and summer.

Potentilla provide several attractive flowering plants for the border. These grow from 18 in. to ft. high, and the strawberry-like blossoms open throughout many weeks in June and July. These plants thrive in ordinary, well-tilled garden soil, preferring that which is well drained; on heavy land that becomes very wet in winter they are liable to perish. They need a position fully exposed to the sunshine and are not happy in shady places. Planting is done preferably in early fall or in spring. An especially good single yellow-flowered kind is P. recta variety Warrenii. It grows 2 ft. high.

Raising Seedlings. A good way to raise an increased stock is by sowing seeds in a flat of sifted sandy soil in March, and placing it in a slightly heated greenhouse or cold frame. Seeds may also be sown out of doors on a prepared border of fine soil in May. The seedlings should be transplanted, about 4 in. apart, to a nursery border before they become crowded.

The double varieties do not come true from seeds. To propagate them the old plants should be lifted in October and carefully divided.

Brilliantly Colored Varieties. Comparatively few species or wild types are now grown in the herbaceous border; reliance is placed on the beautiful named varieties which have richly colored double or semidouble flowers. Some of the showiest of these are Gibson's Scarlet; Tous-

saint l'Ouverture, crimson; William Rollinson, orange-yellow, and Yellow Queen, yellow.

For the Rock Garden. The herbaceous Potentillas which are suitable for the rock garden include a number of hardy kinds. These thrive in well-drained, sandy, loamy soil in a sunny position. The most attractive is Potentilla nitida, a charming little plant, 6 in. high, with gray leaves and pale pink flowers in summer; the variety alba has white flowers. These two plants like gritty soil and do well in a moraine.

Others which are suitable for the rock garden are P. alba, 9 in., white; P. ambigua, 4 in., yellow; P. aurea, 4 in., rich yellow; P. fragiformis, 8-10 in., deep yellow; P. tormentillo-formosa (Tonguei), 6 in., orange-yellow; P. verna, 4-5 in., yellow; P. tridentata, 3-6 in., white, evergreen foliage.

The rose-colored Potentilla named for a Miss

One of the several named varieties of Potentilla fruticosa.

Willmott, a variety of P. nepalensis, grows about 12 in. high and is suitable either for the flower border or the rock garden.

These rock-garden kinds may be increased by sowing seeds in pots of sifted sandy soil in spring, or by careful division of the plants in September or early spring.

Attractive Flowering Shrubs. Of the shrubby Potentillas the chief kinds grown in gardens are varieties of P. fruticosa, a leaf-losing shrub, reaching a height of from 2-3 ft., and bearing large rich yellow flowers, somewhat resembling those of single Roses, throughout many weeks from late in May onwards. It thrives in ordinary garden soil, preferring that which is well drained and even sandy. It occurs natively in a number of varieties throughout the northern parts of the Northern Hemisphere.

There are many varieties of P. fruticosa, all the desirable ones of which are suitable for planting in a large rock garden or near the front of a shrubbery border. Those named below are beautiful free-blossoming shrubs and, with two exceptions, have flowers of some shade of yellow.

Those chiefly to be recommended are arbuscula, 2½ ft.; Farreri, 18 in.; Bowles' Variety, 2 ft.; Kathryn Dykes, 3 ft. Other kinds are Vilmoriniana, 2 ft., gray leaves and cream or pale yellow flowers; Veitchii, 2 ft., white flowers; Friedrichsenii, light yellow.

The shrubby Potentillas may be planted in autumn or spring. If the ground is clayey, sand and compost should be mixed in freely before the plants are put in.

Propagation. The shrubs are propagated, in August, by cuttings of shoots 4 or 5 in. long, inserted in a frame kept close for several weeks to encourage the development of roots, or the cuttings may be rooted in a propagating frame in a greenhouse. The rooted cuttings should be kept in a cold frame for the winter. When well rooted, they should be potted separately in 3-in. pots and planted out of doors in spring or early summer.

If no frame is available, the cuttings may be inserted in a bed of sandy soil in a border out of doors, covered with a hand light or bell jar, and shaded from sunshine.

POTHOS (Po'thos). Evergreen, climbing shrubby plants, from India, China and Madagascar, belonging to the family Araceae. Ornamental plants grown under this name in greenhouses belong to the genus Scindapsus, which see.

POT MARIGOLD. Calendula, which see.

POT MARJORAM. The cultivation of this herb is dealt with under the botanical name of Origanum, which see.

POT OFF. A gardener's term for the operation of transferring a young plant from a seed bed or propagating bed to a small pot.

POTOMATO. This is a name sometimes applied to plants that result from grafting tomatoes on potatoes, and potatoes on tomatoes, When the tomato is grafted on the potato, the resulting plant will often produce both potatoes and tomatoes, but not in sufficient quantities to make the practice profitable. The potato-on-the-tomato grafted plant produces neither potatoes nor tomatoes. The combination plant that results from such grafting is also sometimes called the topato.

POT ON. A gardeners' term for the operation of transferring a plant from a smaller pot to a larger one.

POTPOURRI. A potpourri is a jar of flower petals used to scent a room. There are numerous methods of making potpourris, but they may be roughly divided into two classes—those made solely of dried petals, leaves, etc., and those enriched with essential oils, etc. The fragrance of the first kind is delicate but lasting; the fragrance of the second kind is very rich at first, but not so lasting.

All richly scented flowers do not retain their scent when dried. Jasmine flowers, when fresh, for instance, have an exceptionally strong perfume, but are scentless when dried.

Petals of scented Roses should always predominate in potpourri. The other chief ingredients are Carnation petals, Lavender flowers, Orange flowers, Acacia flowers, Mignonette flowers, Heliotrope flowers, Rosemary flowers, Honeysuckle flowers; leaves of Marjoram, Sweet Balm, Lemon Verbena, Rosemary, Pennyroyal.

When to Gather the Leaves and Flowers. Flowers and leaves should be gathered when there has been no rain for at least 24 hours, and when the dew has dried on them, but before the sun is at its hottest. Methods of drying vary. According to some, the drying should be done in the sun. The majority of people prefer to dry in the shade, preferably in a warm room with the windows open when there is a dry wind blowing.

A great many people spread the petals and leaves on a table to dry. This is a mistake, as it takes too long.

Success depends on quick drying, and the quickest method of drying is to spread the ingredients on fine wire screening or netting, as this enables the air to circulate all around them. It is best to dry a small quantity at a time. Partially or fully dried flowers should never be left exposed on a damp day, for they absorb moisture from the atmosphere and are then apt to decay.

Flowers that are overblown should be avoided, but those selected should be fully expanded, otherwise their full fragrance is not developed. Small rosebuds look attractive in a potpourri, but they are scentless. Blue flowers are always pleasing, and the best for this purpose are Borage flowers. They should be picked before they are fully expanded, otherwise they lose their color. Deep-red Roses are best for potpourri, for other colored Roses fade badly.

An excellent ingredient rarely used is an Orange stuck with Cloves, dried in a slow oven and, when perfectly dry, crushed to powder.

A great many people object to layers of salt in a jar, but it certainly makes a richer potpourri. When layers of salt are put in, the jar should be tightly sealed for a month, as this enhances the fragrance.

Recipes for Potpourri. The following is a recipe dated 1834:

"Put into a large china jar the following ingredients in layers, with bay salt strewed between the layers: 2 pecks Damask Roses, part in bud and part blown; Violets, Orange flowers and Jasmine, 1 handful each; Orrisroot (sliced), Benjamin and Storax, 2 oz. each; ¼ oz. Musk; ¼ lb. Angelica root (sliced); 2 handfuls Lavender flowers; ½ handful Rosemary flowers; Bay and Laurel leaves, ½ handful each; 3 Seville Oranges, stuck as full of Cloves as possible, dried in a cool oven and pounded; ½ handful knotted Marjoram; and 2 handfuls Balm of Gilead (dried). Cover all quite close. When the pot is uncovered the perfume is very fine."

Spices to Be Used. The following is an excellent recipe dated 1890:

"Gather the Roses on a dry day only, and lay them on sheets of newspaper to dry in the sun, then sprinkle them freely with finely powdered bay salt. Pound smoothly together a small quantity of Musk, Storax, gum Benjamin, dried Seville Orange peel, Angelica root, Cloves, Jamaica Pepper, Coriander seed, and spirits of wine.

"Now take the sun-dried leaves, Clove Carnations, Lavender, Woodruff, Rosemary, and any fragrant flowers, such as Orange blossom, Violets, etc., and place them in layers in a china or earthenware jar, alternately with salt and the pounded spices mentioned above. Or, pound very fine 1 lb. bay salt, 2 oz. saltpeter, ½ oz. each of Cloves and Allspice, and mix these thoroughly with a grated Nutmeg, the very finely pared rind of 4 Lemons (being careful to omit all white pith), 1 dr. Musk, 1 oz. Bergamot, 6 dr. powdered Orrisroot, and 1 dr. each of spirits of Lavender, essence of Lemon, and Storax.

"Have ready minced a handful each of Bay leaves, Rosemary, Myrtle, Lemon Thyme and Sweet Verbena. Place these all, when well hand-mixed, into a jar with a close-fitting lid, adding to them, as you can get them, 6 handfuls of sweet-smelling and dried Rose leaves, 3 of Orange blossom, 3 of Clove Pinks, and 2 each of Rosemary flowers, Lavender flowers, Jasmine flowers, and Violets."

The Roses must be gathered on a perfectly dry day, and may then, if liked, be placed in the jar at once, and the same applies to the other blossoms, for all sweet-scented flowers (as long as they are not succulent) can be used for potpourri—stirring them all well into the mixture, for potpourri cannot be too much stirred, especially at first. But no flowers must be added while the least damp, either from rain or dew.

If the potpourri appears to become too dry, add more bay salt and saltpeter; if too moist, add more spice and Orrisroot; but always start your "beau-pot" (as our grandmothers called it) with the quantities given above, adding more flowers from time to time, as the spice retains its strength for years.

The old Cabbage Roses are the most fragrant, but any kinds will do as long as they are dry; still, to have the scent perfect, there should be a strong proportion of the old-fashioned blooms; the more modern Tea Roses are almost too faint to be entirely relied on. The question of drying simply depends on how long it takes to remove any moisture from the Rose leaves. If gathered on a hot, sunny day, when absolutely dry, they need little, if any, exposure to the sun.

The following is a recipe which has been used for years:

"Thoroughly dry the flowers to be used. There must be no particle of moisture left as it would mold and spoil the whole. The best flowers for the purpose are Roses (Damask), Moss Roses, and the old Cabbage Roses best of all, Lavender, Clove Carnations, Woodruff, Rosemary, Violets, Sweet Verbena, and, in fact, any sweet-smelling flowers. Leaves of the Sweet Bay, Sweet Briar, Balm, Lemon Thyme, and even a little Mint, are all good. The rind of a Lemon or two, and the rind of Tangerine and Oranges (cut in strips) may be added.

"Have ready a mixture composed of 1 lb. kitchen salt, ½ lb. bay salt, ½ oz. of Storax, 6 dr. Orrisroot, a grated Nutmeg, ½ teaspoonful ground Cloves, ½ teaspoonful of Allspice and 1 oz. oil of Bergamot.

Old pots should be scrubbed and allowed to dry before plants are potted in them.

"The bay salt must be pounded and all the dry ingredients well mixed, then add the Bergamot and mix again. Put a layer of this at the bottom of your jar, then a layer of dried flowers alternately and keep the jar closed. Turn it over frequently, especially at first."

POTTING. The work of potting and repotting plants is one that concerns every owner of a greenhouse or window garden; unless it is carried out correctly, the plants cannot make satisfactory progress.

The details of chief importance are to choose clean, well-drained pots of the most suitable size, to set the plants in them at the proper depth, and to use a soil compost which meets the needs of the different kinds.

To provide drainage, first place a piece of crock, concave side downward, in the hole in the bottom of the pot.

Then put a layer of smaller pieces of crock in the bottom of the pot.

Some undecayed leaves, straw or moss is then placed over the crocks to prevent the soil from washing down and clogging the drainage.

First of all, old pots must be cleaned thoroughly by washing them with a scrubbing brush and hot water.

It is necessary that new flowerpots be soaked in water for a few minutes before being used. If new pots are not treated in this way they will absorb a great deal of moisture and the soil in the pots will dry very quickly during the first few weeks; as a consequence, the roots of the plants may suffer.

After they have been washed or soaked, the pots should be allowed to dry before soil is placed in them.

Drainage is an important detail in the cultivation of plants in pots, and especially when they are grown in large pots. It is provided by pieces of broken flowerpots which gardeners call "crocks," and the practice of putting in the drainage is called "crocking" the pots. When small pots are used, as for seedlings and rooted cuttings, it is sufficient to place one large "crock" over the hole in the bottom of the pot.

When larger plants are potted, it is usual to set one large "crock" over the hole and then to put in a layer, half an inch or so deep, of smaller "crocks." Coarse cinders, shells or broken brick may be substituted for broken flowerpots as "crocks." When very big pots are used the layer of crocks may be 2-3 in. thick.

To prevent the soil compost from being washed down into the drainage and blocking it up, a layer of coarse material is placed on the "crocks." This may consist of the rougher, fibrous parts which remain after the compost has been sifted; or coarse leaf mold, moss or dead leaves may be used.

A compost which suits most kinds of plants cultivated in pots consists of two parts of loam and one part of peat moss or leaf mold, with a free scattering of sand. Coarse sand, free of fine matter, is generally used and should be regarded as essential in the cultivation of plants in pots. The addition of bone meal at the rate of 1 lb. to each bushel of potting compost is usually advisable, and sometimes other fertilizers are added.

The ingredients of the potting compost must be mixed thoroughly by turning over the heap several times. When used for seedlings, it must

be passed through a fine sieve, one having a half inch mesh. However, in preparing a compost for the potting of plants of larger sizes, sifting is not only unnecessary, but unwise. Large lumps of

Good loam (topsoil) forms the basis of most potting composts.

To the loam should be added some leaf mold, peat moss or other decayed organic matter.

Unless the loam is very sandy some coarse sand should be added to most potting mixtures.

For many plants some dried cow manure added to the potting mixture is beneficial.

Bone meal or other fertilizer may usually be added with advantage to potting soils.

When the ingredients are all assembled they should be mixed together while they are in a slightly moist but not wet condition.

turf should be broken into pieces of a size suitable to the needs of the plants being dealt with. In potting Chrysanthemums, for example, the pieces should be almost an inch wide, and half that size for Cinerarias and Geraniums.

The fibrous part of loam is the most valuable —in fact, when potting vigorous plants, garden-ers sometimes sift out most of the "fine" soil using only the larger, fibrous portion.

The depth at which the plant is placed in the flowerpot is another detail of importance; it must be set so that the uppermost roots are covered with not less than half an inch of soil, but space must be left at the top of the pot for watering. Before the plant is placed in its new pot the old "crocks" should be removed and the soil should be loosened slightly with a pointed stick for the purpose of disentangling the roots and so enabling them to enter the fresh soil more readily.

When to Pot. Some kinds of plants thrive best when their roots are not disturbed. Such kinds are repotted at intervals of several years only. Here belong many bulbous plants which are grown permanently in pots, such as Hippeas-trums, Nerines, Eucharis and Haemanthus. Other plants that get along well with infrequent pot-ting are most Cacti and other succulents and such comparatively slow-growing kinds as As-pidistras, Sansevierias, Rubber Plants, Dracaenas, Palms and most Aroids. In general, as long as plants of the above-mentioned types are prosper-ing and can be provided adequate supplies of nutrients by fertilizing and by top-dressing them periodically, repotting is unnecessary.

Big plants in large pots or tubs require repot-ting (or retubbing) much less frequently than younger specimens of the same kinds in small receptacles. For example, during their first year Fuchsias may be repotted two or three times but large specimen Fuchsias may go five to ten years without this attention. The same holds true for Geraniums, Bay Trees, Aucubas, Oleanders, Oranges, Tree Ferns, Pandanus, Boston Ferns and a host of other favorite kinds.

Certain plants, for instance Calla Lilies, Martha Washington Geraniums and Calanthes, benefit from being repotted annually. Yet others, especially annuals and plants that are raised anew from cuttings each year as are Chrysanthemums and Poinsettias, are potted two or more times each season. Young plants of many kinds that re-quire infrequent repotting when older, may ben-efit from being potted more than once during their first year.

Established plants that are repotted once a

year or less frequently are normally given this attention at the beginning of their new growing season. Plants potted more than once in a season receive this attention during their growing season as well as, if they are more than a year old, at the commencement of that period.

If a plant is obviously suffering from being in an unsuitable soil, possibly one that has been soured or otherwise made unsuitable for growth through overwatering, it is usually wise to repot it at once, even though it be out of season, into a well-drained container of the minimum size that will accommodate the roots, and then to nurse the plant back to vigor by careful attention to watering, shading, humidifying the atmosphere and other details that produce a favorable environment.

How to Pot. Methods of potting vary slightly for different types of plants and often differ somewhat for young plants and bigger ones of the same kinds. For details of how to pot Orchids, see Orchid: It Adds Beauty to the Greenhouse and Garden.

A general rule is, that when leafy plants in active growth are potted as much soil as can be must be retained about their roots and every care must be taken to see that the roots suffer minimum disturbance and injury. When plants are in a dormant state, particularly if they are leafless, or if it is practicable to prune back the tops more or less severely and thus reduce the amount of top growth and leafage, it is permissible to remove some or all of the soil from the roots and sometimes to cut back the roots themselves at potting time.

Hardy shrubs, Roses and other deciduous woody plants can be potted bare-rooted in late fall or early spring. Such plants are centered in the crocked pots, after a little soil has been thrown in to cover the drainage material, and soil is worked in among the roots and is made firm with the fingers or by packing it down with a potting stick. The pots should be of sizes that just comfortably accommodate the roots with just a little room to spare. The surface of the soil is finished off level an inch or so below the rim of the pot to allow room for watering.

Hardy herbaceous perennials, such as Astilbes, Hostas and Delphiniums and such biennials as

To test whether or not potting soil is in a suitable physical condition, squeeze a handful when it is damp but not wet.

If, when the hand is opened, the soil remains together in a tight clod even though tapped lightly with the finger, it is too heavy and needs additional sand, organic matter or both.

If, when the hand is opened, the ball of soil falls apart when tapped lightly with the finger, it is in a suitable physical condition.

A few hours before they are potted, plants should be watered thoroughly.

The plant to be repotted is removed from its old pot by inverting the pot and tapping the rim sharply on the edge of a bench.

Foxgloves, Canterbury Bells and Sweet Williams that are dug from nursery beds and potted for forcing should be lifted in fall or early spring with as large a ball of soil as possible attached to their roots and be set in pots just big enough to hold the roots and soil mass. Soil is then filled in between pot and the root ball and is formed and finished off at the surface in the manner described above for hardy shrubs.

Young plants of annuals and hardy and tender perennials that are potted off from flats or frames are lifted with as much soil as possible attached to their roots and treated as recommended above for hardy herbaceous perennials with the exception that, the plants being small and somewhat delicate, the soil is not pressed so firmly as it would be with larger plants.

Plants transferred from one pot to another, that is specimens that are repotted, may be handled in one of several ways. Most usually the

A Geranium removed from its pot in preparation for repotting. The roots show clearly in the ball of soil. All flowers and flower buds should be picked off at potting time.

The soil at the shoulder of the ball and along its sides is loosened slightly with a pointed stick.

A little potting soil is put in the bottom of the pot over the drainage material.

The plant to be potted is then centered in the pot and the soil around the ball of roots is pressed down in the pot.

operation consists of moving the plant into a larger container but quite often plants are re-potted into pots of the same size as those they occupy and, sometimes, into smaller ones.

When plants are moved into bigger pots (are potted on), the operation may be done usually at the beginning of the growing season or, in the case of fast-growing kinds such as Geraniums, Chrysanthemums, Cinerarias, Cyclamens and Primulas, during the growing season as well.

When potting is done during the growing season great care is taken not to disturb the root ball beyond carefully removing the old crocks and scraping any loose soil from the top of the ball. When potting is done at the beginning of the growing season it is often possible, in addition to removing the crocks, to tease out from the roots some of the old soil. A pot one, or not more than two, sizes larger than the pot the plant is taken from is usually big enough as a new

When potting is finished the soil surface should be leveled and slightly roughened at an inch or so below the rim of the pot to allow for watering.

The newly potted plant is thoroughly watered.

Plants which are in pots too large for them, such as this pruned-back Geranium, may be transferred to smaller receptacles.

The plant is taken out of its pot and as much surplus soil as possible is removed from its roots with the fingers.

stick marks that have been made in the prior step.

Plants are repotted into pots of the same size as those they previously occupied because they have poor root systems or are kinds known to thrive best when their roots are rather crowded. In either case the procedure is essentially the same as for potting on, but because of the limited space available for soil special care must be taken to work it evenly among the roots.

Transferring plants from larger to smaller pots

Additional soil that is not permeated by healthy roots may be removed with the aid of a pointed stick.

Next, a pot just large enough to accommodate the roots is selected and is crocked.

container. Too large a move is likely to be harmful, especially to fine-rooted plants such as Azaleas and Heathers. Over-potting (transferring to too big containers) is a common error of amateurs.

After the plant is made ready for potting by picking off any dead leaves, doing any pruning that may be needed and cleaning it of insects that may be present, it is removed from its pot and the ball is prepared as recommended in the next but one paragraph above. Sufficient soil is then put over the drainage in the pot to bring the top of the ball to the right level (so that when potting is completed the top of the ball is covered with ½-1 in. of soil). The plant is centered, soil is placed around its roots and this is made firm either by pressing it with the fingers or ramming it with a potting stick. The surface is made level and at a sufficient distance below the rim of the pot to allow for easy watering. After firming, the immediate surface is loosened just sufficiently to remove finger and potting

The plant is lowered into the new pot and soil is filled in among and around the new roots.

The soil is made firm with the fingers.

The plant has been transferred from a 4-in. pot to a 2½-in. pot and is now ready for watering.

example Crinums and Hippeastrums, are potted with part of the bulb above the surface, other kinds, for example Eucharis and Hydrosme, are potted with the top of the bulb just beneath the surface.

How Firm to Pot. The question of how firm to pack the soil when potting is not easy to answer. Modern growers tend to press it less firm than was once the practice. For woody plants, those that have a tough shrubby or treelike stem, the soil should be made firmer than for soft-wooded plants. For plants that have very fine roots, such as Azaleas and Heathers, the potting soil is made firmer than for coarser rooted kinds. Even with the firmest potting it should be possible to feel a little "give" when the tip of the finger is pressed very hard on to the surface of the newly packed soil but the finger should not sink in the soil. With moderately firm potting the finger end will sink somewhat into the soil when it is pressed very hard upon its surface. With "light" potting if the finger is pressed hard on the soil surface it will sink into it for an appreciable distance. Light potting is used for very young plants, such as seedlings and cuttings, and for some plants that like a very woodsy soil mixture, such as certain Begonias, Ferns and many plants that are natives of the forest floor.

Water Before and After. Plants should be watered thoroughly a few hours before they are repotted, to make sure that the "ball," that is, the mass of soil and roots, is moist throughout. When potting is finished, the soil should again be watered, with the water applied as a fine spray. Sufficient should be given to thoroughly wet the entire mass of soil. Subsequent waterings, until roots have penetrated the new soil, should be spaced so that the soil becomes moderately dry between applications. Too frequent watering, following potting, is likely to sour the soil and cause the roots to rot.

It is usually advantageous to shade newly potted plants from strong sun until they have recovered from the shock of transplanting and their roots have re-established themselves. Lightly spraying the foliage with water is often beneficial.

POTTING STICK. A piece of wood of convenient size and shape to permit soil to be rammed firmly about the roots of plants in the

is called reducing them. Plants that have inadequate roots for the pots they are in may be reduced and a few kinds, for example Martha Washington Geraniums, are reduced yearly in their routine cultural care. The procedure does not differ from that recommended above for potting on except that, as the plants are returned to the smallest pot that the roots will just fit into, space for new soil is quite limited and every effort must be made to make sure that it is evenly distributed among the roots.

When hardy bulbs for forcing are potted they are often planted several together in a pot or pan and so closely that the individuals touch each other or nearly do. In some cases, as with Lilies, the bulbs are usually potted singly. Stem-rooting bulbs such as most Lilies are set low in the pots with a good covering of soil over them. Bulbs that do not produce roots from their stems, such as Hyacinths, Narcissi and Tulips, are potted with the tips of the bulbs showing above the surface of the soil. Many kinds of tender bulbs, for

With larger plants a potting stick is used to firm the soil between the root ball and the pot.

operations of potting and repotting. For plants being set in larger-sized pots, say those of 6-in. diameter or more, a piece of a broom handle 1-2 ft. long, smoothed to a gradual wedge shape at one end, makes an excellent potting stick. Potting sticks are rarely used when potting in receptacles smaller than 6 in. in diameter. For Orchid potting, special potting "sticks" made of aluminum alloy are manufactured; these are very useful for the special purpose for which they are designed.

POWDER PUFF TREE. See Calliandra.

PRAIRIE BUTTONROOT. Liatris pycnostachya, which see.

PRAIRIE CLOVER. Petalostemum, which see.

PRAIRIE GENTIAN. Eustoma Russellianum, which see.

PRAIRIE MALLOW. Malvastrum coccineum, which see.

PRAIRIE ROSE. See Rosa setigera.

PRAIRIE SUNFLOWER. See Helianthus rigidus.

PRATIA (Prat′ia). Somewhat tender, low-growing or creeping herbaceous flowering plants which belong to the Lobelia family, Lobeliaceae. They are found growing wild in tropical Asia, Java, New Zealand and the Himalayas. These dainty little plants, which are suitable for growing in sheltered places in the rock garden, have slender prostrate stems clothed with small leaves, and bear tiny white, blue or pink-white flowers during the summer. The name Pratia commemorates M. Prat-Bernon, of the French Navy.

For a Sunny Rock Garden. Pratia requires a sunny, well-drained position and a compost of equal parts of peat, leaf mold and sand. Planting is done in spring. The plants must be kept moist if the weather is dry. Little subsequent attention is required as the plants grow together and form dense mats of foliage covered with the small white, blue or pinkish flowers in summer.

Cultivation in Pots. In cold climates some of the kinds must be grown in flower pans in a cool greenhouse or frame. The best flower pans are those 4 in. deep and 6 in. or more in diameter. They are well drained with crocks, over which a layer of the rough siftings is placed, and the remainder of the space is filled with a compost of equal parts of peat, leaf mold and sand. Small plants or seedlings are then inserted 2 in. apart. They are watered and shaded until established, then exposed to full light, but shaded from the fierce rays of the midday sun in summer.

During the summer months established plants must be kept moist at the roots, but throughout the winter the soil is only moistened when it becomes quite dry.

Raising Seedlings. Propagation is by seeds, cuttings or division. Seeds are sown in spring or early summer in the greenhouse. When large enough to handle, the seedlings are pricked out, 1 in. apart, into shallow boxes, watered, and shaded until established. They are gradually hardened off and planted out of doors in the spring, or are transplanted into pots.

Cuttings Are Taken in August. Side shoots are taken off with a heel, the leaves removed from the lower half of the stem and the heel pared smooth with a sharp knife. The shoots are inserted in well-drained pots of sandy soil, which are placed in a close frame until roots are formed. Division is practiced in spring. Small portions are detached from the old plants and replanted in their permanent positions.

The chief kinds are P. angulata, white; P. begonifolia, blue; and P. arenaria, pink-white. P. begonifolia is more tender than the others.

PRAYER. An ancient garden prayer that has

been preserved is to be found in Leonard Mascall's *Booke of the Arte and maner howe to plant and graffe all sortes of trees, howe to set stones and sowe Pepines to make wylde trees to graffe on as also remedies and medicines. With divers other new practises by one of the Abbey of Saint Vincent in Fraunce. Practised with his owne handes, divided into seaven Chapters, as hereafter more plainly shall appeare. With an addition in the ende of this booke on certaine Dutch practises set forth and Englished by Leonard Mascall*, 1572.

The prayer is as follows: "Also, when soever ye shall plant or graffe it shall be mete and good for you to saye as foloweth:

"In the name of God the Father, the Sonne and the holy Ghost, Amen. Increase and multiplye, and replenish the earth: and saye the Lordes prayer, then say: Lord God heare my prayer, and let this my desire of thee be hearde. The holy spirit of God which hath created all things for man and hath given them for our comfort, in thy name O Lorde we set, plant and graffe, desiring that by thy mighty power they maye encrease, and multiply uppon the earth, in bearing plenty of fruite, to the profite, and comfort of all thy faithful people, thorow Christe our Lorde. Amen."

With the exception of "certaine Dutch Practises" Mascall's book is a translation of David Brossard's *L'Art et Manière de semer et faire Pépinières*. Leonard Mascall (1546-1605) was a member of a family said to have established themselves in Sussex, England, shortly after the Norman Conquest. Members of the family were sheriffs of the county in the reigns of Richard Coeur de Lion and John, and the name Mascall is probably a corruption of the Norman "Marescal."

Leonard Mascall's home was Plumpton Place, and in the recently restored moat he is supposed to have put the first carp brought to England. At one time Mascall was clerk of the kitchen to Archbishop Parker, and in his *Government of Cattell* he states he was chief farrier (blacksmith) to James I.

PRAYER PLANT. Maranta leuconeura variety Kerchoveana, which see.

PRETTY FACE. Brodiaea ixioides, which see.

PRICKING OUT OR PRICKING OFF. This term is used by gardeners to describe the work of transplanting seedlings, from the flowerpot, pan or flat in which the seeds were sown, into other flats or to frames; there they are set farther apart so that they shall have room for development. This work must be done carefully, for if many roots are broken or damaged in the process the seedlings will perish. See Seed Sowing Under Glass, in the article on Propagation.

Seedlings that are being transplanted should be handled carefully so that they will not be injured.

A dibble, a short blunt-pointed peg, may be used to make holes to accommodate the roots of the seedlings.

The dibble is also used to press the soil firmly about the roots of the seedlings.

Some gardeners use their finger in place of a dibble in planting seedlings.

PRICKLY ASH. Zanthoxylum americanum, which see.

PRICKLY DATE PALM. Acanthophoenix.

PRICKLY PEAR. See Opuntia.

PRICKLY PHLOX. Gilia californica, which see.

PRICKLY POPPY. See Argemone.

PRICKLY RHUBARB. See Gunnera.

PRICKLY THRIFT. Acantholimon, which see.

PRIDE OF INDIA. Melia Azedarach, which see.

PRIMROSE. See Primula. The color "primrose" is pale yellow.

PRIMROSE, ARABIAN. Arnebia cornuta, which see.

PRIMROSE, CAPE. Streptocarpus, which see.

PRIMROSE, EVENING. Oenothera, which see.

PRIMROSE WILLOW. Jussiaea, which see.

PRIMULA or PRIMROSE
Charming Flowers for Woodland and Greenhouse

Primula (Prim'ula). A large and important group of plants belonging to the family Primulaceae, the Primrose family. The name is derived from the Latin *primus,* first, and alludes to the early flowering of many of the species. Primulas are mostly hardy perennial herbs, natives of Europe and temperate Asia, North America and Java. One kind, Primula magellanica, is the only species found south of the Equator, in southern South America.

The Primulas are divided by botanists into thirty groups or sections, some of which are further divided into subsections. The sections which are of most horticultural interest for outdoor gardening are those named auricula, candelabra, denticulata, sikkimensis and vernales. The sections malacoides, floribunda, obconica and sinensis provide a fine selection of greenhouse Primulas.

Some Primulas, such as P. vulgaris, the English Primrose, bear their flowers singly on stems that rise directly from the bases of the plants. In other kinds, such as P. denticulata, P. obconica and P. elatior, the flowers are borne several or many together in a head or umbel at the top of the scape or flower stem.

In yet a third group the flowers are borne in a number of whorls spaced along the upper portions of the flower scapes, so that a tiered inflorescence results. Notable in this group are members of the candelabra section of Primula, such as P. japonica, P. Beesiana and P. pulver-

ulenta and some members of the malacoides section such as P. effusa, P. malacoides and P. Forbesii.

Primula gives us a wide range of extremely beautiful plants for the rock garden, the bog garden or waterside, for flower beds, the wild and the woodland garden, for the greenhouse, and even for the garden.

For Cool Climates. Over most of the United States the summers are too hot for the successful

The yellow Primrose of English coppice and hedgerow, Primula vulgaris, is one of the easiest of hardy kinds to grow.

Primula obconica comes in a wide range of colors and is one of the most popular of the tender Primulas.

cultivation of many of the Primulas. In the Pacific Northwest and other favored areas a considerable number can be cultivated, but, where hot, dry summers are the rule, only a few of the more tolerant kinds are practicable as garden plants. Among the most satisfactory Primulas for the Northeast are: P. Auricula, P. Beesiana, P. Bullesiana, P. Bulleyana, P. Cockburniana, P. cortusoides, P. denticulata, P. elatior, P. japonica, P. Juliae, P. polyantha, P. rosea, P. Sieboldii, P. Veitchii, P. veris, and P. vulgaris.

For Greenhouse Cultivation. A number of tender Primulas are favorite pot plants for growing in greenhouses for winter and spring bloom. For this purpose the modern varieties of Primula sinensis are a sumptuous and extremely varied race. This is of special interest when it is remembered that all have originated by selection from the original type plant introduced from China a hundred or so years ago; this plant has never been successfully crossed with any other species. It is curious, too, that Primula sinensis has never been found in the wild state, and botanists are uncertain whether the original imported plant from gardens in Canton was from a wild species or garden hybrid.

Primula obconica, another greenhouse plant, has also hitherto withstood every union arranged for it by the hybridist. Crosses with others have been claimed and reported from time to time, but these must be regarded with scepticism. During the last thirty years or so, however, this recalcitrant specimen has been improved out of all recognition by careful selection.

It is curious that these valuable greenhouse Primulas should refuse to cross with any other species with which they have been mated, and there is yet another tender Primula which has behaved in exactly the same way, Primula malacoides. This, when first introduced, was a pretty plant, with light and graceful tiers of smallish pink flowers. Cultivation and selection have already produced a magnificent range of varieties of P. malacoides, with larger flowers of richer coloring.

The only true hybrid greenhouse Primula of any importance is Primula kewensis. This appeared at the Royal Botanic Gardens, Kew, England, as a chance self-sown seedling in a greenhouse where P. verticillata and P. floribunda had been grown side by side.

The management of greenhouse Primulas will be discussed in detail later in this article.

Hardy Primulas

The hardy Primulas may be divided roughly into two main classes: the bog or woodland kinds, and the cliff and rock dwellers. There are also many Primulas which might be called meadow plants, for they are most suitable grown in the garden in beds of loam. Instances of this latter class are the English Primrose, the Cowslip, and the beautiful forms of colored Polyanthus or Bunch Primrose.

For Moist Places. The majority of the bog-loving Primulas, although they grow more vigorously in wet places, such as the bog garden, the pond or streamside, may also be grown quite successfully if provided with a soil so rich in humus or vegetable matter that it acts like a sponge and absorbs moisture readily and retains it long, and if they are watered freely in dry weather. Leaf mold, peat moss, cow manure, or sphagnum moss should be dug in, in liberal quantities. At the same time a position shaded from the strong sunshine should be selected.

The rock- and cliff-dwelling Primulas are best grown in the rock garden proper, in fairly well-drained positions, and in loamy soil that never becomes really dry. Many make admirable subjects for cultivation in the alpine house.

How to Raise Hardy Primulas from Seed. The hardy Primulas of nearly all kinds may be raised from seeds, and these should be sown as soon after they have been harvested as possible. If sown at once, they will usually germinate freely, but if kept for only a few weeks they take much longer to germinate and the seedlings come up irregularly over a long period. The seeds should be sown in pots or pans filled with sifted loam, leaf mold or peat moss and sand. Water thorough-

The surface of the soil is carefully leveled before the seedlings are inserted.

Primula seedlings ready for transplanting.

Holes are made with a dibble and the seedlings carefully planted about 2 in. apart.

Flats to receive the Primula seedlings are prepared by filling them with a suitable soil mixture and pressing it moderately firm.

ly after sowing, and place the pans in a shaded, north-facing cold frame or other shady place, and keep covered with a sheet of glass and a piece of paper.

Prick off the seedlings as soon as they are large enough to handle, and grow in the usual way. If the seeds have not germinated by autumn, the pans may be placed in a shady place in the open air, and exposed to frost and snow all winter. This greatly helps germination, and the seedlings will then usually come up freely

After they have been transplanted, the seedlings are watered with a fine spray and are kept shaded to encourage new growth.

if the seed pans are transferred to a frame in spring. In dealing with the seeds of rare and valuable Primulas, hope of germination should not be abandoned under eighteen months or two years.

The English Primrose. Primula vulgaris (P. acaulis), the common English Primrose, is without a doubt one of the most beautiful of the Primula race, and one of the finest garden plants. The color of the common kind is a lovely shade of soft yellow, which is extremely rare among flowers; the scent, too, is delicious and, like the color, almost unique.

There are several interesting geographical forms or varieties of P. vulgaris. Variety Sibthorpii (P. vulgaris rubra) is an old and valued garden plant, native to Asia Minor. In effect it is an English Primrose with rose-lilac flowers, easy to grow, early-flowering, and free-flowering.

It is probable that from Primula vulgaris Sibthorpii arose all the colored forms of Primrose and Polyanthus Primroses which can be such a brilliant feature of our spring gardening. The Primrose Evelyn Arkwright was found in an English wood by the lady whose name it bears. It is a gigantic form, with leaves larger, stronger and more heavily crinkled than the type, and with flowers three or four times as large. Although still in cultivation in Great Britain. it is extremely rare.

The English Primrose is deserving of extended cultivation in gardens. If massed in rock gardens, by the side of shady walks, and in other cool, moist places, it yields a profusion of fascinating flowers in spring. Although it does not have such imposing flowers as the Polyanthus or bunch-flowered Primrose, which is commonly used in spring beds, it is a delightful plant for less formal settings.

The gardener can increase his stock of English Primroses by lifting and dividing the plants as soon as they have finished flowering or by sowing seeds in spring as recommended below for Polyanthus Primroses. The double-flowered varieties, and choice named single varieties that are propagated to secure young plants absolutely identical with the parent plants, are increased by division.

The English Primroses with flowers of colors other than pale yellow are beautiful spring-blooming plants, those of blue or violet-blue shades being chief favorites. They occur both in single-flowered and double-flowered varieties. The former are quite easily raised from seeds, the latter by division.

There are various strains or types of single-flowered English Primroses, seeds of which are sold in mixture or separately; thus one can purchase seeds which will yield flowers in shades of blue, yellow or crimson.

The first blue Primroses—they are seldom or never truly blue but rather a fine range of violet, violet-blue and purple—were first raised by the late Mr. G. F. Wilson in his garden at Wisley, England, now the property of the Royal Horticultural Society.

Double-flowered English Primroses. The double-flowered Primroses, white, yellow, mauve, crimson, etc., are "antiques" of exceptional charm.

Among them are some charming old-fashioned kinds as double-mauve, double-white, Arthur Dumoulin, (pale purplish), Burgundy (purple-crimson) and others. These thrive best in rather moist, loamy soil, in somewhat shady places and should be lifted and divided annually after the flowering season.

The Polyanthus Primrose. The bunch-flowered Primrose or Polyanthus originated as a cross between the common Primrose (Primula vulgaris),

Polyanthus Primroses, Primula polyantha.

the Cowslip (P. veris) and the Oxlip (P. elatior). From this parentage the modern, large-
flowered Polyanthuses have been developed by
cross-breeding and selection. The Polyanthus
Primrose is one of the most beautiful of all
spring-flowering plants. The modern strains or
types have large blooms in a delightful range of
color, ranging from white, through cream and
yellow, to orange and crimson. The plants are
vigorous and bloom profusely in April and May.

Polyanthus Primroses make a fascinating display when massed in partial shade, as, for instance, by the side of a walk in open woodland,
or in a shady garden border. The plants will,
however, flourish in a sunny place if the soil
is moderately deep and rich, for, like most
members of the Primrose family, they like cool,
moist conditions.

These plants are often used in association
with bulbs for filling spring flower beds. If set
in a sunny border, as, for example, at the foot
of a house wall, they will bloom earlier than
others in the open garden, and, where the climate is mild, flowers may often be gathered in
winter.

The Polyanthus Primrose is propagated either
by sowing seeds or by lifting and separating the
old plants as soon as they have finished flowering. It is wise to raise fresh plants from seeds
frequently, every two or three years, to maintain
a strong and healthy stock. The seeds should be
sown in a slightly heated greenhouse in February
or March, if possible, for the seedlings make
rather slow progress at first, and it is necessary
to sow early to ensure strong, well-developed
plants by autumn. Seeds may be sown in flats
of sandy soil in a cold frame in April, or out of
doors in May.

When the old plants are lifted and divided in
June the rooted pieces should be set in a partially

shaded border and kept moist throughout summer, being finally planted in autumn or, in very cold climates, wintered in a cold frame.

Primula alpicola is a beautiful plant; it has the habit and general appearance of P. sikkimensis, but is not so tall, and the fragrant bell-shaped flowers, borne in a drooping shower from a 12-in. stem, are of a delicate creamy white or pale yellow, and mealy outside. The variety violacea has violet-colored flowers. Both may be raised from seeds and grown in moist, well-drained loam. They flower in May and June.

Primula Auricula is a name which covers a very wide range of splendid Alpine Primulas. The wild type is a cliff-dwelling plant, with a thick hard, trunklike stem, broad leathery leaves powdered with white meal, and heads of beautiful yellow cowslip-scented flowers, with white meal on the stems. It is widely distributed in the central and eastern Alps, and though its natural home is on cliffs, it occasionally seeds down into the soil or the screes below, where it finds abundant moisture in times of drought.

A number of beautiful and distinct forms of

Primula japonica blooming freely in moist soil in a shady location.

P. Auricula occur in the Alps. P. Bauhinii, of the Italian Alps, is a vigorous grower and has very mealy leaves; P. serratifolia has serrated leaves, and P. ciliata, a dwarf and scentless native of the Dolomites, has golden-yellow flowers. All these are plants of great beauty and charm, and may be grown in the rock garden or the Alpine house. They need a compost of fibrous loam, leaf mold, sand, and a little lime rubble or limestone. They may be propagated by division or offsets, and by seeds.

Primula Auricula was crossed with other wild Alpine Primulas—P. viscosa, P. rubra (hirsuta), and P. villosa, as early as the sixteenth century, and gave rise to what are known as garden Auriculas. The garden Auriculas, both the Show and the Border varieties, are classed, together with all the other hybrids from these crosses, under the comprehensive name of P. pubescens.

The Border Auriculas are a strong-growing race, with trunklike stems, broad leaves, and heads of handsome scented flowers in a wonderful range of coloring: purple, red-brown, mauve and yellow.

They are grown in loamy soil, make attractive border or edging plants, and are charming for cutting. They are increased by division of the plants, after flowering or in late summer; or plants may be raised from seeds.

The Show Auriculas are a highly bred race, less hardy than the Border sorts, requiring cold greenhouse or frame cultivation. More attention was given to them a hundred years ago than at the present day, though fortunately the interest in England in these lovely flowers is reviving. The Show Auriculas have been bred for ages to conform to rigid rules as to regularity of shape and carriage of the flowers and symmetry of marking in the blossoms. Each blossom or "pip" should have a perfect round center of white meal, and this is surrounded by concentric rings of other colors: purple, green, brown, red, yellow, etc. The hobby of growing and breeding Show Auriculas is a fascinating one but the plants are scarcely known in America. The other Auricula hybrids are described under P. pubescens.

Primula Beesiana is one of the eastern Asiatic bog Candelabra Primulas, similar to P. japonica.

in habit and requirements, with tiers of flowers of a rather unpleasing hard magenta color. It is fairly easy to grow in moist loam, and is increased by division or seeds. Crossed with P. Bulleyana, it has given rise to a race of beautiful hybrids known as P. Bullesiana; these are described below.

P. Bullesiana is the name given to a race of hybrids resulting from a cross between P. Bulleyana and P. Beesiana. In habit they resemble their parents, but they embrace a wide range of beautiful colors: claret, purple, rose, cream, mauve and cinnabar-red. They are most beautiful when grown in a mass with all the colors mixed. All these Candelabra Primulas,

although superb in the bog garden, can also be grown extremely well in thin woodland, if the ground is well dug and enriched with leaf mold and cow manure.

Primula Bulleyana is a bog plant from eastern Asia and is of the very greatest beauty. It is of the nature of P. japonica, forming big clumps of strong lettuce-like leaves, and sending up tall stems bearing numerous whorls of large handsome blossoms. The buds are red-gold, and open to golden-yellow flowers. The plant is moderately easy to grow in loam, which can be kept moist, or in the bog garden, and may be increased by division or by seeds, which are produced freely and germinate readily.

The rare Primula chionantha, with meal-covered foliage and fragrant ivory-white flowers.

Polyanthus Primroses, Primula polyantha, planted in containers, are here used effectively to decorate the wall of a terrace.

Primula capitata has various geographical forms, more or less distinct, of which the finest is Mooreana. It forms rosettes of green, tooth-edged leaves 6-9 in. across, and sends up numerous erect wiry stems 6-9 in. tall, each carrying a large, roundish, flattened head of bell-shaped, violet-colored flowers; these are fragrant and their beauty is enhanced by the calyces, which are powdered with silver-white meal. P. capitata Mooreana flowers irregularly throughout summer. The plant enjoys a cool and fairly moist position in the rock garden in loam and leaf mold and is easily raised from seeds.

Primula chionantha is a most beautiful plant from Yunnan, with smooth leaves powdered with golden meal, and erect stems, 12-18 in. high, carrying several whorls of large white, dusky-eyed fragrant flowers. It may be grown in a bed of loam and leaf mold, well-drained yet always moist. The only means of increase is by seeds, which are produced abundantly and germinate readily if sown soon after gathering. P. chionantha is a fine subject for massing in the cooler flat places of the rock garden or among choice shrubs.

Primula Cockburniana is a brilliant short-lived Candelabra Primula for fairly moist loam. The flowers are coppery scarlet, carried tier above tier on 12-18 in. stems. The plant is easily raised from seeds, and is well worth growing, especially when massed in bold patches. It is a native of western China.

The magnificent early-spring-flowering Primula denticulata.

Primula cortusoides, a native of Siberia, is an easy kind to grow and flourishes in northeastern America. It grows about 6-12 in. high and has umbels of rose-pink flowers. Its leaves are softly hairy.

Primula denticulata, from the Himalayas, is an old and valued garden favorite. It is a strong grower, forming clumps of big leaves from which, in spring, appear numerous 8-12 in. stems, each carrying a globular clustered head of lilac-colored flowers. There are selected color forms ranging from pale rose-lilac to deep crimson-lilac and white. It is propagated by division of the plants, after flowering, which is the only way with special varieties, and by seeds, which are produced in abundance and germinate freely.

P. denticulata delights in rich, moist loam and is intolerant of drought; it is a showy plant for the waterside, cool spots in the rock garden, shady corners in flower borders, and for the woodland. A variety of P. denticulata with large purple flowers and golden meal upon the flower stems and the undersides of the leaves has been distinguished under the name cachemiriana.

Primula elatior is the true Oxlip. It is not unlike the Cowslip, with larger flowers of paler yellow. It is an interesting and beautiful plant, and valuable for cool corners in the garden. It is increased by division of the roots, or from seeds.

Primula farinosa, the Bird's-Eye Primrose, is a native of northern Europe. It is a small, dainty plant with a rosette of leaves 2-3 in. across, and producing several erect, wiry stems, 4-6 in. high, each carrying a head of bright pink, golden-

A woodland planting of Primula pulverulenta, of the "candelabra" type, with meal-covered stems, at the height of its floral beauty.

eyed flowers. The leaves, stems and calyces are all heavily powdered with silvery white meal, which greatly enhances the beauty of the plant. The plants will often eventually form a clump of a dozen or more rosettes.

In autumn the leaves die away, leaving nothing but a fleshy bud the size of a hazel nut, which sends out fresh leaves and flowers the following spring.

Primula farinosa is a charming plant for the rock garden. This plant will thrive in loam with a fair amount of leaf mold added, or in the moraine; it is necessary to shade and water it in the summer. It is best associated with small plants of its own vigor, such as Gentiana verna,

Androsace lactea or Erigeron leiomerus. It flowers in May and June. It is easily propagated, either by seed or division of the rosettes.

Primula Florindae. This superb Primula was introduced from southeastern Tibet by Captain F. Kingdon-Ward, and is one of the most important additions to the family that have been made for many years. It is a bog plant, and in effect resembles a gigantic Primula sikkimensis with sulphur-yellow flowers. The broad-stalked leaves grow up to 18 in. tall, whereas the stout flower stems will reach a height of 3-4 ft., according to the richness and moisture of the soil the plant is given. The yellow, bell-shaped flowers, each ½ in. in diameter, are pendent in

The fragrant, giant yellow Tibetan Cowslip, Primula Florindae.

The white-flowered Primula helvetica, a gem for the rock garden or alpine house.

heads of thirty or forty at the summits of the stems, and are deliciously cowslip-scented and powdered with white meal.

Primula Florindae enjoys rich loam and a very moist or even boggy position. It is a magnificent plant for the streamside, pondside and the bog garden, where it must be given ample room in which to develop its fine foliage. Two feet apart is not too far to plant these Primulas, if the soil is really good and sufficiently moist.

The best means of propagation is by seeds, which are produced abundantly and germinate readily if sown soon after gathering.

Primula frondosa is closely related to P. farinosa, and is a native of northern Thrace. It is larger in all its parts than P. farinosa, and is easier to grow. The numerous, erect, loose flower heads, in May and June, are lilac-pink and very pretty. It is a valuable plant for loamy soil in the rock garden, and is easily increased by division of the plants in spring, or by seeds sown in a pan of loam, sand and leaf mold in summer in a cold frame.

Primula helodoxa is an introduction from China. It belongs to the Candelabra section of bog Primulas, and resembles P. japonica, with its tiers of flowers one above the other upon tall, erect stems. The flowers are rich golden-yellow.

The plant may be divided, but is most readily raised from seeds, which are produced abundantly. They should be sown as soon after ripening as possible, in a pan of loam, sand and leaf mold, in a cold frame. The plant enjoys rich loam, a sunny position, and a moist or even boggy situation. It grows up to 3 ft. tall and is extremely handsome.

Primula helvetica is really a hybrid of the P. pubescens set. A good rock-garden plant with heads of lilac-pink flowers and delighting in

The hardy Japanese Primrose, Primula japonica.

loamy soil in the rock garden, it is useful, too, for the alpine house. Primula helvetica alba has beautiful cream-white, deliciously fragrant flowers. It has the additional merit of being of easy cultivation.

Primula japonica is one of the showiest and most popular of all the bog Primulas. It forms great clumps of leaves, and in May and June produces numerous stout erect stems 18 in. or more high, and each carrying several whorls, tier above tier, of showy blossoms each as big as a quarter. In the ordinary type of P. japonica the flowers are crimson-claret with golden eye; but there are now several beautiful color varieties of equal or even greater beauty, including white with golden eye, pink, deep crimson, and a wonderful terra-cotta red with golden eye, called sanguinea.

Primula japonica is of the easiest possible cultivation, requiring shade, loamy soil and ample moisture at the root to grow luxuriantly, and flower brilliantly. It is superb in the bog garden, by the pond or streamside, or in half-open woodland; it may even be grown in the flower border, if provision is made for moisture at the roots.

In any naturally moist situation, where the plant is well suited, P. japonica will seed and reproduce itself profusely. Plants of specially good color may be increased by division, and the various color forms—alba, rosea, coccinea, etc.—come almost true from seed, which should be sown as soon after gathering as possible.

Primula Juliae was introduced from the Caucasus in comparatively recent years, and is a valuable addition to the rock garden. It is closely related to the English Primrose, P. vulgaris, and in effect is like a dwarf, widely spreading edition of this Primrose, with smaller, heart-shaped leaves, and similar flowers on much shorter stems, and of a strong claret-crimson or magenta color. The whole plant only grows 2 or 3 in. high, but spreads over the ground with thick rhizomatous roots, soon forming handsome clumps. It begins to flower very early in the spring and, in mild climates, often produces blossoms during mild spells in the middle of winter. Later, when in full bloom, the plant is absolutely covered with flowers. At the time of flowering, few leaves are in evidence, the foliage appearing after flowering is done. A particularly brilliant effect may be obtained by setting among Primula Juliae, bulbs of blue Scillas, Chionodoxa or blue Grape Hyacinth, or early-flowering golden Daffodils. The hose-in-hose variety of P. Juliae is also very colorful.

Primula Juliae is a valuable plant in the rock garden, in the wild garden, half-open woodland, and as spring ground cover in flower beds. It likes loamy soil and may be raised from seeds, but it has generally been found that the easier

A group of Japanese Primroses flowering in moist soil.

way is to lift and divide the plants after flowering.

Primula Juliae has been crossed with P. vulgaris, the English Primrose, and the hybrid is called P. Juliana. By crossing various-colored Primroses with P. Juliae, a fine range of hybrids, each distinguished by a variety name, has been produced. Among the best are: Wanda, crimson-magenta; Pam, ruby-red; Beryl, rich crimson; Vulcan, claret; Bunty, violet; Purple Splendor, crimson-purple; Jewel, crimson; C. R. Janes, pinkish-orange; and Gloria, claret-crimson. The last named is the finest of all, flowering all the winter and well into spring. These hybrids must be increased by division; they repay the labor of splitting every second or third year and planting in rich loamy soil.

Primula Littoniana (P. Viali), from the high mountains of Yunnan, is a singularly beautiful and curious plant. The leaves are ovate, ribbed and downy and, from their midst in June, spring a number of erect wiry stems, 9-12 in. tall, each bearing a conical spike of small lilac flowers set among reddish bracts. The spikes are several inches long, and the topmost flowers taper to a point of brilliant red bracts. This spike of lilac and red is at once startling and beautiful, and

Primula Littoniana (Viali) from Yunnan, one of the most distinct and striking members of this lovely race.

entirely unlike that of any other Primula plant.

The plant is best raised from seeds, sown in spring, and the seedlings grown on in a cold frame and planted out, when large enough, in a bed of well-drained loam, where they should flower the following year. The plant disappears completely in winter, and is rather late in starting into leaf in the spring, for which reason it is apt to be overlooked or given up for dead, and so lost.

There is a giant variety of P. Littoniana which is taller and more handsome than the type.

Primula marginata is one of the most beautiful of the European rock Primulas. It is found locally, but abundantly, on rocks and cliffs in parts of the Alps of Europe.

The plant forms thick trunklike stems which trail down from the rock ledges in long masses; at the end of each stem are the broad leaves, which are silvered with a margin of shining white meal. The flowers, borne in loose umbels of from five to eight or more on 3-4 in. stems in early spring, are cowslip-shaped and cowslip-scented and of soft lavender-blue, rose-lavender, or lilac. The stems, calyces and the centers of the flowers are dusted with white meal.

Primula marginata is easily cultivated in well-drained loam, and a position in the rock garden well raised up among the rocks. It also makes a charming plant for pots or pans in the alpine house, and it blooms in early spring when flowers are especially welcome. It may be raised from seeds; especially good varieties are increased by division or by removing side shoots and planting them as cuttings, after flowering.

This Primula has given several beautiful hybrids, among them being P. Marven (the parent plants are P. marginata and P. venusta). This has smooth-edged leaves, and has violet-colored flowers with white eye. P. Linda Pope has extra-large white-edged leaves, and large lilac flowers of incredible beauty. P. Rehniana, also with silver-edged leaves, has lavender-blue flowers.

Primula Parryi is a Rocky Mountain plant, rare in cultivation and difficult to grow, but of exceeding beauty. It belongs to the nivalis section of the family. The flowers are intense rose-purple with golden eye. It requires loam, sand and peat, ample moisture and perfect drainage and, in addition, something else which no gardener has discovered.

As in the cultivation of many other rock-garden plants which are sometimes difficult to manage, the gardener must carry out experiments to try to find exactly which conditions prove most suitable. This can be done by setting the plants in various kinds of soil and in different situations.

Primula polyneura (Veitchii) has broad leaves and 6-9 in. stems carrying whorls of vivid magenta flowers in early summer. It enjoys a cool position in the rock garden in light loam and leaf mold. It may be increased by division or by seeds.

Primula pubescens is a group name which is properly used for a vast range of hybrid or crossbred Primulas—raised from P. Auricula, P. rubra and P. viscosa. It covers, therefore, all the garden Auriculas, show and border, and all those hybrids some of whose pedigrees are far too ancient and complicated ever to be traced. Many of these "pubescens" Primulas are of value for the flower border, the rock garden and the alpine house in regions where fairly cool summers prevail.

Primula pulverulenta. This is one of the best of the moisture-loving Candelabra Primulas. It is like a slender and graceful P. japonica, with crimson flowers and stems all white with silver meal. It is most easily raised from seed, and may be grown in the bog garden, by the pond or streamside, in moist, half-open woodland, or even in the cooler parts of the flower border if given manure to keep its roots cool. It grows 18 in. or rather more tall. There is a beautiful variety, Mrs. R. B. Berkeley, with soft pink flowers, and a superb pink-flowered race, known as the Bartley Strain, which has the merits of vigor and of producing fertile seed. Crossed with P. Cockburniana, P. pulverulenta has also produced several races of gorgeous orange and cinnabar-red hybrids.

Primula rosea is one of the most brilliant of all the bog or moisture-loving Primulas. It forms strong clumps of smooth pale green leaves, and in early spring, before the leaves, come the flowers, in wide heads, on stems 9-12 in. tall, and of pure rose color. It must be given a really damp position, but otherwise is easy to grow. It is easily raised from seed, which should be sown as soon after it is ripe as possible, or the clumps may be lifted and divided after flowering.

Primula Sieboldii is a Japanese species of which there are many named varieties, in a wide range of colors—pink, crimson, etc. The plant has wide velvety stalked leaves, and heads of large flowers in early summer. It is a plant for cool, half-shady places in the rock garden, margin of the bog garden, or half-open woodland, and enjoys loam and leaf mold. It is increased by division of the plants or by seeds.

Primula sikkimensis, the Sikkim Cowslip, is one of the most beautiful and the most accommodating of all the bog Primulas. It forms big clumps of long leaves, from among which, in early summer, spring many tall, wiry stems. Dangling from their summits are loose showers of cowslip-scented, bell-shaped blossoms, of a clear pale yellow. The plant grows from 18 in. to 2 ft. tall; however, this growth according to

A beautiful Primula of the Sikkim Cowslip type, P. alpicola, which bears clusters of creamy-white meal-covered, fragrant flowers on 12-in. stems.

the general richness and moistness varies.

Although the clumps may be increased by division, the better way is to raise the plant from seeds, which are produced in abundance and germinate freely.

Light, rich soil and ample moisture at the root are the plant's only requirements; it is at home in the bog garden, by the pond or the streamside, or in cool, moist hollows in the rock garden.

The Cowslip. Primula veris, the wild European Cowslip, is one of the best of Primulas. It is easily raised from seeds sown in spring and the plants flourish in loamy soil, especially if it is on the heavy side.

A variety of Primula sinensis, one of the loveliest of the Primroses.

The Cowslip, Primula veris, is an easy kind to grow. It has pale yellow flowers.

There is a strain in cultivation known as Copper Cowslips. Actually the color ranges from the normal yellow through deep gold to the loveliest tawny coppers and orange-reds. They are true Cowslips, with the true Cowslip scent.

Both the type and the Copper varieties are charming when growing, and valuable for cutting.

Greenhouse Primulas

The Primulas suitable for cultivation under glass make very beautiful pot plants for a display during the late autumn, winter, and early spring months. They are indispensable to all who have a greenhouse and wish to keep it as gay as possible during those seasons.

The Chinese Primulas, varieties of Primula sinensis, are favorites; others which are also of great value are Primula obconica, P. malacoides (the Fairy Primrose), P. kewensis, P. verticillata, and P. floribunda. All these are suitable for a cool greenhouse. Many of the hardy Primulas are also good plants for cultivation in pots in the cool greenhouse to bloom a little in advance of those grown out of doors.

Although many Primulas are natives of China, the term Chinese Primulas is commonly applied to those greenhouse flowering plants which have been raised from Primula sinensis. They provide

Primula malacoides.

a fascinating display of bloom during the dullest months of the year and the flowers show a wide range of coloring—from blush to crimson and from lavender to violet-blue, and there are white varieties.

Large-flowered and Star Primulas. There are two chief types of Chinese Primula, the large-flowered and the small-flowered or star (stellata) varieties. The former produce imposing clusters of large flowers and are of value for purposes of display. The star-flowered plants are of tall and graceful growth, bear tier on tier of blooms throughout many weeks in winter and early spring, and are easier to cultivate than the giant-flowered type.

The secret of success in the cultivation of Chinese Primulas is to provide them with perfectly cool, moist conditions. They do not need much warmth, even in winter; an average temperature of 50 degrees suits them perfectly, and if it falls to 45 degrees on cold nights no harm will be done.

When to Sow Seeds. By sowing seeds in March–May, plants will be obtained which will provide flowers from late in the year—November or early December—until the end of February or March. The seeds should be sown in flower pans, cleaned, drained with crocks, and filled to within 1/4 in. or so of the rims with finely sifted compost of loam and leaf mold in equal quantities, together with a free scattering of sand. The seeds are very small and care is necessary in sowing them so that they will be distributed evenly and thinly over the surface of the seed pan. The soil ought to be thoroughly moistened with a fine spray before the seeds are sown.

As the seeds are so small, the merest sprinkling of fine soil or sand provides sufficient covering. When the seeds are sown, the pans should be covered with pieces of glass and shaded with brown paper or other material. If placed in a greenhouse having a temperature of 55-60 degrees they will germinate in a few weeks.

Managing the Seedlings. As soon as the seedlings show through the soil, the paper and glass must be removed.

Watering the seedling Primulas must be done carefully or they may be attacked by the damping-off disease, a trouble which is likely to spread quickly if not checked, and may soon cause the collapse of all the seedlings. They should not be watered from above. The only safe way is to immerse the seed pans almost to the rims in a vessel of water; as soon as the moisture is seen on the surface of the soil it will be known that sufficient water has been taken up.

If the soil was thoroughly moistened before the seeds were sown, little, if any, water will be needed before the seeds germinate. It is most important, however, that the soil be not allowed to get dry; if it appears to be moderately dry the seed pans should be watered in the way explained.

Transplanting. As soon as the seedlings are large enough to be handled conveniently—that is to say, when they are 1½ in. high—they should be transplanted and placed separately in small pots of soil, or 2 in. apart in flats of soil. A similar compost to that already recommended is used, though it should be passed through a coarser sieve.

If the seedlings are placed in small pots—which is an advantage, because potting or repotting will be a simple matter—great care must be taken that the soil is not overwatered. The safe rule is not to give water until the soil is fairly dry, then to fill the pots to the rims and to give no more water until the soil is again fairly dry.

When the seedlings are established in the small pots or flats, they should be grown in a night temperature as near 50 degrees as practicable.

Shade from Bright Sunshine Is Necessary. When risk of cold weather at night appears to be over, the pots or flats of Primulas should be put in a cold frame facing north and stood on a bed of sifted ashes or sand with the plants not more than 12 in. from the glass sash. If the frame is too deep for this, the pots or flats should be set on boards laid across inverted flowerpots. or other supports to bring them nearer the glass. The bed of sand or ashes is kept moist and helps to maintain the cool, humid atmospheric conditions that are so favorable to the growth of Primulas.

If the seedlings have been transplanted to flats instead of small pots, they must, before they become crowded, be potted individually in 3-in. or 4-in. pots. Sometime during the summer, when they are well rooted in the small pots, they should be repotted in pots that measure 5 or 6 in. in diameter.

The Final Potting. At this, the final potting, the compost should consist of two parts of fibrous loam and one part of leaf mold or peat moss, with a free admixture of sand and some bone meal and dried cow manure or other fertilizer added. Primulas delight in leaf mold.

In potting, care must be taken to set the plants at such a depth that the ends of the stalks of the lowest leaves are slightly embedded; if the plants are set too high in the pots they will fall over and require supporting by sticks. Placing the plants too high in the pots is one of the commonest faults in the management of Chinese Primulas.

Throughout the summer months the frame must be ventilated freely; during rainy weather, when it is unwise to pull the sashes off because the soil in the pots might become sodden, they should be raised by means of blocks of wood. The more fresh air the plants have the finer they will be. Shade from bright sunshine must be provided. All flower stems which develop during the summer months ought to be picked off to encourage the plants to make good growth.

Towards the end of September, or earlier if there is danger of frost, the Primulas should be removed to a greenhouse or conservatory in which a night temperature of 45-50 degrees is maintained. There the plants from the earliest sowing will begin to bloom towards the end of November, and those from a later sowing will flower in the new year.

Primula obconica is another splendid winter-flowering plant. In the newer varieties the blooms are large and of rich and varied coloring; the leaves and leafstalks are less hairy than those of the older varieties.

This is the Primula that causes a dermatitis in some people. It is well to use gloves when potting and watering the plants, to prevent the possibility of their causing an irritation of the skin.

This Primula needs the same treatment as Chinese Primulas. The seeds, however, should

This attractive tender Primrose is Primula floribunda, a golden-flowered parent of the hybrid Primula kewensis.

be sown rather earlier; the first lot should be sown in February and a second lot in March.

The earliest plants will begin to bloom in autumn and the others will be in full beauty in winter.

Primula kewensis is a charming winter- and early spring-blooming plant, and is of particular value because it has yellow flowers. P. floribunda is a similar plant with smaller yellow flowers. P. verticillata, which blooms in spring, is a beautiful plant with grayish leaves, and bears 18-in. stems with pale yellow, pendent flowers.

The Fairy Primrose, P. malacoides, is a first-rate plant for the amateur's greenhouse; it is

Primula verticillata, one of the parents of the hybrid Primula kewensis, has meal-covered leaves and pale yellow flowers.

A specimen plant of Primula malacoides.

easily grown and may be had in bloom from fall to spring. The modern, large-flowered (tetraploid) varieties are very beautiful; the plants grow quickly, soon forming large specimens, and bear a profusion of rose, lilac, pink, or crimson blooms on stems 12 in. or more high.

Seeds should be sown in March, April, May, and June to provide plants which will yield flowers from autumn until late spring and early summer. All these need the same treatment as the Chinese Primulas—cool, moist conditions in summer and a slightly warm greenhouse in winter.

After they have flowered, these Primulas are not worth keeping; it is the common practice to raise them fresh from seeds every year.

PRINCE ALBERT'S YEW. Saxegothaea conspicua, which see.

PRINCE'S-FEATHER. See Amaranthus hybridus variety hypochondriacus, Polygonum orientale and Saxifraga umbrosa.

PRINSEPIA (Prinsep'ia). Little-known, hardy, leaf-losing (deciduous) shrubs, with spiny branches, and bearing small flowers, produced singly or in small clusters from the leaf axils in spring; the flowers are followed by showy fruits which ripen in August. In some respects they resemble small-fruited Plums.

Prinsepia belongs to the Rose family, Rosaceae. The few kinds known are natives of Asia, from the Himalayas northwards. The name honors Macaire-Prinsep, a renown Swiss botanist.

P. sinensis is the best-known kind. It forms a loose shrub 6 ft. or so high; the flowers are yellow and are followed by red fruits. It is a native of Manchuria.

P. uniflora, from China, has white flowers, produced one to three together, which are followed by black fruits.

A third kind, P. utilis, from the Himalayas, grows up to 12 ft. tall, with very spiny growth and fragrant, creamy-white flowers followed by purple fruits.

The Prinsepias require a sunny position in well-drained, loamy soil, and are increased by seeds, or cuttings of short shoots placed in a frame in July.

PRITCHARDIA. See Eupritchardia.

PRIVET. See Ligustrum.

PROBOSCIDEA JUSSIEUI—*Unicorn Plant, Proboscis Flower* (Proboscid'ea). This native American plant grows wild from Delaware and Indiana to New Mexico. It belongs in the Martynia family, Martyniaceae. The name is derived from *proboskis,* and refers to the proboscis-like beak of the fruit. This plant is often grown as P. fragrans and as Martynia fragrans. The former name rightfully belongs to an allied kind that is a native of Mexico. By some botanists it is named P. louisiana.

The Unicorn Plant is an annual and is of simple cultivation. In the South, seeds may be sown outdoors in spring where the plants are to mature; in the North they may be raised indoors early, in the same way as are Tomatoes, and be planted out in the garden when the weather is warm and settled. They grow in any reasonably good soil and appreciate a sunny position.

Because these plants are of sprawling habit and need considerable room when they are fully developed, they should be spaced at least 5 ft. apart. The young fruits are pickled in the same manner as young Cucumbers.

PROBOSCIS FLOWER. Proboscidea Jussieui, which see.

PROLIFERATION. A term used to describe multiplication of growth in excess of that which is normal, as, for instance, in the Hen-and-Chicken Daisy and Marigold (Calendula), when

[9—13]
Polyanthus Primroses
(Primula polyantha with blue Forget-me-nots)

subsidiary flower heads are produced from the main inflorescence.

PROMENAEA (Promenae'a; Promen'aea). Attractive, dwarf-growing Orchids which are frequently included under Zygopetalum. All are epiphytal (grow on trees) and have small, light green pseudobulbs and evergreen leaves. They are found wild in Brazil. See under Zygopetalum.

PROPAGATING CASE. An apparatus used for the purpose of rooting cuttings and raising seedlings. In its simplest form the propagating case consists of a flowerpot or box covered with a sheet of glass. Specially constructed propagating cases are made on the same principle as the hardy plant frame, with a sliding or hinged "sash" or top, the sides being either of wood or brick.

The purpose of the propagating case is to provide a moist atmosphere which will prevent cuttings from wilting until they are rooted. Without this protection many cuttings would quickly wither. To facilitate the formation of roots, bottom heat is often provided by means of hot-water pipes or electric soil-heating cables.

Bottom heat is necessary or at least very helpful in the propagation of plants which are grown in a greenhouse; it ensures the production of roots much more quickly and so minimizes the risk of losses, for the longer the cuttings take to form roots, the greater is the risk of failure.

PROPAGATION
The Various Methods by Which Plants Are Increased

Worthwhile Work. Amateur gardeners should master a variety of methods of propagating plants. Nearly all gardeners engage in the practice of raising plants from seed, many are familiar with the method of division or separation, and some practice the art of propagating plants from soft wood cuttings or slips, but beyond that the majority of amateur gardeners do not venture. Even with these methods of securing increase, the amateur is very apt to limit himself to a few kinds of plants that are commonly propagated in home gardens.

Too rarely do home gardeners propagate trees and shrubs or even ground-cover plants; they rely upon the professional nurseryman for many plants that they could with little trouble raise themselves. Not only is plant propagating work of great interest, but it also provides stocks of plants most economically and, when desired, stocks of plants that are difficult or impossible to obtain from commercial sources. It is true that it takes longer to raise one's own plants than to buy them ready grown. However, doing the work at home and tending the youngsters through their early stages and on to maturity provides a satisfaction that the buyer of ready-grown plants never knows.

The above is not to be interpreted as a suggestion that amateur gardeners should rely upon their own efforts at propagation for all the plants they need. It would be obviously impractical for a new home owner with an empty lot and need for a shade tree to wait until he had grown one from seed, or for the person in need of a screen of shrubs to hide an unwanted view, or of evergreens to use in a foundation planting, to start with cuttings and grow them on in nursery rows until they are large enough for the purpose for

A propagating bench in a small greenhouse. Cuttings of Coleus, Impatiens and many other kinds are here rooting in a bed of sand.

which they are actually needed immediately.

None but the keenest amateur propagators will normally undertake to bud their own Roses or raise young fruit trees by grafting and budding (although they may engage in the latter arts to change the variety of an established tree). In these cases the Roses and fruit trees obtained from a reliable nursery are usually likely to be better in quality than those propagated at home.

Planning Ahead. It is often possible to anticipate the need for plants some months or even years in advance. If you would like a hedge in a certain place someday but do not wish to go to the expense of purchasing nursery plants, it is a simple matter to raise the required number of Yews or Privets from cuttings, or of Hemlocks or Barberries from seeds, and in two to four years to have plants big enough to set out as a young hedge.

In most gardens there are places that would be improved if they were planted with Pachysandra, English Ivy, evergreen Euonymus, Vinca, Epimedium, Sedum or some other ground cover instead of grass. Such plants can be raised in large numbers and relatively quickly at home by following the simplest of propagating techniques. The great majority of shrubs and evergreens are easy to increase and so are the vast majority of herbaceous perennials (including bulbs) and of greenhouse plants and house plants.

The suggestion made here is that every serious gardener should undertake a certain amount of plant propagation each year and that he should not confine himself to run-of-the-mill items. Almost always there are unusual plants that attract interest in one's own garden, in the gardens of friends, in botanical gardens and in other public places. In most cases propagating material can be obtained from these, at least in small amounts, with little effort. To grow sturdy plants from such "starts" is an inspiring challenge to the true gardener.

The Home Nursery. Wherever any appreciable number of hardy plants are being propagated it is advisable to set aside a special area for the purpose. This nursery ground may cover but a few square yards or be as extensive as the gardener desires. But it should be a propagating

area, a space given over to raising young plants and growing them on until they are of sufficient size to be planted in their permanent locations. Good results are not ordinarily possible if young seedlings, newly rooted cuttings and other propagations are set out in beds and borders that are chiefly filled with mature plants. The young plants cannot compete with these, and are likely to be starved or crowded out.

In the propagating area the young plants (seedlings, rooted cuttings, layerings and so on) should be planted in nursery rows (straight rows in which the plants are to grow until ready for their next transplanting). The rows should be spaced so that the plants have room to develop for a year or two (or sometimes more) and so

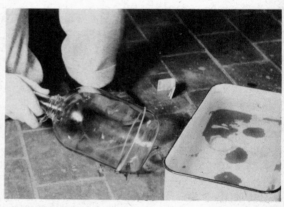

To make a bell jar from a cider bottle, soak a piece of string in kerosene, tie it around the bottle lightly, an inch or two above the bottom, set the string on fire and slowly revolve the bottle.

When the string has burned completely around the bottle, plunge the bottle in cold water and its base will break away cleanly.

that the ground between them may be cultivated to keep down weeds.

A cold frame, even a simple one, and some
bell jars (gallon cider bottles with their bottoms
cut out make good bell jars) are great aids in
the amateur's nursery ground. For propagating
greenhouse and house plants, as well as some
hardy plants, a terrarium or a greenhouse propagating case (a cold-frame-like structure inside a
greenhouse for the purpose of maintaining high
atmospheric humidity about the plants it contains) is invaluable.

Sexual and Asexual Methods of Increase. All
methods of propagation may be classed as sexual
or asexual (or vegetative). Sexual reproduction
includes those methods in which the development of the young plant depends upon the com-
bining of a male and female element (fertilization). Here belongs propagation by seeds and by
spores (see Ferns). All other methods of propagation, including cuttings, division, layering,
budding, and grafting, are asexual or vegetative.

Plants raised from seeds and spores have,. in
effect, two parents, or at least are the result of a
recombination of heredity factors. Because of
this, they frequently differ to a greater or lesser
degree from the plant from which the seeds or
spores were gathered, just as puppies, kittens and
human children differ from their mothers and
fathers.

In many cases seeds and spores are unsatis-
factory or even impossible means of raising new
plants of particular kinds. Many double-flowered
plants, as well as some other kinds, do not produce seeds. Improved garden varieties of most
kinds, such as the Baldwin Apple, the Peace
Rose, the Hicks Yew and the Charles Dickens
Rhododendron, will not breed true from seeds;
their progenies raised from seeds are totally unlike, and generally markedly inferior to, their
parents. In yet other cases, reproduction by
means of seeds is considered too slow for practical purposes. In such circumstances vegetative
methods of propagation are resorted to. The
same remarks apply to raising certain Ferns
from Spores.

Propagation by seed is, however, absolutely
necessary in many cases—for example, with Carrots, Cabbage, Spinach and most vegetables,
and with the vast majority of annuals such as
Clarkias, Sweet Peas and Calendulas. In many
other cases it is a great convenience, enabling
the gardener to raise large numbers of plants
quickly and easily.

Most natural species—that is to say, plants as
they occur in the wild, unimproved by hybridizing or selective breeding—may be satisfactorily
raised from seeds, and so it is quite practicable
to raise plants of Malus coronaria (the Wild
Sweet Crab Apple or the Garland Crab Apple),
Rosa multiflora, Taxus baccata (the Japanese
Yew) and Rhododendron catawbiense in this
way.

Vegetative propagation makes it possible to
secure increase of many plants that it is not
practicable to raise from seeds or spores. In
many cases stocks can be increased more rapidly
by vegetative means.

One of the great advantages of vegetative
propagation is based on the fact that a plant so
raised is not, from a genetical or heredity stand-
point, a new individual, but is, in reality, an
extension of the parent plant from which it was
taken, and so (except in a few very special
cases) reproduces exactly the parent plant. By
using vegetative methods of propagation, choice
horticultural varieties are increased and are kept
true to their types.

Exceptions to the rule that vegetative propagations exactly duplicate their parents are found
in the cases of Yews and many conifers. If side
branches of these are taken as cuttings, the resulting plants retain the lateral growth habit of
a branch and do not, usually, develop the typical
erect, symmetrical habit of growth of the leading
shoot of a plant raised from seeds or of one raised
from a cutting made from a terminal shoot.

Other examples are to be found in English
Ivy and certain other plants in which, if cuttings
are made of flowering shoots, the new plants retain the characteristic habits, leaf shapes and
flowering propensities of flowering shoots and
do not produce the vine shoots or other more
juvenile type of growths.

Yet another example of cuttings failing to
produce plants identical with the parents is to
be found in the variegated-leaved Sansevieria or
Snake Plant. In this case the cuttings made of

sections of the leaves (except the section containing the base) give rise to plain green-leaved plants. In some cases, for example with some Bouvardias and Pelargoniums (Geraniums), root cuttings do not reproduce the parent plant true to type.

Cuttings

Horticulturally, a cutting consists of a piece of a plant from which, if a favorable environment is afforded, a new plant can be grown. A cutting differs from a division or separation in that the latter are in effect complete plants when they are removed from their parents; they consist of roots and tops, or roots and established buds from which new tops will develop in proper season, or young complete bulbs or other underground organs.

Propagation by cuttings is one of the commonest methods of increasing plants. In many cases it affords a very rapid means of securing a stock of desirable kinds and it has the advantage of being an easy method.

There are several different types of cuttings. The naming of the various kinds is based upon the parts of the plant from which they are formed and upon the softness or firmness (maturity of the parts) at the times the cuttings are made.

In theory, it may be possible to propagate all plants by cuttings, and cuttings may consist of any part of the plants with active living cells. In practice, there are many plants that do not root, or do not root readily from cuttings, and for which there are more convenient methods of propagation. It is most satisfactory to take cuttings of those parts of the plant which generate new plants soon and make healthy growth.

Cuttings are, therefore, normally taken of (a) the stem or branch system, (b) the root system, and (c) the leaves. Some plants root readily from cuttings of all three types, but the choice of cutting materials is usually dictated by the season and by the readiness with which the part of the plant will root.

Not all plants are suitable for propagation by cuttings. Most plants of the Prunus (Plum) and Malus (Apple) genera, for instance, are difficult to root from cuttings. In the case of other plants,

such as Roses, it may be more useful to obtain increase by budding or grafting.

In the case of leafy greenwood cuttings, evergreen cuttings, and cuttings of difficult-to-root species, special techniques of propagation are necessary. These are concerned with the provision of the proper rooting medium, a close atmosphere, and the warmth needed for optimum results.

Rooting Mediums. Some plants, such as Willow, Oleander and Rambler Roses, are such moisture lovers that their cuttings root readily in water, and can be transferred from there to the soil. For the majority of cuttings, however, a well-aerated rooting medium, kept moist, is to be preferred. Most plant cuttings can be readily rooted in sand, preferably sharp gritty sand. This contains little nutriment, however, and, once rooted, the cuttings need moving into more fertile soil. A mixture of sand and peat moss is an excellent rooting medium for many kinds of plants, particularly those that like somewhat acid soil.

An alternative modern material is a horticultural grade of vermiculite. This mica-like, finely fragmented material gives good aeration with better moisture retention than sand, and is

A cutting of Chinese Evergreen Aglaonema modestum, rooted in water.

Vermiculite, when used as a rooting medium for cuttings, is not packed firm. The cuttings are stuck into the vermiculite and then are watered to firm them.

highly suitable for use in frames, pots, pans or propagating cases. Once the cuttings are rooted, they must be fed or set out in more fertile soil.

Cuttings which take rather long to root may be placed in a rooting medium of finely chopped sphagnum moss or a mixture of sphagnum moss and sand in the proportions of 1 to 2.

In the case of most rooting mediums it is essential that the cuttings be planted firmly, and, to ensure this, the medium is well firmed before the cuttings are planted and is then packed about the base of each cutting. Such firm planting is not necessary in the case of vermiculite —the cuttings are merely pushed into it and watered with a fine spray.

Cuttings in the open and in cold frames root readily in sandy soil. On heavier soils, they may be inserted in trenches or holes filled with coarse sand. The soil in frames may consist of a base of fertile, sandy loam with a surface layer of coarse sand, 2-3 in. thick.

Water Loss. It is easy to realize that if a cutting loses water too rapidly it will wilt and die. The chief loss is by transpiration. This can be partly checked in greenwood (leafy) cuttings by removing some of the foliage, and partly by shading, especially during the hottest part of the day. But the greatest safeguard lies in the provision of a close atmosphere during the period of transition from unrooted cutting to rooted plant.

A close atmosphere for cuttings planted in the open can be provided by placing bell jars or even Mason jars over them. For the more difficult species, a propagating frame or case is needed. The outdoor propagating frame should have a sheltered location, shaded from hot sun. The soil bed should consist of a base of 3 in. of weathered ashes, 2-3 in. of sandy soil and 3-4 in.

The bell jar that has covered these cuttings has been removed to show a small pan with its drainage hole blocked sunk inside a larger pan. The smaller pan is kept filled with water. Moisture seeps through the walls of the smaller pan and keeps the rooting medium, which is packed between the two pans, evenly moist.

of sharp sand, well firmed and watered, and the surface should be within 4-6 in. of the glass. Or cuttings can be inserted in pots, and these plunged to their rims in ashes in the frame. With the help of such a frame most species native to the temperate zones of the world can be propagated successfully by cuttings.

For Tender Plants. To propagate tender plants, greenhouse plants, tropical or semitropical species and the more difficult subjects, a greenhouse is desirable. Some kinds of cuttings will root readily in an open bench but for the

A propagating device made from a box, a wire framework and polyethylene film.

The polyethylene pulled back to show the cuttings planted in a bed of firmly packed sand.

majority a propagating case is most useful. This consists of a small frame used inside a greenhouse, and usually placed over a source of heat or provided with electric soil-heating wires. The value of the propagating case lies in its provision of soil warmth or bottom heat as well as in a warm, close atmosphere.

Cuttings of many kinds of plants may be rooted

in a sunroom or window garden. To provide the necessary close atmosphere and thus improve the chances of success, cuttings put to root in such locations should be kept covered with a bell jar, Mason jar or similar glass container. Or they may be kept in a terrarium or in a propagating device made by fitting a shallow box with a superstructure framework of wire or wood and covering this with polyethylene plastic film—to form, in effect, a miniature greenhouse. The cuttings should be kept shaded from direct sun until they have rooted.

Bottom Heat. Soil warmth, or bottom heat as the gardener calls it, is an invaluable factor in

Bottom heat is supplied to this propagating bed by a grid of electric heating cables placed beneath the sand.

stimulating quick rooting. It is the warmth of the outdoor soil in autumn that favors hardwood cuttings.

The provision of a steady bottom heat in a propagating case, however, is needed for the more difficult cuttings. It is desirable that the temperature of the rooting medium should be about 10-12° F. above what is normal for the growth of the mature plants. A rough but ready guide to the needs of cuttings is afforded by the temperature range, humidity and soil of the plants' native habitat.

Mist Propagation. One of the newer methods of inducing cuttings to root is called mist propagation. With this technique, the cuttings are planted in a very porous rooting medium, such as coarse sand, in a well-drained bench or other container, and are constantly or intermittently bathed in a foglike mist of water.

The mist is produced by special nozzles attached to water lines and so spaced that all the cuttings are kept constantly wet from the time they are planted until they have rooted. For the best results the relative humidity about the cuttings should be maintained at above 90 per cent. With the intermittent method, timing devices turn the water on and off every few minutes. No shading is provided, and so the cuttings receive

minate on the surface of a leaf or stem and cause infection.

Preparation for Planting. Cuttings are best made with a razor blade or very sharp knife, as the smoother the cut surface, the less chance for parasitic fungi to invade. Cuttings of succulent or woolly plants (for example, Cacti, Zonal Pelargoniums) should be allowed to lose some moisture and the leaves to become limp before planting. Cuttings of most plants, however, should be well watered with a fine spray as soon as they are inserted.

Root-inducing Hormones. Rooting can be quickened by the use of a root-inducing, growth-

A propagating greenhouse at the Montreal Botanical Garden, Canada, fitted with a water system and special nozzles to produce an intermittent mist.

In preparing a cutting of a Geranium some of the lower leaves are first removed.

The base of the stem is cut squarely across just beneath a node or joint in the stem from where the leaf was produced.

Geranium cuttings being planted in a pot of sand. A wooden peg or dibble is used for making the hole into which the cutting is placed.

maximum light and are able to carry on photosynthesis at a maximum rate. The high humidity of the atmosphere about the cuttings prevents them from losing water by transpiration to the extent that they wilt.

Mist propagation can be practiced in greenhouses or outdoors. In the latter case, canvas or other types of screens are erected about the propagating beds or benches to prevent the mist from blowing away.

Contrary to what might be expected, cuttings under mist propagation suffer very little from disease organisms. Apparently the mist washes spores of fungi off the leaves and out of the air promptly and they never have a chance to ger-

By dipping cuttings in specially prepared hormone powders before they are planted, more rapid formation of roots is encouraged.

and food supplies, the problem of the propagator is to keep the cutting alive while stimulating satisfactory rooting.

To some extent, the cutting can live on its own accumulated reserves for a time. This capacity, and the readiness with which cuttings root, vary greatly according to the age of the cuttings and the species from which they are taken.

Cuttings root through the development of the specialized layer of cells known as the cambium, a thin ring of creamy green tissue lying between the outer bark and the firm wood. These cells heal a cut by forming a callus from which roots emerge. Satisfactory development depends chiefly on the control of three factors: moisture, temperature, and aeration. Moisture losses through transpiration must be reduced to a minimum. Warmth and aeration are essential to the chemical and biological activity of the cells which form roots. Food supply, although important, is not urgent until the cuttings have rooted.

Stem cuttings should be taken from healthy shoots which are fully characteristic of the species or variety. Flowering shoots are seldom suitable, and shoots of a specialized character like the horizontal laterals or fastigiate shoots of conifers should be avoided, except for special purposes, as they tend to reproduce the nature of their own specialized growth and not that of the parent plant as a whole. Stem cuttings are broadly of two classes, those of greenwood or soft growth, and those of hardwood or dormant growth. In either case they may consist of terminal pieces of shoots with the tip buds intact or sections of stems cut across both at their tops and bottoms. Greenwood or soft-shoot cuttings are most usually made of terminal growths, hardwood cuttings of sectional pieces of stem. Some indoor plants, such as Dieffenbachias and Philodendrons, are often propagated from short sections of stem each containing only one or two "eyes" or growth buds and many other plants can be increased from such short sectional cuttings if the need for rapidly increasing a limited amount of stock arises.

Hardwood cuttings consist of mature, ripe wood approaching or in a dormant condition. They are usually taken in late autumn or early winter, or in early spring, before growth begins

regulating substance or hormone—by dipping the base of the cutting in a powder or liquid preparation. This quickens the formation of the roots, but thereafter the rooted plant behaves as a normally rooted cutting. As the cuttings begin to grow, they should be watered and ventilated like other plants and, when well rooted, they should be lifted with the root soil ball intact for transplanting.

Sanitation. Strict sanitation of the cutting bed is extremely important. By this is meant the prompt picking off of all decaying and dead leaves, the taking of effective measures if mold appears (dusting with sulphur or applying some other fungicide, ventilating more freely, and avoidance of too much watering and syringing), and the use of disease-free media in which to plant the cuttings. If the cutting bed is suspected of harboring disease organisms it should be discarded and replaced with fresh sand, sand and peat moss, or whatever other rooting medium is being used, or the old medium should be sterilized by using some soil-sterilizing agent such as formaldehyde, Semesan or other mercury compound prepared for the purpose.

Stem Cuttings. Cuttings of the stems of plants may be taken at various stages of growth and seasons. Once they have been detached from the parent plant, however, and so deprived of water

Potentilla fruticosa, like many shrubs, is easily propagated from terminal shoots of the young growth in mid-summer.

Cuttings are prepared by removing some of their lower leaves and slicing the stem across just beneath a node.

With a blunt-pointed dibber or a pencil, the cuttings are planted firmly in a pan containing well-packed sand.

Immediately after planting, the cuttings are thoroughly watered with a fine spray.

The pan containing the cuttings is then buried to its rim in cinders or peat moss in a cold frame and is protected from drying drafts by being covered with sash.

Within a very few weeks the cuttings will have rooted and then may be planted individually in small pots. Here is a sturdy plant of Potentilla produced in a few weeks from a stem cutting taken in August.

Hardwood cuttings consist of short lengths of current season's growth prepared after the leaves have dropped from them in the fall.

again. Probably the best time in the case of deciduous trees and shrubs is immediately before the leaves fall in autumn. The cutting has the chance to form a callus before the soil becomes colder, and is then in a perfect state to resume active growth the following spring.

The absence of leaves on hardwood cuttings means that moisture loss through transpiration is very low. Such cuttings, where winters are not particularly severe, can usually be rooted in the open, given well-drained soil. They consist of

Trenches for the reception of the cuttings are made in a bed of fine well-drained soil outdoors.

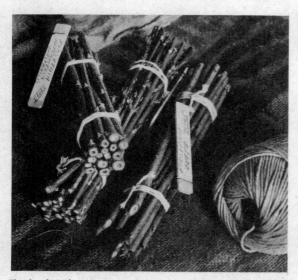

The hardwood cuttings are tied into bundles, carefully labeled, and are buried in cold frames or out-of-doors beneath 6-8 in. of sand. In early spring the bundles of cuttings are removed from the sand. By that time the bases of all of them will have callused over and new roots may even have started to develop.

The cuttings are inserted individually, 2-3 in. apart, with their tips just protruding above the surface of the ground.

Then soil is shoveled against the cuttings.

The soil is made firm against the cuttings by treading and its surface is then raked and leveled.

sand. In spring, before new growth begins, they are dug up from the sand and are planted in nursery rows in sandy soil outdoors, being placed vertically, butt ends downwards with their tips just protruding from the soil.

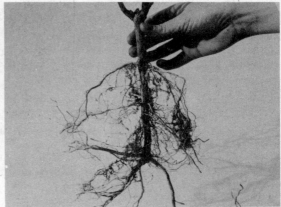

This plant of Viburnum was raised from a hardwood cutting. Note that the roots have developed from almost the entire length of the original cutting.

This is a year-old plant of Stephanandra propagated from a hardwood cutting. Note that the roots in this case have all developed from the base of the original cutting.

sturdy shoots, with from two to six buds, planted firmly in the soil, some of the buds projecting above the surface. Hardwood cuttings should be made of young but fully ripened shoots of the current season's growth.

In severe climates hardwood cuttings are made in fall or in early winter and are buried in sand out of doors or in a cold frame for the winter. They may be tied in bundles of a dozen to twenty-five each and laid horizontally or they may be placed vertically with their butt ends up. In either case they are covered with 6-8 inches of

Making a cutting of Coleus. After the lower leaves are removed the stem is cut across cleanly beneath the node.

Coleus cuttings planted in a bed of sand in a propagating greenhouse.

In about a month the Coleus cuttings will be well rooted and ready for transplanting into small pots.

Soft-shoot cuttings are most often taken (that is, prepared and planted) during the season of most active growth from spring to fall, but in some cases—as for instance with Begonias, Geraniums, English Ivy, Philodendrons and many other plants—cuttings made in winter root with equal ease, provided proper conditions for rooting are maintained.

The exact season at which cuttings are taken often depends upon when the new plants are wanted to be of a certain size for a particular purpose. For instance, if Geraniums in 5-in. pots are needed for planting in window boxes in May, cuttings taken in September will give good results; however, if Geraniums in 3½- or 4-in. pots are wanted in May, then cuttings taken in January or February will prove satisfactory.

The degree of softness of the stem tissues that is most desirable for soft-shoot cuttings varies with the kind of plants. In a very few cases, for example with Lilacs, extremely soft shoots root best, but in the vast majority of cases the shoots from which cuttings are made should be moderately firm, certainly not sappy and immature. In many cases, for example with most hardy deciduous shrubs such as Forsythias, Weigelas and Privets, the shoots used as cuttings should have reached that state of firmness and approaching maturity that gardeners call half-ripe.

Soft-shoot cuttings are made from current season's growth, and hence consist of parts of leafy stems. The shoots from which they are made may be basal ones that spring directly from the crown or rootstock, as is the case with such herbaceous perennials as Phlox, Asters, Chrysanthemums and Heleniums when they are propagated from cuttings taken in early spring; terminal growths (the ends of branches) of older shoots, such as are most often used in propagating Geraniums, Fuchsias, Abutilons, Begonias and Cacti; or short new side shoots that arise from older branches (usually branches of the previous year's growth) and which are often favored for use as cuttings when propagating deciduous shrubs such as Viburnums, Deutzias and Forsythias and such tender shrubs as Lantanas and Plumbagos.

When short side shoots are used as cuttings, they are often taken with a heel (a thin slice of the branch from which the shoot arises) of older

From this old stock plant of Lantana short side shoots are being removed to form heel cuttings.

Heel cuttings of Lantana. The heel consists of a small piece of the main stem which is left attached to the base of the cutting.

wood attached to their bases, and this is trimmed smooth with a sharp knife to form the base of the cutting. In other cases the base of the cutting is formed by cutting the stem cleanly across just beneath a node (joint). In all instances the lower leaves are cut off so that the bottom part of the stem which is planted in the rooting medium is without leaves.

A sectional cutting of Dieffenbachia kept in a suitable environment soon develops roots below and a stem bearing leaves above.

Some plants, such as this Dieffenbachia, can be propagated from short sections of a stem laid horizontally in sand or other rooting medium and placed in a warm moist atmosphere.

Cuttings of Evergreens. Most evergreens can be rooted from cuttings. Some, such as Kurume Azaleas, Boxwood and Yews, root quickly and with great ease. Others, such as Rhododendrons, Hollies and Thuya, take longer to root and are somewhat more exacting in their needs. Yet others, such as Kalmia (Mountain Laurel), are, for all practical purposes, impossible to root from cuttings.

Here in the nearer pans of sand sectional stem cuttings of Dieffenbachia are planted vertically. In the rear, pans of leaf cuttings of Peperomias are planted in a mixture of peat moss and sand.

Cuttings of Boxwood root readily and develop roots from all parts of the stem.

Midsummer or slightly later, after the new growths have become firm and lost their immaturity, is a good time to take cuttings of evergreens. At that time they can be rooted in a frame outdoors. The frame should be in a shaded place and be kept close. Another good time to take cuttings of most evergreens is in late fall, but before really severe freezing weather has arrived. Cuttings taken then should be planted in a propagating case or a propagating bench in a cool greenhouse.

Rooted cuttings of evergreens. At left, Yew, at the right a Thuja. In these cases the roots all develop from the bases of the cuttings.

Most evergreens root well in either well-packed sand or in a mixture of sand and peat moss that is packed down firmly. The sand should be coarse, and it is very important that the propagating bed be well drained. Excellent drainage, so that water that is applied runs through quickly and does not stagnate, and watering rather freely so that the rooting medium is kept always quite moist, are important details in rooting cuttings of evergreens. Whenever the conditions are such that the foliage will dry before nightfall, it is helpful to syringe the foliage lightly with plain water.

Cuttings of evergreens will vary in size according to kind. Plants with short shoots and crowded leaves, such as Heaths and Heathers, may be propagated from cuttings 1-1½ in long. With Yews, Boxwood, Junipers and similar plants, the cuttings may be 2-4 in. long, and with Aucubas, Laurus and other large-leaved plants that have their leaves rather widely spaced they may be 4-6 in. long. In all cases they should be set firmly in the rooting medium after they have been prepared by removing some of their lower leaves and cutting their bases cleanly across just beneath a node with a sharp knife. Their general care is the same as that given above for soft-shoot cuttings. They need shade from direct sunshine until they have rooted.

Leaf Cuttings. Certain plants with more or less thick or succulent leaves can be propagated from cuttings consisting of single leaves and, in some cases, of part of a leaf. These plants include all members of the family Gesneriaceae, such as Achimenes, Gloxinias, Haberleas, Ramondas, Saintpaulias, Sinningias, Smithianthas and Streptocarpus; all members of the family Crassulaceae, such as Cotyledons, Crassulas, Echeverias, Kalanchoes and Sedums; a considerable number of Begonias, especially the Rex Begonias (B. Rex-cultorum) and the Christmas Begonias (B. cheimantha); and a variety of other plants including Hyacinthus, Lachenalias, Sansevierias and Lewisias.

In some cases leaf cuttings must consist of entire leaves, and in all cases they may do so, but with members of the family Gesneriaceae, with Begonia Rex-cultorum varieties and with Sansevierias, Lachenalias and some others, portions of

In a warm, moist atmosphere, leaf cuttings of Christmas Begonias soon root if planted in sand or a mixture of sand and peat moss.

a leaf give equally satisfactory results. When parts of leaves of Sansevierias, Lachenalias, Hyacinthus and other plants that have veins running parallel up and down the leaf are used, the leaf

If leaves of Begonia Rex-cultorum are sliced across at the junctions of the main veins and are then laid flat on a mixture of peat moss and sand in a warm, moist atmosphere, a new plant soon develops from each incision.

A young plant of Begonia Rex-cultorum growing from a leaf cutting.

is simply cut across horizontally into sections 2-4 in. long, and these are inserted vertically, or nearly so, with their bases about 1 in. deep in the rooting medium. Leaves that have veins forming a network pattern and are suited to this method of propagation may be cut into wedge-shaped pieces in such a manner that the base of each wedge includes the junction point of two major veins (the point where two main veins meet). The wedges are then inserted in the rooting medium vertically, or nearly so, with their bases buried to a depth of about one inch.

The Panda Plant, Kalanchoë tomentosa, like many succulents, is easily propagated from leaf cuttings.

When whole leaves are used as leaf cuttings, either the petiole (leafstalk) or, if the leaf has no stalk, the bottom of the leaf itself, is inserted in the rooting medium. Usually the leaves are set more or less vertically, but with some succulent plants, with Tolmeia (Pickaback plant) and some others it is more convenient to set them nearly horizontally.

Leaf cuttings of Peperomia that have developed roots and young shoots.

The rooting medium in which leaf cuttings are planted and the care they need after planting are the same as for soft-shoot cuttings. For most kinds a mixture of peat moss and sand is a satisfactory rooting medium; for succulents, such as Kalanchoes, Sedums and other members of the family Crassulaceae, plain sand is better.

Leaf cuttings of succulents such as Crassulas, Kalanchoes and Sedums root well under ordinary atmospheric conditions, but those of other kinds of plants require the humid atmosphere of a propagating case, terrarium or bell jar and shade from direct sunshine for their successful growth. The rooting medium should be kept just moist but not constantly saturated.

Begonia Rex-cultorum varieties are often propagated by taking a single leaf, cutting the main veins through at intervals of 1½-2 in., and then laying the leaf flat, underside down, on a suitable rooting medium in a propagating case. The leaf is weighted down by placing a few pebbles on it or is held down with hairpin-like pegs fashioned from wire. Under suitable conditions each slit made through the veins gives rise to a new plant. The best time to take leaf cuttings is when the leaves are fully developed. Immature leaves are not satisfactory.

Bulb Cuttings. This method of propagation is not well known among gardeners, yet it is a way of securing increase, with considerable speed, of certain plants that can only be propagated comparatively slowly by other means. Because it is a vegetative process, the progeny are identical with the parent plant.

Choice varieties of Hippeastrum (Amaryllis) are the bulbs most usually increased by means of bulb cuttings, but good success has also been had with Albuca, Chasmanthe, Cooperia, Haemanthus, Hymenocallis, Lycoris, Narcissus, Nerine, Pancratium, Phaedranassa, Scilla, Sprekelia and Urceolina. Undoubtedly there are many other bulbous plants which can be increased in this fashion.

The procedure is as follows. A large mature bulb is quartered with a sharp knife lengthways. Then each quarter is divided lengthways into two or more wedges, care being taken that each section includes a part of the bottom or basal plate of the bulb. Next the wedges are further

To make bulb cuttings, the bulb, in this case a Hippeastrum, first cut into pie-shaped (wedge-shaped) segments.

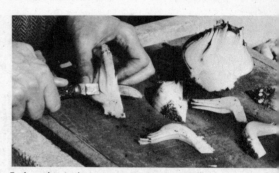

Each wedge is then cut into two or more bulb cuttings by slici down between the scales of the bulb. Each final fraction m· have a small piece of the basal plate of the bulb attached it.

Bulb cuttings of Hippeastrum planted in a mixture of peat m· and sand. They are put in a warm, moist place to root.

cut up by slipping a knife down between eve third or fourth of the concentric fleshy scales which the bulb is formed and slicing throug the basal plate at the bottom. Each of the fin pieces is a bulb cutting. Each consists of portio of a few bulb scales (that is, a sliver of th

[9—14a]
Preparing cuttings

—14]
king cuttings of Iresine

—14b]
serting cuttings in sand

[9—14c]
Plant from which cuttings were taken and pan showing cuttings inserted

[9—15]
Propagating bench almost filled with cuttings

[9—15a]
Mist system in operation over propagating bench

[9—15b]
Roots on Boxwood cutting planted under mist system

[9—15c]
Propagation: seedlings in greenhouse

After a few weeks each bulb cutting will have developed a small bulb with one or more leaves and roots from the base of the bulb. The young plants may then be potted individually.

bulb itself) with a small piece of the basal plate attached.

The bulb cuttings are planted vertically or nearly so, with their lower halves buried and their upper parts in the air, in flats or in a propagating case containing a mixture of peat moss and sand. The rooting medium is kept just moist but not constantly wet, and the temperature is maintained at a slightly higher level than bulbs of the types being propagated normally require. Slight bottom heat is helpful but not necessary in encouraging the bulb cuttings to form roots and to produce from between their scales young new bulbs. This they do in a few weeks or at most a few months' time.

August and September have proved good times to make and insert bulb cuttings, but the method is comparatively new and there is ample opportunity for gardeners to experiment with it both with regard to the kinds of plants that can

be increased in this way and the best time of the year to make the cuttings.

Once the young bulbs are well formed, they should be transplanted to flats of sandy, peaty soil and be kept growing under environmental conditions favorable to their kinds. Unless the young bulbs naturally go to rest when their normal dormant seasons come around, it is best to keep them actively growing without resting them until they bear their first bloom. With Hippeastrums this can be done; with some other

Thick roots are removed from a plant of perennial Cynoglossum in preparation for making root cuttings.

Root cuttings, about 3 in. long, are made with a sharp knife. Their upper ends are cut square, their lower ends slanting.

Root cuttings are planted vertically and close together with peg or dibble in a sand bed, then covered with an inch of sand.

The following spring, vigorous top growth develops. This indicates that the root cuttings have also substantial root growth.

When good roots and a sturdy top have developed from the root cutting, the young plant is transplanted in a nursery bed for further growth.

kinds it is necessary to allow them to go dormant each year.

Root Cuttings. Many plants with stout roots can be increased from root cuttings. The method consists simply of cutting the thick roots into 1-2 in. lengths and inserting them upright in a compost of half peat moss and half sand in early spring or in fall. Plants which can be treated in this way include Anchusa italica, Oriental Poppy, Anemone japonica, Echinops, Eryngium, Phlox; vegetables such as Sea Kale, Horse-radish, and Rhubarb; and other plants such as Fatsia, Rhus typhina, Romneya, Tecoma and Yucca.

Propagation by Division

Division is one of the simplest methods of propagation; it is employed in increasing many hardy herbaceous perennials and rock-garden plants, and a few shrubs as well as a good many pot plants.

Division consists of breaking up old plants or clumps into several rooted pieces, and replanting them at once, or potting them, as may be necessary. The best and most vigorous pieces are found on the outer parts of the old plants, and they alone should be chosen; the inner, old parts should not be used.

The way to divide many kinds of plants with the least damage to the roots is to use two garden

Clump-forming herbaceous perennials, such as the Stachys pictured here, may be divided by cutting them into pieces with a sharp spade.

Fall and early spring are the best times to divide most herbaceous perennials. This clump of Day Lilies is being lifted for propagation.

After it is dug, two garden forks, back to back, are thrust vertically into the clump.

Final divisions of the Day Lily clump. Before they are planted the leaves may be cut back somewhat.

forks; these are thrust, back to back, in the clump, and the tops of the handles are prized outwards.

Most of the hardy herbaceous perennials can be propagated by division. It is, however, unwise to disturb some kinds for this purpose,

The handles of the forks are forced apart to break the clump into pieces with minimum damage to the roots.

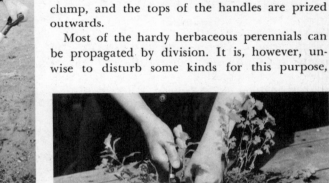

Chrysanthemums and some other fast-spreading perennials may be divided into single-shoot divisions.

The pieces formed by dividing the clump with forks may be further divided by cutting them into pieces with a sharp knife.

Each single-shoot division should be well rooted. Before planting the tops of the shoots may be pinched back.

because they become established slowly and are only seen at their best when left undisturbed year after year. Japanese Anemone, Oriental Poppy, Peony, Sea Holly, Gypsophila, Delphinium and Lupine are examples.

The kinds which are generally propagated by division are such vigorous plants as Michaelmas Daisy or perennial Aster, perennial Sunflowers, Artemisia lactiflora, Achillea or Milfoil and Rudbeckias or Coneflowers. Such kinds benefit by being lifted and separated into rooted pieces every year, or certainly every two years—work which may be done in autumn or spring. But it is wise to leave most other kinds undisturbed and propagate them by seeds, cuttings or offsets.

Of pot plants that are commonly propagated by division the following are examples: Aspidistras, Boston Ferns, Liriope and Sansevierias.

Separation

Separation is a term often used as being synonymous with division. Thus, gardeners refer to dividing or separating Asters, perennial Sunflowers, Artemisias, Achilleas, Rudbeckias and the like and of separating African Violets, Aspidistras and Snake Plants when they cut or pull them into pieces, each piece having some roots and some stems, leaves or part of the crown of the plant.

But separation also has a more specialized meaning. It especially refers to propagating plants by the use of naturally detachable vegetative parts such as bulblets and other offsets,

Next, the root ball is pulled apart with the hands into suitably sized pieces.

Pots, just big enough to accommodate the pieces without crowding the roots, are crocked and leaves are placed over the crocks to prevent the drainage from becoming clogged.

Sansevierias and plants of similar habits of growth are divided by first removing them from their pots and cutting through the stoutest rhizomes and roots.

Soil is worked around the roots and made firm and each division soon establishes itself as a new plant.

Separating Narcissi bulbs. This is best done in late spring, as soon as the foliage has died down.

bulbils and plantlets. Many kinds of plants produce such naturally detachable parts. The names given to these parts vary according to the position they occupy in relation to the parent plant, but all are essentially young plants produced on or near the parent. The act of removing the young plants from the parents is called separation. Separation, as used in this special sense, is akin to division and sometimes is referred to as such. More precisely, in separating plants, the breaks or cuts are made along natural lines of cleavage; in dividing plants, on the other hand, specimens that have no natural tendency to split into separate units are forcibly made to do so by cutting or breaking them apart.

Most bulbs, corms and tubers produce against or close to themselves young bulbs (bulblets), young corms (cormels) or young tubers (tubercles). When these, which are often called offsets, are to be used for propagating purposes, they should be removed from the parent plant during the dormant season. In the case of deciduous plants such as Narcissi, Freesias, Hippeastrums, Gloriosas and Gladioli, this may be done as soon as the foliage dies down, and the parts to be used for propagation stored under suitable cool conditions until planting time, or the separation may be done just before new growth starts after the resting (dormant) season.

In the case of plants that retain their foliage throughout the year, such as Eucharis, certain Crinums and Hymenocallis, separation should be done at potting or planting time, just before new growth is resumed after a period of partial dormancy.

Offset is used as a synonymous term for bulblet, cormlet and tubercle (see above), and also to describe a young plant that grows from the base of a parent plant and is easily detached. Offsets of this latter kind are produced freely by such plants as Sempervivums (Hen and Chickens), Gasterias, Haworthias and many kinds of Cacti. They may be separated and started as new plants at any convenient time when they are large enough, but, normally, the beginning of a new growing season is the best time to do this.

Bulbils. Some bulbous plants, such as certain Lilies (for example, the Tiger Lily), bear young bulbs (bulbils) in the leaf axils of their stems or clustered around the bases of their stems just above the parent bulb; certain others, such as the Top Onion, bear bulbils in their inflorescences (flower clusters) or in place of the flowers. Bulbils may be removed when the stems are mature and are about to die down naturally. They may be stored under cool, slightly moist conditions for planting at the beginning of the next growing season, or they may be planted

Bulbils of the Top Onion grow in a cluster at the top of the flower stem, where other Alliums produce their flowers and seeds.

Plantlets of this Kalanchoë are produced freely at the ends of its leaves.

immediately in flats, cold frames or in sheltered nursery beds outdoors.

Plantlets (tiny, easily detachable plants that develop on the leaves or other above-ground parts of the parent) are freely borne by some kinds of plants and always afford a very ready means of securing increase. All that is necessary is to remove the plantlets, as soon as they are big enough to handle easily and are of sufficient size to establish themselves when planted separately, and plant them in light, sandy soil in pots, flats, cold frames or outdoors, depending upon their kind.

Among plants that produce plantlets on their leaves are Tolmeia Menzeisii (Pickaback Plant), Kalanchoe pinnata (Air Plant or Life Plant), Kalanchoe Daigremontiana and certain tropical Nymphaeas (Water Lilies). Among plants that bear plantlets in their inflorescences (clusters of flowers) are Crassula multicava and certain Agaves.

Grafting and Budding

These methods of propagation are dealt with in detail under their respective headings in other parts of this Encyclopedia. For Inarching or Approach Grafting, see Inarching.

Layering

Layering is a most useful and certain method of propagation that provides a well-developed

plant or shrub in the shortest possible time. It is a method well suited to the needs of the amateur who is without greenhouses or other special propagating facilities. See Layering and Air Layering.

Seed Sowing Under Glass

To be successful in raising plants from seed, whether under glass or in the open, the gardener must appreciate the conditions essential to their free germination. In their dormant state they contain insufficient moisture to stimulate them into growth; supply this, and a change will immediately take place in the seeds. They will swell, and burst their coats or testas, but this does not mean that they will germinate, for, in addition to adequate moisture, warmth and air are also necessary. Give these three in the right degrees and the majority of seeds will germinate, provided of course they are fertile.

Ready for sowing seeds indoors—soil compost, pans, crocks, sieve for sifting soil over seeds, and labels.

Filling a pan in preparation for sowing seeds indoors. The soil is pressed firm with the tips of the fingers.

The surface of the soil is leveled off a little below the rim of the pan and is pressed lightly with a tamper.

As soon as the young plants appear above the soil the paper is removed and the seedlings are given adequate light.

The prepared seed pans are watered thoroughly with a fine spray.

A pot of sturdy seedlings, the result of proper sowing and of growing in a favorable environment.

The seeds are scattered thinly over the soil, pressed lightly in and, unless they are dust-fine, are covered lightly with fine soil. A piece of glass and sheet of paper are placed over the pan, which is then put in suitable temperature to encourage germination.

Advantage of Sowing Under Glass. The great advantage of sowing in pots, pans and flats in a greenhouse, frame or other structure is that the gardener is better able to control the conditions that induce quick germination—moisture, warmth and air. Of course, with the hardiest subjects, such as most vegetables and hardy annuals, which require less warmth than the others, such artificial methods are a waste of time unless very early germination and growth are desired, or the seeds are so few that the possibility of losses must be reduced to a minimum.

Germination Temperatures. Many seeds usually sown out of doors will germinate in a minimum temperature of 45 degrees F. If these are sown under glass, however, better results will be obtained in an average temperature of 50 to 55

These seedlings received adequate light as soon as they germinated and so are strong and sturdy.

Seedlings that do not receive enough light become weak and drawn. If the light comes chiefly from one side they lean towards it.

degrees, while for tender subjects the ideal is between 55 and 65 degrees according to the subjects. A few tropical plants need higher temperatures.

In a greenhouse in which suitable winter temperatures can be provided, January is the time to start raising tender plants from seed, of kinds that need a long season of growth. Otherwise it is best to wait until the days are longer and the light stronger before sowing seeds of even such slow-growing summer-flowering plants as Begonias and Lobelias.

In many cases sowings made later than January—well on into spring in fact—will be more desirable. These will produce plants of suitable size for planting outdoors as soon as the weather is warm enough, whereas plants from earlier sowings would be too large.

Seed-sowing Composts. For the general run of flowering plants and vegetables commonly raised from seed in pots or flats under glass, the John Innes seed compost is excellent, although by no means essential to first-class results. As lime is one of the ingredients, it is useless for raising

A demonstration of starting seedlings by using sphagnum moss and vermiculite.

all kinds of Ericaceous (Heather, Rhododendrons, etc.), and other lime-hating plants.

The John Innes seed compost, formulated after considerable research work at the John Innes Horticultural Institution in England, is not difficult to prepare (see John Innes Seed and Potting Composts). The formula is: 2 parts (by bulk) of loam, 1 part of peat, and 1 part of sand, to which are added 1½ oz., superphosphate and ¾ oz. ground limestone per bushel of soil.

For Rhododendrons, Azaleas, Heaths, and other acid-soil plants, also Gentians and hardy Primulas, a compost containing 3 parts of peat or leaf mold to 1 part each of lime-free loam and clean, sharp sand is desirable.

The Soil Ingredients. If you intend to raise seedlings under glass in any quantity, and to grow pot plants in your greenhouse, it will pay you to prepare some good-quality loam. The best type is of medium texture, the product of 4-5 in. turfs from pasture, which have been stacked until the grass has rotted. Such loam will be fibrous and slightly greasy when rubbed between fingers and thumb. If loam prepared in this way is not available, fertile top soil, preferably neither excessively sandy nor very clayey, may be substituted for it.

Granulated horticultural peats are naturally sterile, and for seed composts are valuable on account of their moisture and air-holding qualities. Peat should never be used in a dry state.

Well-rotted leaf mold is an excellent ingredient for seed-sowing and transplanting composts, and may be used in preference to peat where a home supply is available.

The sand should be fairly coarse, clean, and sharp or gritty to the touch when rubbed between fingers and thumb.

Sterilizing the Loam. To rid the loam of any pests and diseases that might harm the seedlings, heat sterilizing is beneficial. A simple method of dealing with small quantities of sifted loam is by steaming in a large saucepan. Half an inch or so of water is placed in the bottom and brought to a boil. The pan is then filled with soil and left to simmer for 20 minutes. This sterilizing process may cause an excess of nitrogen to be released in the loam and the superphosphate is added to the seed compost to correct the acidity thus caused. Heat sterilization of soil may also be accomplished very easily in electric sterilizers which are made especially for this purpose.

If leaf mold is used in composts for seed sowing and pricking off, it is advisable to sterilize this also, separately, before adding it to the loam. Peat and clean sand do not need to be sterilized.

Alternatives to Heat Sterilization. Although generally considered advisable, the heat sterilization of loam and leaf mold used in seed sowing composts is by no means essential. Almost always, excellent results may be had without doing this. As an alternative to sterilization many gardeners treat their seed soils with formaldehyde, chloropicrin (sold as Larvacide) or other commercial preparations sold for the purpose or they treat the seeds before sowing with commercial preparations, such as Arasan, Spergon and Semesan as an anti-damping off precaution. See Damping Off under Pests and Diseases.

Other Seed Sowing Media. Seeds can be successfully germinated in media other than soil composts and in recent years some of these have gained considerable favor among gardeners. Among the most popular are vermiculite, sand and finely sifted sphagnum moss. The latter is sold as milled sphagnum moss. It may be prepared at home by rubbing sphagnum moss, either living or dead, through a fine sieve.

None of the above-mentioned media contains sufficient nutrients to support the young plants that develop from the seeds sown in them, therefore it is essential either to transplant the seedlings while they are quite small or to apply nutrients by watering the medium with dilute complete liquid fertilizers at regular intervals after the young plants have germinated.

A great advantage, apart from saving the work and trouble of preparing soil composts for seed sowing, is that seedlings growing in sterile sand, vermiculite and sphagnum moss are less likely to damp off (be killed by the damping off disease fungus) than those sown in soil mixtures. A method sometimes favored, is to fill the seed sowing receptacles (pots, pans or flats) with soil to within about an inch of the level where the finished surface is to be and then top off with a layer of vermiculite, sphagnum moss or sand. This saves the necessity for applying fertilizer solutions later, because the young plants soon root down into the soil layer, however, the surface layer of sand, vermiculite or sphagnum moss does much to discourage damping off.

Sowing the Seeds. Shallow earthenware pans and pots of 4-in. to 6-in. size are ideal containers in which to sow small quantities of seeds, but make sure they are washed clean or, better still, sterilized, as there is little point in using disease-free compost if the pots or pans remain a possible source of infection. New pans and pots should be soaked in water for a few minutes and then be allowed to dry before being used.

So that there will be no danger of the seed compost becoming sour, or remaining too wet and so causing the seeds to rot, it is important to provide good drainage. First place a large crock over the drainage hole, then fill to one third the depth of the pot or pan with small crocks (broken pots, tiles or brick), and cover these with a layer of loam fiber, half-decayed leaves or sphagnum moss.

The sifted compost is then put in and pressed down evenly with the tips of the fingers to make it moderately firm, but not hard, and the surface then leveled and pressed flat, very lightly, with a round board made specially for the purpose, or with the bottom of another pot.

Thin Sowing Avoids Losses. The chief danger to the young seedlings is damping-off disease, a fungus encouraged by damp conditions. It infects the seedlings at soil level and causes them to topple over. The more crowded the seedlings are, the greater the chances of infection and rapid spread of the disease. Therefore, reasonably thin sowing should be the rule in all cases, especially as crowded seedlings quickly become spindly and seldom make sturdy plants.

Various methods of sowing have their exponents, but with the majority of the fine to medium-sized seeds, provided the operator is steady-handed, the simplest method is to sow directly from the packet by shaking it so that the seeds slide out slowly.

Spacing the Larger Seeds. With some seeds, as for instance Grevilleas, Nasturtiums, and Sweet Peas, spacing the individual seeds well clear of each other is recommended to ensure sturdy and unfettered growth right from the start. This method is most satisfactory with choice subjects like Lupines and Delphiniums if the seeds are few.

How Deep to Cover Them. As a general rule, when sowing seeds in pots or flats, a safe guide is to cover them with fine compost to their own depth, which means that the majority will require only a very light sprinkling. With the larger seeds, a slightly thicker covering is more satisfactory—a ¼-inch, for instance, for Sweet Peas—while for the very fine seeds no covering at all is necessary.

In the latter category, with sand- or dust-like seeds, come the Gloxinias, Calceolarias, Achimenes, Begonias, Primulas, Heaths, Rhododendrons, etc. The raising of these fully tests the skill of the amateur, though failure is as likely to result from mishandling of the seedlings as from faulty sowing. With these seeds, the soil surface should be dusted with fine compost before the seeds are sown.

Watering. Opinions are divided as to the best method of watering pots of seeds, but for practical purposes it is best not to rely on any hard and fast rule. For most vegetable seeds raised under glass, and medium-sized flower seeds, it is quite sound practice to water the compost-filled pots or flats thoroughly the day before sowing, so as to give time for surplus water to drain away. After the seeds are sown, a light sprinkling with a can fitted with a fine spray will settle the covering soil.

For large seeds, which are not likely to become displaced, overhead watering with a fine spray after sowing is satisfactory.

The finest seeds, however, need very careful watering, and the time-honored method of submerging the pots to their rims in water until it soaks to the surface, but avoiding flooding, is the safest, as any attempt at overhead watering would wash the seeds out of position. The pots should be removed from the water as soon as the surface of the compost appears moist and surplus water should be carefully drained off.

Prewarm the soil and water. To assist in providing the right degree of warmth for the seeds, and later for the seedlings at the transplanting stage, it is always an advantage to prewarm the compost by bringing it into the greenhouse a week or two before sowing. For the same reason tepid water, not cold water direct from the main, should be used for watering.

To Conserve Moisture. Once the seeds have been sown, the pots watered, and arranged on the benches of the greenhouse or in the frame, steps must be taken to ensure a humid atmosphere and prevent the compost from drying out completely. The ideal method in the greenhouse, unless it is devoted solely to seed raising (in which case it can be kept closed except for occasional slight ventilation in the mornings of mild days), is to cover the pots with small squares of glass, and spread newspapers over these.

If glass is not available, then paper alone will serve, but it should be damped over lightly on sunny mornings. A paper covering should also be provided in frames, or the whole frame covered with burlap or other material, but not so thickly as to exclude the sun's warmth.

When the Seeds Germinate. The pots should be inspected every few days, or every morning if covered with glass, for signs of germination, the glass being turned to prevent the condensed moisture from dripping on to the seeds. A light spraying with a very fine spray will help to prevent drying out, at the first signs of which the pots should be watered by the immersion method.

As soon as the seedlings commence to appear, the pots should be removed to a position close to the glass, but in sunny weather it may be desirable to shade them lightly to prevent rapid drying out. Early in the year it may be necessary to cover the seedlings on frosty nights or move them away from the glass.

Irregular Germination. In the majority of cases seeds will give a high percentage of germination fairly rapidly if sown while fresh, but the amateur must not blame the seedsman if in some cases germination is irregular. Primulas and Gentians especially are inclined that way, while some seeds, as for instance Irises and Peonies, often take a year or more to germinate. In the case of Primulas, a good tip is to cover them with a thin layer of damp moss, to prevent any possibility of drying out, a frequent cause of irregular germination.

Best Way with Alpines. Bearing in mind the conditions under which most alpine plants exist in Nature, good germination can often be obtained by subjecting the seeds to frost and snow before placing them in the greenhouse or frame.

Gentians, hardy Primulas, Meconopsis and other "difficult" subjects will often germinate as freely as weeds if sown in autumn or winter, while the seed is fresh. The pots should be

When filling flats for seed sowing, the drainage slits are first covered with coarse leaves.

plunged in ashes (to prevent cracking) at the foot of a north wall, and covered with panes of glass to protect them from heavy rain. Here they may be frozen solid, and, if snow occurs, this should be heaped over them. After such treatment, on being transferred to the greenhouse or frame in March or early April, they will germinate freely in a week or two. Seeds of many hardy trees and shrubs also respond well to this freezing treatment.

Then the flat is filled with prepared soil which is leveled even with the tops of the sides.

The soil is pressed moderately firm with the finger tips; care is taken not to miss the corners or edges.

The soil surface is stroked with the edge of a piece of wood to level it a little below the rim of the flat.

The soil is next watered with a fine spray. Boiling water is used if possible.

When the surplus water has drained away the seeds are scattered thinly. If more than one kind is sown in a flat, they may be separated with pieces of cane.

Some kinds of seeds tend to clump together; if they do, they may be separated and spaced with a pencil point.

To prevent the seeds from bouncing when soil is sifted over them they are pressed lightly into the surface.

Soil is sifted over the seeds to a depth of two or three times their own diameter. Extremely fine seeds need no covering.

The flats should be examined daily for signs of germination. Glance along the surface of the soil for the first evidence of growth.

Labels are inserted bearing variety names, sowing dates, etc. To conserve moisture, the flat is covered with a sheet of glass.

As soon as seedlings are up and before they have elongated, the glass and paper are removed.

Paper is placed over the glass to keep out light and, with the glass, encourages uniform environmental conditions.

Some gardeners prefer to sow seeds in flats in closely placed parallel shallow drills rather than to scatter them broadcast.

Sowing in Flats. For flower and vegetable seeds to be raised in any quantity, shallow wooden boxes are very handy. These are called flats. A good size for seed sowing is 2½ in. deep x 14 in. long x 9½ in. wide, with a slit or some holes in the bottom, for water to drain through. In preparing the flat for sowing, the slit or holes are covered with large crocks, and a layer of small crocks then spaced over the bottom and covered with a layer of compost siftings or half-decayed leaves. Flats for seed sowing can be bought, but are easily made by any handyman.

Filling the Flats. The flat is filled to the top with the fine soil compost (sifted through a ¾-in. or ½-in. sieve), and this is pressed down lightly, making it slightly firmer at the corners and sides. For leveling the surface a flat board ½ inch or so thick and slightly longer than the width of the flat is very handy. Soil is heaped into the flat and leveled off by drawing the board, with its edge resting on the sides, from one end of the box to the other, after which the soil is pressed down flat with the board to about ¼ in. from the top. For fine seeds that will not be covered, the flattened surface may be covered with a dusting of fine sand or compost passed through a ¼-in. sieve.

Homemade Sieve for Seed Sowing. For covering small seeds with fine compost a homemade sieve of window screening is very handy. An ordinary cigar box, with the lid and bottom removed, makes a suitable frame, the screening being cut to measure and then tacked to the bottom of the box. Later in the season a sieve of this type may prove very useful for cleaning home-saved seed.

Management of the Seedlings. Once germination has commenced, the aim of the gardener must be to keep the seedlings as sturdy as possible, by exposure to light, although, to prevent rapid drying and wilting, it may be necessary to shade them lightly from direct sunshine. They should be kept close to the glass of the greenhouse or frame, provided the atmospheric temperature is sufficient to keep frost from them, and should be given an increasing amount of fresh air as weather conditions improve.

While the seedlings are in the seed pot or flat, care must be exercised in watering, especially if the seedlings are at all crowded; otherwise they may quickly fall a prey to damping-off disease, a fungus which attacks them at soil level and will destroy a whole potful of seedlings in a day or two. This disease is encouraged by damp, close conditions, hence the importance of careful watering and free ventilation. Large seedlings may be watered overhead, but for small seedlings it is best to continue watering by immersion until ready for pricking off.

Damping off Disease. The chances of attack are lessened by the use of sterilized compost, but if, in spite of all precautions, the disease does appear, the infected patches of seedlings should be removed, with the soil, and the pot or box then watered with Semesan dissolved in water, or with other suitable fungicide.

Transplanting. Once the seedlings have fully developed their seed leaves, it is time to transplant or prick them out into other pans or flats; otherwise they will soon become drawn and weak. A compost similar to that used for sowing is suitable for most seedlings, though it may be slightly coarser for the larger types. If flats are used, these are prepared in just the same way as for sowing, but pans and pots do not require quite so much drainage material.

A small blunt-pointed stick, of little more than pencil thickness, makes a handy dibber, and the seedlings should be set with their seed leaves just clear of the soil, which is made firm with the dibber, taking care, however, not to bruise the stems of the seedlings. They should be spaced 1 to 2 in. apart according to their natural vigor.

For very small seedlings, which are difficult to handle, as those of Begonia, Saintpaulia, Primula, etc., the difficulty can be overcome with the aid of a thin tapering stick, with a notch cut in the end to form two short prongs, with which the seedlings can be lifted and set in the dibber holes.

After being pricked out, the seedlings should be watered in with a spray, then returned to the same temperature and kept shaded and rather close for a day or two to assist their recovery from the move.

Potting Large Seedlings. With large seedlings, like those of Tomatoes, Brooms, etc., it is generally best to transfer them direct from the seed pot to 3-in. pots. A few small cinders in the bottoms of these will suffice for drainage if fairly coarse potting compost is used. The seedlings should be put in with their roots at full length and the soil pressed only moderately firm.

Hardening Off. If the seedlings, whether of flowers or vegetables, are intended for planting in the open garden, they must be grown as hardily as possible. Once they have recovered from the transplanting, they must be given more and more air as growth advances. If raised in the greenhouse, in a few weeks they can be transferred to a frame, which should be ventilated each day, and, as the season advances, at night also, until a week or two before it is intended to plant them. The frame sash can be removed completely in fine weather.

Seed Sowing Under Cloches. The introduction of the modern continuous cloche or P.M.G. (Portable Miniature Greenhouse), as these are called, has placed within the reach of all amateur gardeners a ready means of raising many kinds of hardy plants from seeds with a minimum of trouble and with little risk of losses. For this purpose the types of cloches most favored are the long tent, 24 in. long, with a span of 11 in., and, better still, the long barn, which gives more headroom and a span of 18 in.

For Early Crops. Perhaps the greatest value of the cloches is for raising vegetable and salad-green crops early where they are to grow. It should be noted that the barn cloches are especially economical for early cropping, as with their height and width a greater variety of crops can be grown under them at the same time. For example, if a row of dwarf Peas or Snap Beans is sown down the center, there will still be room on either side for a row of Lettuce, Radish, Spinach, or Carrots.

Seedlings for Transplanting. The protection that cloches afford from cold winds, frost and excessive wet, while at the same time giving ample ventilation to ensure hardiness, makes them ideal for overwintering autumn-sown annuals for early cutting, especially Larkspur, Calendula, Scabious, Nigella, etc.

Preparing the Seedbeds. A little extra care in preparing the soil for cloche sowings is well worth while, although ordinary preparation as for open-air sowings will serve. To improve the moisture-holding capacity of the surface soil a generous dressing of peat or sifted compost may with advantage be mixed with it, and it is always wise, especially for the early sowings, to prewarm the bed, and at the same time dry the soil, by setting the cloches in position a week or two before sowing.

To assist germination, the ends of the cloches, whether they are used singly or in rows, should be closed with sheets of glass or boards, but once the seedlings are growing freely, and provided the weather is favorable, these may be removed to give freer ventilation. For the late spring sowings some shading may be necessary, in the form of a light spraying of limewash on the underside of the glass.

Sowing Seeds in the Open Ground

Bearing in mind the conditions necessary for the quick and free germination of seeds—warmth, an adequate amount of water, and a free supply of air—the gardener's chief problem, in preparing his ground for seed sowing, is how best to provide these conditions in the right degree.

As regards warmth, he must rely largely on the heat of the sun to provide this, and here the cultivator of light soil has the advantage over the owner of heavy clayey soil, in that the latter takes much longer to warm up in the spring. It also takes longer to dry out sufficiently, and an excess of moisture in the soil is even more harmful to seeds, in causing them to rot, than the lack of it, which generally will delay germination rather than destroy the seeds.

Light soils, on the other hand, tend to dry out quickly. Although they may provide ideal conditions for the immediate germination of the seeds, unless they have been sufficiently consolidated, and enriched with moisture-holding materials, the seedlings may suffer in consequence.

Preparing the Soil. Whether you are sowing the seeds of flowers or vegetables, it pays to go to some trouble to prepare the soil for them a week or so before sowing. The finer the seeds, the

When sewing in drills, the first step, after the soil has been forked over and raked fine, is to insert stakes or pegs at appropriate distances apart at the ends of the drills.

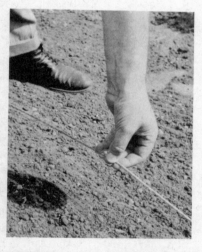

A garden line is then stretched between the stakes. Its tautness is tested by lifting it at its middle an inch or two above the ground level to make sure it snaps back and maintains a straight line.

Various methods are used to make the shallow trenches called drills. A draw hoe is a common and convenient tool used for this purpose. It is especially useful for making fairly deep drills for large seeds.

finer should the surface soil be in which they are sown, so that they will come into direct contact with the soil particles and the risk of irregular germination will thus be minimized.

For the general run of vegetables and annual and biennial flowers, the application of a good complete fertilizer to the soil at the initial preparation for seed sowing, to provide the seedlings with a supply of readily available food, is sound practice, even if the plot has received a dressing of organic manure during the fall or spring. Any balanced fertilizer of about a 5-10-5 analysis is excellent, broadcast over the plot at the rate of 4 ounces to the square yard.

The first step in preparing the ground is to break up the lumps, and at the same time assist surface drying. This is best accomplished by forking the soil through, 6 in. or so deep, mixing the fertilizer well in and leaving the surface as level as possible.

Although a fine level surface is desirable, it is equally important that the undersoil should be firm, so that the seedlings will be able to obtain secure anchorage, and also to prevent rapid drying out by overaeration; for this reason it is wise, especially on medium to light soils, to tread the plot evenly all over before commencing to rake it. This is done most thoroughly by stepping sideways, pressing with each foot alternately, so that the whole area receives equal pressure.

Making a Fine Soil Surface. For large seeds, as for instance of Beans and Peas, a light raking is sufficient to level off the surface for sowing, but for the smaller seeds it is necessary to reduce the surface soil to a fine condition, remove the larger stones, and leave the bed as level as possible.

On the large plot, a wooden hayrake is very handy for quickly leveling and reducing the soil to a fairly fine state, being light and easy to use, but on plots of average size an ordinary iron rake is the best implement, and with its aid, after a little practice, the least-skilled novice will be able to produce a seed bed fine and level enough for the very smallest seeds.

If a large area has to be prepared for seed sowing, and forking would take too long, equally good results can be achieved in breaking up the soil and mixing in the fertilizer with a rototiller, cultivator or harrow.

A stout stake with a V-shaped notch cut in its end is a useful implement for making shallow drills.

The V-notch in the end of the stake is saddled over the garden line and is pushed in short back-and-forth strokes along it.

In this way the notched end of the stake cuts out a drill up to an inch and a half in depth, depending upon the pressure exerted.

Improving Light Soils. Soils that tend to dry out quickly, with consequent harm to the seedlings in really hot weather, can be improved by raking a generous quantity of thoroughly rotted compost or moist granulated peat into the surface of the bed immediately prior to sowing.

On clayey soils the addition of sand, old potting soil, peat, and other loosening materials will help in the production of a finer surface for seed sowing, and such materials may be used for filling the drills after the seeds have been sown, to encourage rapid germination of the seeds.

Seedbeds for Small Sowings. To raise Cabbage, Cauliflower and other Brassica seedlings of all kinds, and Leeks, for transplanting, together with Foxgloves, Canterbury Bells, Sweet Williams, and other biennials, and the larger-seeded perennials, it is desirable to prepare a small seedbed for them, 3 to 5 ft. wide, and as long as necessary. It should be in an open position, and prepared as advised for ordinary outdoor sowing. It is an advantage, if the soil is clayey, to raise the surface of the bed slightly above the normal level, by making narrow temporary paths around it and shoveling the soil from these on to the bed. Such a bed is easy to protect with net or threads if birds are troublesome.

Making the Drills. There are various methods of making seed drills for outdoor sowings. For the general run of vegetables and flower seeds the amateur will find the draw hoe the handiest implement, as after a little practice, drills can be

Yet another convenient method of making shallow drills is by pulling a rake handle or similar piece of wood along the side of a garden line stretched tightly across the ground surface.

When shallow drills of short length are needed they may be made by pressing the handle of a rake or hoe into the newly prepared seed bed surface.

If the soil is at all dry it is advantageous to water the bottom of the seed drills before sowing.

An alternative method of making short shallow drills is by sliding the edge of a narrow board along the surface.

made quickly to any given depth. For sowing in rows it is always best to work with a taut garden line, to keep the drill straight. The edge of the blade, not the back, should be held against the line (an important point if accurate spacing is desired), and as the hoe is drawn towards the operator the fine soil is drawn out, leaving a V-shaped drill of even depth.

A simple method of making short drills for small seeds, such as Lettuce, is with the handle of a rake or hoe, laid across the bed and pressed down lightly.

Yet another method is to cut a deep V-shaped notch in the end of a broom handle or stout stake, saddle the notch over a garden line stretched taut across the ground and then push the stake along the line.

Flat-bottomed drills are convenient for sow-ing garden Peas, and are sometimes favored for Beans. These flat-bottomed drills can be made with either a draw hoe or spade.

Broadcast sowing of seeds, although essential in lawn making, is not generally to be recommended for garden crops, although it is satisfactory for Turnips sown in late summer for "greens" and for green manure crops generally. The seed is scattered lightly over the soil and then raked in, or, if the sowing is on a small scale, the seed is lightly covered with a sprinkling of fine soil.

Thin Sowing Is Important. It is a mistake to sow seeds very thickly, as this is not only wasteful of seeds, but unless the seedlings are thinned quickly at an early stage they will soon become weak and spindly and fall a ready prey to pests, diseases and drought. It is equally important,

Large seeds such as Beans may be sown directly from the hands.

Smaller seeds may be sown directly from the packet.

As an aid to even distribution the seed packet may be held tilted slightly forward and tapped with the forefinger to cause the seed to dribble out.

however, if unbroken rows of crops are the aim, not to sow the smaller seeds too thinly, as there is little doubt that the seedlings find benefit, and to a certain extent shelter, in the close company of neighbors. The aim, therefore, should be to sow the seeds thinly enough to give the seedlings sufficient space right from the start, and to thin the seedlings early enough to prevent any overcrowding.

Covering the Seeds. The final operation, after the seeds have been sown, is to fill in the drills with the topsoil that was removed from them. This is done by pushing it in with the rake, or feet in the case of the larger seeds, and gently firming it, leveling off the surface with a few strokes of the rake held almost upright.

On very light soils it may assist rapid germination if the seed drills are filled with moist peat, or, in the case of small beds, the whole surface is covered with this material, especially for seeds sown in late spring. If the soil is clayey, it is good practice to fill the drills for the early sowings with old sifted potting compost containing plenty of sand, or with a mixture of equal parts of soil, peat moss and sand.

Sowing in Dry Weather. When seeds are sown in summer, watering the drills well before sowing is desirable if the soil is dry. If not watered,

An alternative method that ensures sowing thinly is to tip the seeds into the cupped hand or saucer and then sow a pinch at a time from the fingers and thumb.

Larger seeds may be covered by walking along the drills and pushing the soil into the drill from alternate sides with the feet.

Small seeds may be covered with the head of a rake, with its teeth pointing upwards.

After the drills are covered, the soil above them is firmed lightly by tapping it with a rake.

Finally, the seed bed is raked very lightly by pulling the rake back and forth in the same direction as the drills.

germination may be slow and irregular. After the drills have been made they should be filled several times with water, and the seeds sown when this has soaked away.

For Patches of Annual Flowers. Of all plants raised from seeds sown out of doors, perhaps it is with the hardy annuals that the greatest waste takes place through sowing the seeds too thickly. A simple way to avoid this when sowing patches of annuals, and reduce seedling thinning to a minimum, is to make drills with a pointed stick diagonally across the bed, 6 to 12 in. apart according to the height and habit of the subject. Then make drills at right angles to these, the same distance apart and, at the points where they

Clumps or patches of annuals may be sown at the intersection points of a criss-cross pattern of shallow drills made with the end of a stake.

The drills are watered before the seeds are sown and, after sowing, the soil is pulled over the seeds with the back of a rake.

cross, set a small but adequate pinch of seeds.

The common method of sowing edgings of dwarf annual flowers is in a single drill, 6 in. or more from the edge of the bed. In most cases a band 1 ft. or so wide would give a more colorful effect, and the best way to achieve this is to sow thinly in drills, about 6 in. apart, running diagonally from the edge of the bed.

Protection from Mice and Birds. If you are sowing Peas and there is any danger of mice eating them, the safest precaution is to shake the Peas well in a can containing a little red lead (poisonous) and kerosene before sowing.

How to protect Peas and Brassica seeds of all types from birds is often a problem. Various types of wire and net protectors are available for covering individual rows, and small beds can be protected by covering them with small-mesh wire or string netting, or by inserting sticks around the bed, and stretching black thread between them to form a network a few inches above the soil.

Treatment of Seedlings. As soon as the seedlings can be discerned in the rows, the cultivator or hoe should be brought into use, to loosen the surface soil. This hoeing will let in air and moisture, and at the same time destroy weed seedlings. Thereafter regular hoeing should be the rule, if only for the purpose of keeping weeds in check, but not so close to the seedlings as to damage their roots. Hoeing or cultivating among seedlings that have been sown broadcast is not practicable; hand weeding must be done with these.

With vegetables and annual flowers sown where they are to grow, early thinning should be the rule, to prevent overcrowding. If the plants are sown in continuous rows, thinning should be done in two operations, first singling them to half the final distance, or less, and completing the job when the seedlings have become well established and are growing freely.

With some crops, such as Carrots, Turnips, Spinach, and early Lettuce, the final thinning need not be done until the seedlings are of usable size. Thinning should be done in showery weather if possible; otherwise, if the soil is dry, it should be done in the evening, and the rows then watered well to settle the soil.

Sowing a hill of Squash seeds; five to seven seeds are set in each cluster or hill.

Sowing in Hills. Gardeners often speak of sowing their seeds in hills, and cultural directions frequently advise that seeds be sown in hills.

This is most often the case with certain vegetables, notably Corn, Cucumbers, Squash and Pole Beans. Melons are also often sown in hills.

Simply stated, sowing in hills merely means planting the seeds in small groups or clusters, with the clusters rather distantly spaced from each other. When planting Corn, for instance, the hills, each consisting of about six seeds, may be spaced from 2½ to 3 ft. apart. In the case of Cucumbers the hills should be 4-5 ft. apart.

It is important to remember that hills may or may not be raised above the surrounding soil level. When Corn is planted in hills it is usual to make a shallow depression with a hoe, sow the seeds and cover them with soil without any raising of the surface.

Hills for Cucumbers, Melons, Pole Beans and some other plants are usually made by drawing up the soil to form a low, broad-topped mound, which ensures the seeds and young plants of excellent drainage.

For plants that enjoy rooting in rich, organic material, as do Cucumbers, Squash and Melons, the best plan is to make a shallow hollow in the soil surface, heap into it two or three good-sized pails of rotted manure or rich compost, and then cover with the excavated soil.

Always, when sowing in hills, a few more seeds are set in each than the number of plants that it is intended to let remain. When the young plants begin to crowd, the weakest and least desirable are pulled out and the correct number of the most promising, usually 3-4, are allowed to remain and develop to maturity.

Transplanting. Hardy biennials and perennial plants raised in prepared beds should be transplanted to nursery rows as soon as the seedlings are large enough to handle conveniently. As a general rule, the seedlings may be spaced 6 in. apart, in rows 9 to 12 in. apart. If the weather is dry they should be watered in well.

PROPHET FLOWER. See Arnebia echioides.

PROSTANTHERA — *Mintbush* (Prostanther'a; Prostan'thera). Tender, evergreen flowering shrubs, from Australia, which belong to the family Labiatae. They grow about 4 ft. in height, have slender, twiggy branches clothed with lanceolate (lance-shaped) or linear (long, narrow), entire (undivided), pale green leaves, ½ to 1½ in. in length. The purple or white flowers which are terminal (in the tips of the shoots), or axillary (in the axils of the leaves), are produced in racemes (loose spikes); they average ½ in. in diameter, and have short corolla tubes

which spread out into broad campanulate tips. The name Prostanthera is derived from *prostithemi*, to append, and *anthera*, an anther, and refers to the appendages on the anthers.

Summer and Winter Treatment. In California and similar mild climates these shrubs may be cultivated outdoors. When grown in greenhouses, they require a minimum winter temperature of 45 degrees, and the best soil compost consists of equal parts of turfy loam and peat with sand freely added. Repotting is done in March. The plants are taken out of their pots, the crocks and loose soil are removed from the roots with a pointed stick, and the plants are then set in slightly larger pots. The new pots must be carefully drained, as the plants are liable to die off in stagnant soil, and the compost must be made firm with a potting stick.

After potting, the soil is not moistened until it becomes moderately dry, but then it is thoroughly saturated. This system of watering must be followed until the plants are well rooted; excessive dampness or dryness of the soil is fatal. Well-rooted plants are kept moist at the roots for the remainder of the summer, but throughout

Prostanthera rotundifolia, the Mintbush, an evergreen shrub for a cool greenhouse, bearing purple flowers in summer.

the winter the compost is only moistened when it becomes moderately dry.

Newly potted plants are lightly syringed twice a day and the atmosphere is kept moist by damping the floor and benches until the plants are established. They are also shaded from bright sunlight. When well rooted, less damping and syringing are required and the plants are exposed to all but the fiercest rays of the sun.

Propagation Is by Cuttings. Half-ripened shoots are removed with a heel in July–August. The leaves from the lower half of the stems are taken off and the heels are pared smooth with a sharp knife. The cuttings are then inserted in a propagating case or in a bed of sand, sand and peat moss or vermiculite covered with a bell jar. The moisture is wiped from the inside of the glass each morning until the roots are formed. The rooted cuttings are potted separately in 3-in. pots and subsequently in larger pots. Bushy plants are obtained by cutting back the main shoot to 4 in. and treating the resulting side branches similarly.

The chief kinds are P. nivea, 3 ft., white, June; P. denticulata, 2-3 ft., pale purple, May–June; and P. rotundifolia, Mintbush, 4 ft., purple-blue or lilac, July.

PROSTRATUS. A botanical term meaning of prostrate habit of growth.

PROTEA (Pro'tea; Prote'a). Tender, evergreen flowering plants from South Africa which belong to the family Proteaceae. These plants, which are very beautiful and distinctive, are rarely cultivated and are chiefly to be found in botanical collections. They grow up to 8 ft. in height, and have simple (undivided), ovate (egg-shaped), lanceolate (lance-shaped), or linear (long and narrow) leaves.

The flowers are handsome, mostly terminal (borne at the ends of the shoots), and are solitary (not in clusters); they are large and conspicuous, surrounded by numerous bracts, and are of various colors including red, pink, and whitish-green. The flower heads somewhat resemble those of the Globe Artichoke (Cynara), the flowers of which are also surrounded by overlapping bracts.

The kind which is named after the Globe Artichoke (P. cynaroides) produces a large amount of honey in its flower heads and these

The large-flowered Proteas are handsome evergreen shrubs from South Africa.

are known to the natives as honey pots; from them sugar is made. The name Protea is derived from Proteus, the sea god who had the power of self-transformation, and alludes to the diversity of appearance of the flowers.

Summer and Winter Management. When grown in greenhouses, these plants require a minimum winter temperature of 45 degrees, and a soil compost of three parts of sandy loam, one part of peat, and one part of equal quantities of sand, crushed bricks, and charcoal. Very little syringing, damping, or shading is required.

Repotting is done in March or April. The plants are taken out of their pots, the crocks and loose soil are removed from their roots, and the plants are then set in slightly larger pots. The new pots must be exceptionally well drained; about one third of the depth should be filled with crocks, and these covered with a layer of rough siftings from the compost. The compost must be made firm, but it should not be moistened until it becomes moderately dry. This system of watering is continued throughout the year, as these plants do not thrive in soil which is perpetually moist.

After they have been repotted and until they become established they are shaded from the fierce rays of the sun, but afterwards they are exposed to full light. They are freely ventilated at all times of the year, and during the summer months benefit greatly by being plunged out of doors in a bed of sand or ashes.

Propagation by Cuttings. Well-ripened shoots are taken off in summer. The leaves are removed from the lower half of the stems and a clean cut is made below the bottom node. The pots are prepared by half filling them with crocks, which are covered with the rough siftings from the compost, and the remainder of the space is filled with a finely sifted compost of sand and loam in equal parts.

The cuttings are inserted firmly, and after the compost has been moistened they are covered with a bell jar. Each morning the bell jar is removed, and the moisture wiped from the inside. This treatment is continued until roots are formed, which is a slow process, and the bell jar is then removed. The plants are potted separately in small pots and subsequently in larger pots. Seeds may also be used as a means of propagation.

The chief kinds are P. grandiflora, May, white; P. cynaroides, August, purple; P. cordata, April, purple; and P. rhodantha, June, red.

PROTECTING PLANTS
Methods of Keeping Plants Healthy and Unharmed

Many cultural practices have as their objectives the protection of plants from conditions and enemies that are likely to harm them. Among the most important of these are excessive cold, too-high temperatures, sun, snow, water and wind, as well as diseases, insects, birds, animals, humans and weeds. (For further information concerning these subjects see also Shelter Planting, Pests and Diseases, and Weeds.)

Protection from damage by humans is usually best achieved by means of effective fencing; thus a hedge or other barrier, suitably placed, may prevent harm from being done to a lawn by people walking across it and forming worn paths, and the likelihood of damage being done to planted areas by automobiles.

Fences afford good protection, too, against damage by the larger domestic animals such as cattle, sheep, horses, hogs and dogs and against some wild animals, especially deer and rabbits. To be effective, fences must be strong and of sufficient height. To protect trees and shrubs in winter this means fences sufficiently high above the surface of any snow that may accumulate on the ground. Fences must also be impenetrable by the particular animals they are to keep out. To keep out rabbits, chicken wire having a half-inch or three-quarter-inch mesh is practicable.

To keep the bark of trees from being gnawed by animals such as rabbits and mice (this is especially likely to occur in winter) encircle the trunks with a guard (see Tree Guards) or a girdle of galvanized-wire hardware cloth or half-inch mesh chicken wire. The girdle should extend to a depth of about 6 in. beneath the ground level and sufficiently far above the ground to prevent the animal from reaching unprotected bark when a thick layer of snow makes it possible for it to reach far higher than it otherwise could.

Certain bulbs, such as Crocus and Tulip, are especially likely to be eaten or otherwise damaged by rodents such as mice, chipmunks and moles. These pests may be circumvented by

A bed in which bulbs are to be planted is lined with wire mesh.

Baskets made of wire-mesh hardware cloth may be sunk in the ground and bulbs planted in them to protect them from mice.

planting the bulbs inside baskets or cages made of wire mesh, or by surrounding the whole bed with a vertical wall of the same material carried to a depth of 8-9 in. below ground and extending an inch or two above ground.

Shooting and trapping are effective ways of controlling damage by squirrels, chipmunks, mice, rabbits, moles, woodchucks and other animals, but gardeners should carefully check local laws covering these practices before engaging in them. Only traps of humane types should be used, and they should always be placed where neither persons nor domestic animals, wild animals and birds that are not pests will be harmed by them. In some cases, permission to shoot or trap can be obtained from the State Game Warden after lodging a complaint with him of the damage done.

Against cats, dogs, deer and some other animals, repellents that may be sprayed on the plants have some limited value. Their disadvantage is that they must be frequently renewed. Commercial preparations are available from dealers in horticultural supplies.

Crows, English sparrows and a variety of other birds may harm gardens by damaging fruit, picking off buds, scratching up seedbeds, and in other ways, so that sometimes it is necessary to curb them. Care should always be taken not to destroy birds that are harmless or that in general are useful even though they occasionally damage a little fruit or scratch up a few seeds. Most birds are desirable in gardens and more than "pay for their keep" by aiding in suppressing insects and other pests; they also delight the eye and ear. Check carefully before taking steps against them.

Shooting and trapping are the best ways of eliminating birds that must be killed, but check local laws carefully before attempting either of these. If proper precautions are taken, poisoned grain may sometimes be used effectively, but, unless carefully handled, it is very liable to endanger the lives of desirable birds, animals or even of children. None of these means are practicable against domestic birds such as chickens and ducks. Fencing is the only satisfactory means of keeping these out of gardens. Scarecrows and other bird scares are sometimes effective in

This permanent cage built of wood and wire net protects Blueberries from the attentions of birds.

keeping birds away. (See Birds Detrimental to Gardens.)

Small areas, such as seedbeds, or even a few fruit bushes, may be protected from the attentions of birds by enclosing them in cheesecloth, fine netting or metal screening. As some insurance against injury, the maintenance of bird feeding stations and the provision of drinking water has much to recommend it; some birds damage garden crops when other sources of food are lacking and take juicy young buds and soft fruits to quench their thirst.

Protection from Sun and Heat

The gardener must at times give plants protection against too intense light and against excessively high temperatures.

Damage from intense light is most likely to occur when naturally shade-loving plants are exposed to direct, strong sunshine; when sun-loving plants, comparatively soft and tender

from being grown in a greenhouse or cold frame, are transferred outdoors; and after plants are transplanted. The trunks of trees that have been growing closely together in woodland or nursery may be damaged by sunscald on their south-facing sides following their transference to sunnier locations; by heavy pruning, branches previously shaded by foliage may be exposed to sunshine sufficiently strong to sunscald them. Damage by sun occurs not only in summer; in winter, when the ground is frozen, evergreens, especially, are likely to suffer from this.

The provision of shade is the obvious method of avoiding damage by light that is too intense. Shade-needing plants should be grown in naturally shaded areas, such as woodland, under solitary trees or groups of trees, and areas shaded by high walls or buildings or in locations artificially shaded by lath houses, lath or burlap screens or other appropriate means.

The trunks of trees may, with advantage, be wrapped in burlap or in special tree-wrapping

Wooden slat shades being placed over newly transplanted seedlings to provide temporary shade.

Flowerpots, with a stone placed under the rim of each to ensure ventilation, are here used to shade newly planted annuals.

paper for a season or two following transplanting. When annuals, vegetables, young biennials and perennials are set out in hot sunny weather they should be shaded for a few days following the transplanting operation.

Not a great deal can be done to lower summer temperatures; but in every garden some locations are noticeably warmer than others. At the base of a south-facing wall, for example, the temperature is very noticeably higher than at the base of a north-facing wall; it is likely to be cooler near a pool or other body of water than elsewhere; parts of the garden that receive reflected heat from walls and pavements are warmer than those where plants grow alone in more open areas; in enclosed, "pocketed" spaces temperatures are higher than in more open locations through which breezes blow; and in the shade it is always much cooler than in the sun.

In selecting locations for plants known to prefer cool summer conditions, all these factors should be borne in mind. It should also be remembered that moisture has a cooling effect, and so plants should not be permitted to suffer from lack of water during dry weather.

As a temporary measure, shading may be used to offset some of the ill effects of temperatures that are too high. Spraying the foliage lightly with water lowers its temperature somewhat and has a refreshing effect on plants.

Many plants—Clematis and Lilies, for example —can withstand high atmospheric temperatures, provided the soil is kept reasonably cool and moist. In really hot weather an even temperature at the roots and a steady supply of water go far to ensure success with a great many kinds of plants, especially those that are surface-rooters such as Azaleas, Blueberries and Rhododendrons. Summer mulching is an excellent garden practice designed to conserve moisture and keep the soil temperature moderate and even.

Summer Mulching. An even temperature around the roots and a steady supply of moisture

Hay, weighted along the sides of the row with boards, may be used to shade newly sown seeds until they push through the ground.

in the soil are all-important to growing plants. A mulch, applied in early summer after hot weather begins, tends to maintain these conditions as well as to control harmful weeds.

Mulch materials suitable for summer use are numerous, and the choice will often depend on which is most easily or most economically obtainable. Among kinds commonly used are tobacco stems, peat moss, buckwheat hulls, salt-marsh hay, straw, strawy manure, coarse compost, and leaves (preferably Oak or Beech or a mixture of various kinds, although Pine needles form an excellent mulch beneath Pine trees and around really acid-soil plants). Sawdust may also be used, in which case an application of a fertilizer containing nitrogen should be made at the same time. Pebbles, gravel or rock chips are employed as mulch materials in rock gardens. Flat stones are sometimes used around individual difficult-to-grow plants that revel in a cool root run.

Newly planted trees and shrubs benefit from being mulched immediately after planting. This practice conserves soil moisture, promotes root growth and reduces the likelihood of the plants' suffering from lack of moisture during their first summer.

Protection from Cold

In winter, low temperatures as well as too intense light, lack of water (when the soil is frozen the moisture in it cannot be absorbed by the roots), and wind may cause damage. Some harm is directly due to the effects of below freezing temperatures on the tissues of tender plants; other damage is indirect—for example, the tearing and drying of roots that follows heaving of the soil as a result of alternate freezing and thawing.

It is well known that plants in poorly drained soils are more susceptible to winterkilling than specimens of the same kinds growing in well-drained places. Plants located in hollows or "frost pockets" are much more likely to be damaged than those planted where there is free air drainage. Selection of favorable planting sites is important as a protection against damage by cold.

Importance of Fall Watering. Trees and shrubs, particularly evergreen kinds, are less likely to suffer winter damage if the soil in which they grow is kept moist throughout the autumn. If this is done, their tissues go into the winter well supplied with moisture and they are better able to withstand the dehydrating effects of sun and wind when the ground is so cold that it is difficult or impossible for them to absorb adequate supplies of needed moisture.

If fall rains are inadequate, evergreen shrubs should be soaked thoroughly each fall before the soil freezes. A mulch of leaves or coarse compost applied immediately after the final watering is beneficial in cold climates.

Mulching for Winter Protection. Very fine protection against cold is provided if an insulating layer of more or less loose material is spread over the surface of ground occupied by the roots of many plants. Such a layer either may prevent the underground portions of the plants from freezing or may simply prevent the ground from freezing as deeply as it otherwise would. In the latter case, at least some of the roots are likely to be in unfrozen soil and, if the plant is evergreen, it may still absorb at least some moisture to compensate for that lost from the above-ground foliage.

Winter mulching is really resorting to Nature's way of protecting plants. When leaves fall they are blown among shrubs and other

Leaves and other mulch materials provide protection against fluctuating soil temperatures and rapid loss of moisture.

Littery manure is a good mulch to use around shrubs at the beginning of winter.

perennial plants. Before they decay and return plant food to the soil, they serve as a protection for roots and other below-ground parts by keeping a more even temperature in the soil over which they lie. Many gardeners, instead of taking a lesson from Nature, are inclined to neatness and artificiality and so rake up these leaves in fall. This is not always good practice. If it is done, in many areas it is desirable to replace them with a winter mulch. (See also Winter Covering, below.)

Small shrubs, especially those that have been recently planted or are not reliably hardy, can be protected by placing a layer of dry leaves, several inches thick, around them. The leaves should not be packed down so that air is excluded but should be left loose. Chicken wire may be used to contain them and prevent them from being blown away.

Larger shrubs and evergreens benefit greatly from having the soil covered with a 3-6 in. layer of half-rotted compost, loose, strawy manure, half-rotted leaves or any other appropriate mulch material that remains fairly loose and does not pack down and exclude air.

Winter Covering. In part, this term is interchangeable with winter mulching, but not wholly so. Winter covering includes the various types of protection that cover the tops, the above-ground portions, of plants. Winter covering is normally removed with the coming of spring; winter mulches are often left in position to decay gradually and form nourishment for the plants, or are forked into the ground to decay beneath the surface.

Among plants that are winter covered in cold regions are trees, shrubs and evergreens likely to be injured by cold, perennials and bulbs likely to be damaged by low temperatures and deep freezing of the soil, and young or newly transplanted specimens that may be harmed by heaving of the soil due to alternate freezing and thawing.

Salt hay is convenient to use as a winter covering and is sold in bales.

A light covering of salt hay over young perennials checks damage by heaving during winter.

Brushwood laid over salt hay prevents it from being blown about by the wind.

Young plants of many perennials and biennials are not thoroughly winter hardy in all regions. Where they are somewhat tender, or where there is danger of the small plants being heaved out of the ground by alternate freezing and thawing, they are benefitted by a light winter covering. Plants such as Foxgloves and Canterbury Bells that retain their foliage during winter will not survive, however, if a heavy layer of winter-covering material is spread over them. It should be just thick enough to shade the soil, and so check too frequent alternate freezing and thawing. Branches from Pines, used

Branches of evergreens or discarded Christmas trees provide effective winter protection for perennials.

Christmas trees or other evergreens are very satisfactory as a winter covering, as also is salt-marsh hay.

Delphiniums are sometimes protected by having sand or coal ashes heaped around and over their crowns. This is especially worth while in gardens that suffer from excessive moisture.

Irises and Peonies may not need winter protection if they were planted early. However, young plants set out rather late in the season may suffer injury from heaving by frost unless it is prevented by a light covering. This is especially desirable if the soil is clayey.

Bulbs. Some hardy bulbs such as Daffodils (Narcissi) may suffer damage from severe frost if they are planted late in beds or borders. They should therefore be planted as early as obtainable or be covered with 4-5 in. of straw, salt-marsh hay, leaves, branches of evergreens or similar material. Hardy bulbs planted in grass sod do not require this protection.

Bulbs that are on the borderline of hardiness in any given region, and even many that are usually regarded as tender, may survive the winter outdoors if they are covered. For nearly hardy kinds, those that are just slightly tender —as, for example, Brodiaea uniflora, the Spring Starflower, in southern New York—a covering 4-5 in. thick of any of the materials recommended above for hardy bulbs will prove sufficient. For more tender kinds—such as Gladioli and Montbretias, in southern New York—a layer about a foot thick will usually enable them to survive by preventing the frost from striking deeply enough to harm them. Even Dahlias may be kept alive through the winter by this method in regions where they would otherwise surely perish.

When winter covering is used, it is important not to put it into position too early, not until the ground has frozen to a depth of an inch or two, and it should be removed gradually, not all at one time in spring. If put on too early, many winter-covering materials attract mice and other rodents that may take up winter quarters under their protection; these are likely to damage the plants. Too early or too rapid removal in spring may result in severe damage to tender shoots by sun, wind and late frost.

In the North, protecting a Boxwood against winter damage. First, a wooden framework is erected around it.

The finished job. The Boxwood is protected from sun and wind.

Burlap is then wrapped well around and over the framework.

Shelters and Wrappings. In addition to materials laid directly upon the ground or the plants, there are types of winter covering that involve building a shelter of burlap or similar material about the plants and wrapping the above-ground parts in hay, straw, paper and other protective materials.

Evergreens, even kinds considered fairly hardy, are much more susceptible to winter injury than are leaf-losing (deciduous) trees and shrubs. They transpire moisture through the leaves in winter as well as in summer, and

Next, the edges of the burlap are sewn together where they meet.

In the vicinity of New York City, it is common practice for home gardeners to wrap and tie Fig trees in burlap, old blankets, waterproof paper, and other insulating materials to protect them from excessive cold.

protection from high winds and bright sunshine may be very necessary in cold regions, especially for those evergreens that are not natives. Burlap, neatly nailed to 2 by 4-in. supports on the exposed sides of the plants, is helpful. A few branches of Pines or other evergreens stuck in the soil so that they give protective shade may be all that is needed for some of the smaller, growing evergreens liable to winter damage.

Deciduous trees and shrubs, the tops of which are somewhat tender, as are, for example, Fig trees in the vicinity of New York City, and Hydrangea macrophylla rather farther north, may be successfully brought through the winter by tying their upper parts together, wrapping them in a thick layer of straw, hay, newspaper, old blankets or other material that provides good insulation, and encasing the whole in a layer of waterproof building paper. This is done before very hard frost, and the covering is removed in spring after danger of severe frost has passed.

Roses. In regions of cold winters Roses need protection. Hybrid Tea and Floribunda bush Roses will withstand a temperature of about 12 degrees F. but are likely to be damaged by alternating mild and cold spells. They can be protected by mounding soil, buckwheat hulls, or peat moss around the base of the plants, covering them to a height of at least 8 in. Where the temperature drops below zero F., they should

have soil mounded up to them and, after the ground is frozen to a depth of an inch or two, a thick covering of strawy manure or leaves should be placed over this.

Tree or standard Roses will tolerate about 15 degrees F. Where temperatures drop below this, they should be laid along the ground and covered with soil and a layer of leaves, straw or other winter covering. In the most northerly regions they must be lifted and buried in a trench in the ground.

Large-flowered and everblooming climbers will survive at 5 degrees F. but are best mounded as recommended for Hybrid Teas where the temperature goes lower. In colder regions it is safest to lay the shoots down on top of the ground and cover them with soil.

Climbing Hybrid Teas and Floribundas should be mounded with soil in similar fashion and, in colder regions, laid down along the ground and covered with soil and mulch.

Wintering Plants Indoors. It is common practice to protect many tender plants by growing them over winter in greenhouses, window gardens and in cold frames. In the former locations the plants usually continue to grow through the winter and need attention in the matters of watering, fertilizing and other cultural care in order to flourish.

Plants wintered in cold frames grow little or not at all until warm spring weather arrives.

Soil, heaped around the bases of Rose bushes, protects the stems from critically low temperatures.

A light layer of salt hay affords shade and insulation to plants in cold frames.